# Industrial Economics

# Industrial Economics

**Dr. Ranjana Seth**
*Associate Professor in Economics*
*Vasanta College for Women*
*(Benares Hindu University)*

**Ane Books Pvt. Ltd.**
New Delhi ♦ Chennai

**Industrial Economics**

Dr. Ranjana Seth



First Edition : 2015
Reprint : 2018, 2019, **2020, 2023**

*Published by*

**Ane Books Pvt. Ltd.**

4821, Parwana Bhawan, 1st Floor, 24 Ansari Road, Darya Ganj,
**New Delhi** - 110 002, Tel.: +91(011) 23276843-44, Fax: +91(011) 23276863
e-mail: kapoor@anebooks.com, Website: www.anebooks.com

*Branch Office*

- Avantika Niwas, 1st Floor, 19 Doraiswamy Road, T. Nagar,
**Chennai** - 600 017, Tel.: +91(044) 28141554, 28141209
e-mail: anebookschennai@gmail.com, rathinam@anebooks.com



ISBN : 978-93-8015-681-1

***Dedicated to***

*my reverened parents*

**Late Dr. S.N. Mehrotra, Smt. Kanta Mehrotra and Late Hari Krishan Das Seth**

# Preface

The Indian Economy has been witnessing structural changes in industrialisation. The present book is a modest attempt to provide a compact, coherent and consistent analysis about certain major aspects of industrialisation. It has been attempted to present in a systematic manner the market-behaviour of business firms under different market structure, the problems and progress of industrial development during the planning era and emergence of global competition and Indian Industry.

Every endeavour has been made to incorporate the latest facts on various spheres of industrial economy from published works of eminent Scholars, journals and magazines. Conceived thus the present book should be of value to students of Economics, Commerce and of other Competitive exams.

I owe my intellectual debt of gratitude to Dr. Vijai Shivpuri, Prof. P.K. Bhargav and to my collegues who encouraged me in writing this book. My special thanks to my husband Dr. S.K. Seth and to my son Abhishek Seth and Vedansh Seth who always provoked me to write this book.

I owe thanks to the whole publication team of Ane Books Pvt. Ltd. and my special thanks to Mr. J.R. Kapoor who took all pains and efforts in the publication of this book.

I hope the readers of this book will favour me with their valuable suggestions and pin point the shortcomings.

**The Author**

# Syllabus

| Sr. No. | Paper-IX B.H.U. | Hrs. |
|---|---|---|
| **Unit–I** | Industry and Economic Development; problems of Industrialisation in Developing Countries, Industrial classification and Data Information, concepts of plant, firm, industry. market : Market structure; Market Power; and Market Conduct. | |
| **UNIT–II** | Weber's Theory of Location; Factors affecting location of an Industry; Localisation and Decentralisation of Industries; Dispersion and problem of regional imbalence in India. | |
| **UNIT–III** | Industrial Organisation and Ownership Structure–Public, Private, Joint and Cooperative sectors, Industrial Competition and Monopoly, Factors Determining Optimum Size, Economics of scale. | |
| **UNIT–IV** | Rationalisation in Industries– Automation and Standardisation; Industrial productivity–Measurement and Determinants Introduction to cost benefit Analysis. | |
| **UNIT–V** | Industrial progress under the plans, Industrial Policy; Problems of large and small scale industries, sickness in Indian Industries; Multinationals in India; Emerging Global Competition and Indian Industry. | |

# Contents

CHAPTER 1

# Industry and Economic Development

## 1.1 INTRODUCTION

Industrial development has a necessary and ultimately a large role to play in almost any sound development programme[1]. Industrialisation has come to be regarded as synonymous to economic development and if an under-developed country wants to raise its economic development then of course it must initate programmes of industrialisation. The Soviet delegation to the U.N. Economic and Social council in 1963, stated that industrialisation is a system of economic development in which major part of natural resources are used to develop a technically up-to-date, diversified national industry capable of assuring a high rate of growth for the economy as a whole and of overcoming economic and social backwardness"[2].

As a matter of fact we see that the essential criteria that are being used to distinguish developed economy from an under-developed economy always relates to the proportion of work force engaged in industrial activity, the proportion of national output originating, in industrial sector. No doubt both the terms industrialisation and economic development are used interchangeably. Industrialisation is taken thus as a concomitant of development.

## 1.2 THE MEANING OF INDUSTRIALISATION

Industrialisation in the Marxist literature is used in two different meanings. In the narrow meaning, it refers to the establishment and development of the production of the means of production. In the broad meaning, it refers to the completion of the industrial revolution and the transfer of the economy to

1. Murray D : *Industrial Development* p. 5.
2. This definition was submitted to the Soviet Deligation to the U.N. Economic and Social Council in 1963 and was quoted by Shirokov, *Industrialisation of India*, P.8.

industrial methods of production. Taken together these meanings imply that industrialisation begins with the setting of the heavy industries for the production of the means of production and that when an adequate industrial production has been created the entire economy is transferred to the industrial methods of production. These two meanings correspond to the initial and concluding stages of industrialisation. This idea of industrialisation owes its origin to the specific character of economic development in the erstwhile U.S.S.R. According to Shirokov, when the Soviet Union initiated the process of industrialisation it had a definite industrial potential including several light and heavy industry, transport and communication, skilled labour and technical know how. As against this the developing countries were faced with a different situation that is; with a backward social and economic system which was **not** conducive to large scale industrialisation[3].

"Industrialisation in its wider sense is the key to economic progress and higher living standards". "Industrialisation may be defined" as a process in which changes of a series of strategical production functions are taking place. It involves those basic changes that accompany the mechanization of an enterprise, the building of a new industry, the opening of a new market and the exploitation of a new territory. This is in a way, a process of deepening as well as widening of capital"[4]. **Prof. A.H. Hansen** defines the deepening process as one where more capital is used per unit of output while the widening process means that capital formation grows *pari passu* with the increase in the output of final goods"[5]. In other words, this process raises the productivity per worker in the country. Eugene Staley, marks an association between industrialisation and the high productivity which makes high average incomes. "The two are parts of an interlinked process one does not proceed very far without the other. It is equally true to say that (*i*) high productivity produces industrialisation and that industrialisation produces high productivity"[6]. It is in this context that Condliffe and Rosenstein Rodan have viewed industrialisation as an alternative to emigration for solving the problem of over population and of raising the national income in economically less developed areas.

Industrialisation means thus the establishment and development of manufacturing industries along with bringing about a change in the whole economic structure. Industrialisation is thus a process by which the "Centre of Gravity" of the economy shifts from agriculture to industry. It involves two things basically that is adoption of technologically superior technique of production that helps to transform basic raw material and intermediate goods into manufactured goods and secondly leads to the application of modern technique of management and organisation.

3. P.T. Bauer and B.S. Yamey, *The Economics of Under Developed Countries.*
4. Pei-Kang Chang, *Agriculture and Industrialisation,* p. 69.
5. A.H. Hansen, *Fiscal Policy and Business cycle,* p. 355.
6. E.Staley, *The Future of Under Developed Countries,* pp. 394–395.

Industrialisation as such involves the organisation of production in business enterprises characterised by specialisation and division of labour both within and among themselves, this specialisation is based on the application of technology and on mechanical and electrical power to supplement and replace human effort and motivated by the objective of minimising cost per unit and maximising returns to the enterprise. This leads to realisation of industrial progress and promotion of economic growth rate in the country.

Industrialisation may thus be termed as "a precursor to economic development and social change".

### 1.2.1 Characteristics of Industrialisation

Certain basic features of industrialisation can be gathered from the definition of industrialisation They are pin-pointed as such:

1. Industrialisation and economic development are synonymous.
2. There is deepening and widening of capital.
3. Development of a new process takes place.
4. Industrialisation is related to take-off stage of development.
5. Mobility of factors of production takes place.
6. Social changes occurs.

### 1.2.2 Pattern of Industrialisation

**Pattern of industrialisation** varies from **country to country** (*i*) According to the amount of initiative taken by the government or private enterprises, industrialisation may be individual or private initiated, state initiated, jointly initiated (mixed economy). Infact in the initial stage of industrialisation efforts of both government and individuals are involved. India may be categorised as mixed economy.

(*ii*) Industrialisation can also be classified as revolutionary and evolutionary. The process of industrialisation undergone in Soviet Russia is described as **'Revolutionary'** to distinguish it from **"Evolutionary"** type as marked in U.K. But these two terms are mutually overlapping. The period of evolution of modern industry in England was designated Industrial Revolution while the revolutionary process of industrialisation adopted by U.S.S.R. was most evolutionary in character as it began with imported technology. To these forces personal freedom along with restrictions are added.

The pattern of industrialisation is also based on intensity *i.e., as labour intensive and capital intensive*. In labour intensive pattern labour is used *viably* as compared to capital in the process of production while in capital intensive pattern capital plays a vital role.

Pattern of industrialisation is also based on *size and location.* on the basis of size it may be large or small and on the basis of location the enterprises may be either localised or diversified in different areas. In localised pattern industry are located in a particular area while in *decentralised pattern industry* gets diversified into different areas promoting regional balance as such. **The pattern of industrialisation can be viewed with the help of chart (*see* chart 1):**

**CHART 1**

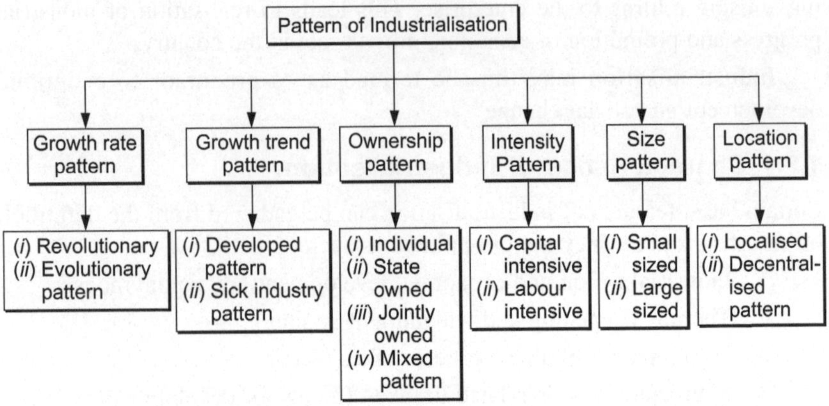


### 1.2.3 Agriculture and Industrialisation

It is unreal to consider agricultural development as separate or conflicting. Debates have centered around the relative importance to be assigned to agriculture *versus* Industry. But this dichotomy is often overdrawn. The concern today is to understand the inter-relationship which exist between agriculture and industry and the contribution that each can make to the other.

In the Less Developed Countries more people are engaged in agriculture for their livelihood than in the industrial and other sector. Agriculture growth provided food for the growing non-agricultural labour force and raw material for agro-based industries this domestic demand for industrial goods stimulates increases saving and tax revenue to be utilised for further development, earns more foreign exchange to finance imports of capital, intermediate goods and raw materials for industrialisation and facilitates the development of labour intensive village, small and medium industries in rural and urban areas.

Since agriculture provides employment to more than 70% of the population in the early stages of development, increase in agriculture production and productivity raises rural income. Rising rural incomes have strong multiplier effects in that they increase the demand for domestic non-agricultural goods and services which in turn increases the income of those providing the goods and services. This rise in the demand for industrial goods brings gains in industrialisation.

When there is agricultural progress some of the resources for industrialisation come from agriculture. Infact, increase agricultural productivity implies a large marketable surplus and a redistribution of income in favour of rural sector. Industrialisation requires the reallocation of funds towards the modern sector along with the rising agricultural income. Rising farm incomes are mopped up through raising land taxes and betterment levies and the mobilisation of rural saving through saving drives and also through such financial institution as cooperative and rural banks. They play an important part in channelising rural saving for industrialisation.

Industrialisation favourably affects agricultural development in a number of ways. *Firstly*, with industrialisation incomes rises rapidly which increases the demand for such agricultural commodities as milk, vegetables, etc. This in turn raises work for rural population and raises income.

*Secondly*, industrialisation raises the availability of capital for the agricultural sector which helps in modernising agriculture and raising farm output.

*Thirdly,* industrialisation followed by urbanisation opens vast job opportunities to the rural people who remit money back to the home this is used to buy inputs for farming or raising cattle, poultry, fisheries etc. With the improved means of transportation due to industrialisation markets expand which facilities the sale of such agricultural products in the towns raising their income thereby. *Fourthly*, when urbanisation follows industrialisation it provides larger facilities for education, travel and contact with new things and ideas which widens horizon of the rural people, changing their attitude toward life and leading to modernisation.

Industrialisation provides a wide and expanding range of consumer good which encourages the agriculturist to increase farm produce. This in turn tends to raise their incomes to enable them to buy consumer goods.

Thus, both agriculture and industrial development are intended and each effects the growth of the other. Therefore, harmonious development of both the sectors are necessary for steady growth of the economy. Because of this interdependence of agriculture and industry, we say that they are complementary and not competitive.

## 1.3 URGE/ROLE OF INDUSTRIALISATION

Industrialisation is a "precursor to economic development and social changes". The effects of industrialisation on the economy of a nation are many and varied. *They can be studied as such:*

### 1. Structural Changes in the Economy

The most important structural change in the economy introduced by industrialisation is in the occupational pattern. Most of the developing countries are characterised by heavy dependence of their population on the agricultural sector. Incomes in this sector being low the economies of these countries remain stagnant and backward. Industrialisation brings about a marked change in the occupational pattern by opening up new avenues of employment opportunity in the industrial sector. The pressure of population on agriculture declines and the disguised unemployed people earning only as subsistence livelyhood in agriculture are able to move out to industries where incomes are higher and prospects of progress brighter. Thus, industrialisation brings with it strong forces and dynamism that help the developing countries in breaking the shackles of stagnation.

### 2. Beneficial Effects on Agricultural Development

Industrialisation helps in accelerating the pace of agricultural growth in a number of ways. For instance, it increases the demand for wage-good of which initially food is the most important. This results in favourable market for agricultural good and tends to break down the relatively stagnant subsistence character of agriculture. The production of each crop is stimulated, the development of agriculture processing industry encouraged and the integration of the rural and urban economies made possible. Industrialisations also makes a wider range of consumer goods available to agricultural worker, raises their level of want and encourages greater productive effort. By encouraging the reorganisation of agriculture on a more efficient, large scale, mechanised basis industrialisation creates conditions which leads to rise in agricultural productivity.

### 3. Changes in the Social Outlook

The social outlook of the people undergoes a drastic change. The traditional village life with its communal bond is completely transformed as large number of villagers move to cities to work in industries. New progressive ideas changes the outlook of the workers. A new entrepreneurial class in born, capital formation rises, technical innovation takes place and new skills emerge. All these developments have far reaching effect on social relationship and this brings in fact a new modern and vibrant society.

### 4. Rise in per Capita Income

Due to industrialisation total national income rises rapidly. Progress of industrialisation is accompanied by an increment in national and per capita income. In the industrially developed countries GNP is high in relation to developed economies. The **Table 1.1** reflects the situation in India. It may be noted that the share of manufacturing sector, construction electricity and water supply in 1999-2000, Gross Domestic Product (GDP) rose from Rs. 41,0646 crores to Rs. 707845 crores in 2006-07. (Quick Estimate). In service sector *i.e.,* trade hotel, transport and communication the share surmountly rose from Rs. 387514 crores in (1999-2000) to Rs. 778895 crores in 2006-07 and to 875398 crores in 2007-08 (Quick Estimate).

**Table 1.1:** Gross domestic product at factor cost by industry of origin

| Year | Agriculture, forestry & fishing, mining and quarrying | Manufacturing, construction, electricity, gas and water supply | Trade, hotels, transport & communication | Financing, insurance, real estate and business services | Public administration & defence and other services | Gross domestic product at factor cost (2 to 6) |
|---|---|---|---|---|---|---|
| 1 | 2 | 3 | 4 | 5 | 6 | 7 |
| | | **At 1999-00 prices** | | | | |
| 1950-51 | 127062 | 30618 | 25409 | 17238 | 23771 | 224786 |
| 1951-52 | 129301 | 32008 | 26097 | 17635 | 24485 | 230034 |
| 1952-53 | 133349 | 31992 | 26940 | 18374 | 24989 | 236562 |
| 1953-54 | 143349 | 34011 | 27943 | 18637 | 25763 | 250960 |
| 1954-55 | 147657 | 36952 | 29738 | 19318 | 26686 | 261615 |
| 1955-56 | 146475 | 41144 | 31907 | 20094 | 27512 | 268316 |
| 1956-57 | 154424 | 44790 | 34262 | 20423 | 28567 | 283589 |
| 1957-58 | 147941 | 44217 | 35392 | 21194 | 29858 | 280160 |
| 1958-59 | 162542 | 47412 | 37206 | 21795 | 31083 | 301422 |
| 1959-60 | 161184 | 50767 | 39532 | 22628 | 32420 | 308018 |
| 1960-61 | 172433 | 56143 | 42885 | 23096 | 34012 | 329825 |
| 1961-62 | 172889 | 60124 | 45687 | 24089 | 35610 | 340060 |
| 1962-63 | 170253 | 63932 | 48421 | 24900 | 38139 | 347253 |
| 1963-64 | 174276 | 70729 | 51833 | 25670 | 40642 | 364834 |
| 1964-65 | 189832 | 75930 | 55287 | 26374 | 43322 | 392503 |
| 1965-66 | 170413 | 78300 | 56385 | 27171 | 45039 | 378157 |
| 1966-67 | 168275 | 81077 | 57880 | 27648 | 47116 | 382008 |
| 1967-68 | 192382 | 83659 | 60424 | 28401 | 48970 | 413094 |
| 1968-69 | 192316 | 87992 | 63485 | 29786 | 51152 | 423874 |
| 1969-70 | 204555 | 95024 | 66613 | 31024 | 53976 | 451496 |
| 1970-71 | 217862 | 96642 | 69816 | 32321 | 56950 | 474131 |
| 1971-72 | 214135 | 99171 | 71445 | 33987 | 59493 | 478918 |
| 1972-73 | 204288 | 102603 | 73226 | 35301 | 61439 | 477392 |
| 1973-74 | 218482 | 103498 | 76297 | 36165 | 63063 | 499120 |
| 1974-75 | 215726 | 104773 | 81054 | 36049 | 66051 | 504914 |
| 1975-76 | 243462 | 111336 | 88357 | 38534 | 68384 | 550379 |
| 1976-77 | 230363 | 121639 | 92449 | 41590 | 70284 | 557258 |
| 1977-78 | 252740 | 130519 | 98356 | 43626 | 72171 | 598885 |
| 1978-79 | 258605 | 140668 | 106338 | 46708 | 75290 | 631839 |
| 1979-80 | 227147 | 135755 | 105939 | 47163 | 80793 | 598974 |
| 1980-81 | 256342 | 141420 | 111997 | 48067 | 84095 | 641921 |
| 1981-82 | 269309 | 151968 | 118888 | 51972 | 85895 | 678033 |
| 1982-83 | 270340 | 152734 | 125343 | 56926 | 92518 | 697861 |
| 1983-84 | 296514 | 165954 | 131718 | 62510 | 95974 | 752669 |

| 1 | 2 | 3 | 4 | 5 | 6 | 7 |
|---|---|---|---|---|---|---|
| 1984-85 | 301144 | 173466 | 138069 | 67182 | 102623 | 782484 |
| 1985-86 | 302970 | 180794 | 149032 | 73741 | 108512 | 815049 |
| 1986-87 | 304012 | 189987 | 158041 | 81510 | 116666 | 850217 |
| 1987-88 | 300271 | 201059 | 166349 | 87487 | 125102 | 880267 |
| 1988-89 | 347344 | 217602 | 176066 | 96024 | 132666 | 969702 |
| 1989-90 | 353038 | 236017 | 189043 | 107962 | 143119 | 1029178 |
| 1990-91 | 368907 | 251868 | 198770 | 114670 | 149357 | 1083572 |
| 1991-92 | 363245 | 251633 | 203897 | 127079 | 153219 | 1099072 |
| 1992-93 | 385685 | 260668 | 215271 | 133999 | 162400 | 1158025 |
| 1993-94 | 397916 | 277143 | 230141 | 148962 | 169654 | 1223816 |
| 1994-95 | 418084 | 302872 | 252876 | 154751 | 173493 | 1302076 |
| 1995-96 | 417378 | 339845 | 286232 | 167276 | 186244 | 1396974 |
| 1996-97 | 455458 | 364725 | 309328 | 177627 | 201241 | 1508378 |
| 1997-98 | 448241 | 376071 | 332580 | 198423 | 213902 | 1573263 |
| 1998-99 | 475201 | 392170 | 358014 | 213902 | 239123 | 1678410 |
| 1999-00 | 488109 | 410647 | 387515 | 23549 | 266707 | 1786526 |
| | | **New Series at 1999-2000 prices** | | | | |
| 1999-00 | 488109 | 410646 | 387514 | 233550 | 266707 | 1786526 |
| 2000-01 | 487992 | 438372 | 415650 | 243048 | 279239 | 1864301 |
| 2001-02 | 516584 | 450723 | 453847 | 260737 | 290715 | 1972606 |
| 2002-03 | 486134 | 481758 | 496691 | 281550 | 302153 | 2048286 |
| 2003-04 | 531302 | 519322 | 556370 | 297250 | 318514 | 2222758 |
| 2004-05 | 535501 | 574072 | 615849 | 323080 | 340266 | 2388768 |
| 2005-06 | 566278 | 635223 | 690399 | 359888 | 364313 | 2616101 |
| 2006-07 | 591353 | 706280 | 778895 | 409472 | 385118 | 2871118 |
| 2007-08(Q) | 619121 | 766358 | 875398 | 457584 | 411256 | 3129717 |

**Source:** Central Statistical Organisation.

P: Provisional estimates. Q : Quick estimates.

**Note:** For the year prior to 1980-81 totals under col. 7 may not add up to totals of individual item under col. 2 to col. 6 due to splicing technique applied independently at the level of each industry and at the total level.

## 5. Promotes Employment Opportunity

Industrialisation promotes employment opportunity. The sectoral employment share by current daily status reflects that in manufacturing sector the percentage was 11.27% in 1983 and it rose to 12.90% in 2004–05, the share of workforce deployed in agriculture declined from 65.42% in 1983 to 52.06% in 2004–05 while the manufacturing sectors share rose marginally. Trade hotel and restaurant sector contributed significantly higher (from 6.98% in 1983 to 12.62% in 2004–05) to the overall employment than in the earlier year (*see* Table 1.2).

**Table 1.2:** Sectorial Employment shares by Current Daily Status (CDS Basis)

| Industry | 1983 | 1993-94 | 1999-00 | 2004-05 |
|---|---|---|---|---|
| Agriculture | 65.42 | 61.03 | 56.64 | 52.06 |
| Mining and Quarrying | 0.66 | 0.78 | 0.67 | 0.63 |
| Manufacturing | 11.27 | 11.10 | 12.13 | 12.90 |
| Electricity, water etc. | 0.34 | 0.41 | 0.34 | 0.35 |
| Construction | 2.56 | 3.63 | 4.44 | 5.57 |
| Trade, hotel and restaurant | 6.98 | 8.26 | 11.20 | 12.62 |
| Transport, storage and communication | 2.88 | 3.22 | 4.06 | 4.61 |
| Fin., Insur., Real est., and busi. service | 0.78 | 1.08 | 1.36 | 2.00 |
| Comty., social and personal services | 9.10 | 10.50 | 9.16 | 9.24 |
| **Total** | **100.0** | **100.0** | **100.0** | **100.0** |

**Source:** Various rounds of NSSO survey on employment and unemployment/Planning Commission.

### 6. Industrialisation Resolves Many Problems

Industrialisation is actually an effort to find out solution to the various problems of poverty, insecurity, overpopulation and backwardness etc.

### 7. Industrialisation and Capital Formation

Industrialisation also helps in boosting capital formation with raising of national and per capita income.

## 1.3.1 Determinants of Industrial Growth

There are various factors determining industrial growth. They can be classified as Economic and Non-Economic factors (*see* chart 2).

**CHART 2**

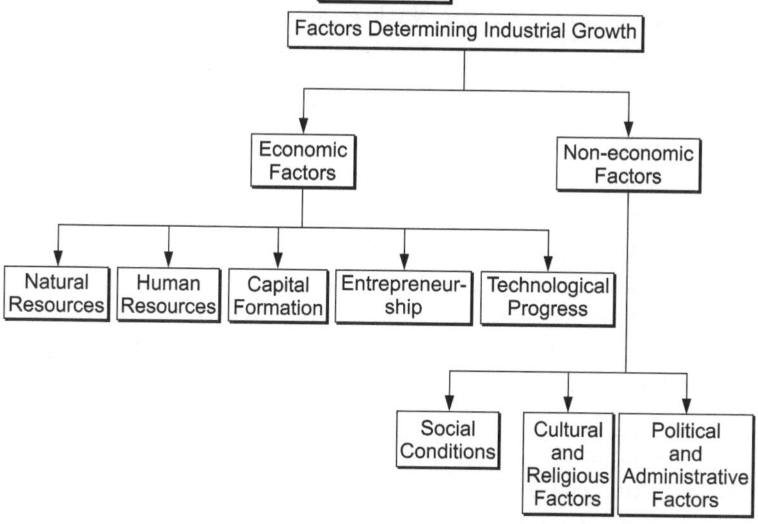

### 1.3.2 Economic Factors

1. **Natural Resources:** Natural resources play an important role in the process of industrialisation .**W.A.Lewis** stated that other things being equal we can make better use of rich resources than we can of the poor"[7]. A country which is rich in its natural resources has a high impetus to promote development although there are countries like Japan which has added a new dimension to the path of industrialisations despite lack of natural resources.
2. **Human Resources:** If population is less with skilled manpower, literate forces then it would result in promotion of industrialisation since human capital formation is the process of increasing knowledge, skill and the capacities of the people of the country. Good human resources backed by skilled literate personnel leads to promotion of industrialisation.
3. **Capital Formation:** Without adequacy of capital industrialisation lays no where Proper banking facility is also necessary since it enables industries to acquire cheap resources for its development. Capital is therefore an impetus to promote industrial growth.
4. **Entrepreneurship:** A good skillful entrepreneur adds to the promotion of industrial rate of growth. Entrepreneur is the chief pivot of any industry.
5. **Technological Progress:** Good, and efficient technique is a determinant of industrial growth. Efficient technology helps to boost up the rate of productivity and economic progress.

### 1.3.3 Non-Economic Factors

Industrialisation is determined not only by economic factors but also by non-economic factors. **Prof. Ragnar Nurkse** said that "Economic Development has much to do with human endowment, social attitude and political conditions and historical accidents". **Richard T. Gill** also expressed the fact that "Economic Development is not a mechanical process it is not a simple adding of assorted factors. Ultimately it is a human enterprise and like all human enterprises its outcome will depend finally on the skill, quality and attitude of the man who undertakes it"[8].

1. **Social Conditions:** These include social organisation and social attitude of the people. Replacing old traditional idea by new innovative thought would initate in the process of progress of the economy. Ideas and promotion of new technological ideas would help to promote industrialisation.

---

7. W.A. Lewis: *The Theory of Economic Growth* p. 52
8. Richard. T.Gill *'Economic Development'* p. 12

2. **Cultural and Religious Consideration:** This also determines the pace of industrialisation. If the attitude of the people becomes optimistic and is nullified by traditional religious thought then growth will take place speedily.
3. **Political and Administration Set up:** A stable government promotes increament of investment and thereby raises the rate of growth. People willingness to invest in an unstable government is less since nobody wants to bear risk.

Thus, both economic and non-economic factors promotes industrialisation.

## 1.4. FACTORS INHIBITING INDUSTRIALISATION/ PROBLEMS

Industrialisation as we have seen so far is the most pivot sector which raises income, standard of livings and promotes economic progress.

The LDC are facing many a problem in their effort to promote industrialisation. Hence, it is necessary to focus our attention on the major obstacles which come to the path of industrialisation.

1. **Under Utilisation of Resources:** Plenty of resources available internally alone cannot speed up industrialisation. Proper use of available resources should be there[9]. Infact, in most of the under-developed countries the rate of industrial growth is poor not because of lack of natural resources but only due to under utilisation of the available resources[10]. Without adequate utilisation of natural resources it is highly difficult for an economy to embark upon bigger industrial projects since it is not always possible to import raw material from other countries. Dependence on foreign resources will prove dangerous in time of crisis. Further problem regarding import of bulky and perishable material may also arise. Therefore, under utilisation of resources stands as a crucial problem.
2. **Low Capital Formation:** The under-developed countries are under-equipped with capital in relation to their population and natural resources [11]. In all the under-developed countries the per-capita income and the per capita real income are very low[12]. This low real income

---

9. Gerald. M. Meir, *The Problem of Limited* ***Economic Development*** *in Economics of under-development* Ed.A.N Agarwal and S.P. Singh, Oxford University Press, 1966 p. 65, 66.
10. Paul .A. Baran, On *political Economy of Backwardness in Economics of Under-development* p. 81.
11. Atan. B. Mountjoy, *Industrialisation in Under-developed Countries,* Hutchinson University, London, 1968, P.24.
12. Kenneth E.Boulding, *The Skills of the Economist,* Hamish Hamish London 1958, pp.106 - 107.

operates itself in a vicious circle. As such low capital formation hinders the process of industrialisation.

3. **Infrastructural Facilities:** Growth of a network of infrastructure like transport, power, communication etc is an essential pre-requisite for rapid industrialisation. But in case of under-developed countries lack of proper infrastructure leads to slow pace of industrialisation. When infrastructure is sound investment rises in industries.
4. **Market Imperfection:** In an under-developed economy since per-capita income is less therefore standard of living too is low. Most portion of the income is spent on fulfilling the basic needs of life that is on consumer goods and less amount of money is left to be spent on capital goods and as such industrial activity is low. Further, information relating to market, market imperfections stands on the path of industrialisation.
5. **Low Level of Technology:** To promote industrialisation, availability of modern technical know-how is essential[13]. **Dewhurst** writes ; "Technology in fact can be thought of as a primary resource"[14]. There is lack of proper technology in under developed countries. They are more labour intensive in technology. Therefore, technical know-how trained personnels are absent from under developed countries. This is a barrier to promotion of industrialisation. Mechanisation is a requisite for promotion of productivity.
6. **Population Explosion:** An under-developed country is inhabitated by dense population. Therefore, it makes use of labour intensive technology. The productive efficiency in these process tends to be lower than that of capital intensive process. Hence, low rate of industrailisation. Further due to large expansion of population saving resources are utilised more in consumer good industry rather than capital good industry Further the quality of the work force in these less developed countries is also poor and this effects productivity.
7. **Problem Associated with Labourers:** If the laboures are illiterate not trained, they fail then to understand the modern technique of production. Further, due to family bondage, mobility is poor and limited. The people from rural belt are attached to their homeland and therefore this restricts their mobility. Further the labourers are under-nourished due to low per capita income in under developed countries. And this effects the productivity of the labour force. All this processes as a hurdle in the path of industrialisation.

---

13. J.A. Schumpeter, *The Theory of Economic Development,* Harvard Cambridge, Massachusetts. 1949. P. 68.
14. J.F. Dewhurst, *America's Needs and Resources: A Survey,* 20th century Fund, New York, 1955 p. 834.

**Prof. A. K . Cairncross** said that "Development is not a matter of having plenty of money nor is it purely an economic phenomena. It embraces all aspects of social behaviour, the establishment of law and order scruplousness in business dealing, including dealings with revenue authorities, relationship between the family, literacy, familiarity with mechanical gadgets and so on"[15]

8. **Lack of Proper Entrepreneurs:** An under-developed country is backed by illiterate enterpreneur who lacks skillfulness and is unable to take quick decision. This effects the working of industry and thereby restricts the growth rate.
9. **Administrative Hurdle:** Bureaucracy, corruption and red tapism in administration lead to wrong decisions being taken. All of these prove as a hurdle to industrialisation.
10. **Political Instability:** In the absence of political stability industrial production would be affected especially in the initial stages of industrialisation, as the masses are apt to organise for political action in their own interest, rapidly working of industry would not be possible. Industrial growth is handicapped by political instability and political disintegration. The policy framed for industrialisation is actually influenced by the philosophy of the prevailing political party. Due to political instability when parties change their philosophies, this also hinders the policies of industrialisation and industrial progress.
11. **Change Social Attitude:** Industrialisation is influenced by the attitudes of the people in the society. But in U.D.C. people are not so ambitious and whole hearted. The aspirations of the people and their efforts should be such as to achieve miraculous industrial progress. Therefore, change in social mind set is essential to raise industrialisation.
12. **International Hurdle:** International situation is an important factor which affects industrialisation. The global economy has been categorised into advanced countries and less developed conuntries. The decisions taken by advanced countries are basically in their own benefit this affects industrialisation. Dependence upon certain industrially advanced countries for capital equipment also implies certain technical disadvantage for less developed countries because plant design and automatic devices may suit more to the conditions of advanced industrial countries than in under developed countries. Restraints may also be exercised by means of Patents taken by the producing concern in industrially advanced countries. The fiscal policies in capital exporting countries may also exercise a deterrent effect on the outflow of industrial capital to U.D.C. The combination of fiscal and exchange controls has probably militated against the foreign financing of secondary industry in less developed countries.

---

15. A.K. Cairncross, *Factors in Economic Development* p. 26.

### 1.4.1 Measures Conducive to Industrialisation

Several measures and policies have been designed to speed up the process of industrialisation their applicability and effectiveness however depending among other things upon its industrial status, its size and resources, the relative incidence of the obstacle and the extent to which governmental policy can help to remove the obstacles. An effective programme of industrial development is likely to require the adoption and simultaneous carrying out of several of the appropriate polices. The various measures conducive to industrialisation can be examined under two heads (*i*) Domestic, (*ii*) International. Under domestic measures steps can be taken up to solve the problems related to the technological improvement, flow of factor of production, improvement of manpower resources etc. While international measures comprise the attitude of industrially advanced countries and the interest taken by international organisations.

### 1.4.2 Domestic Internal Incentive Measures

**I. Accelerating the flow of the factors of production:** The acceleration of the factors of production depends upon:

1. Capital, 2. Entrepreneurial ability, 3. Labour, 4. Raw material and natural resources.

1. **Capital:** Inadequate capital effects the establishment of industry. The shortage of capital is due to low savings and capital formation. Most of the under-developed countries witness inequality in distribution of income. It is essential that every encouragement should be given to institutional developments parallel to industrial development; public debt policy, deficit financing, can help in raising up of income and thereby speeding industrialisation.
2. **Enterepreneurial Ability:** It should be borne in mind that the assumption of the entrepreneurial role to promote industrialisation is a pre-requisite. But in an under developed country the shortage of managerial and entrepreneurial ability is crucial one. Therefore, attention must be given to train the managers and this can be feasible through opening up management institutes and development corporations.
3. **Raw Material and Natural Resources:** Lack of natural resources is an effective barrier to intensive industrialisation. The Government steps to stimulate development of local raw material resources which is likely to facilitate the process of industrialisation.
4. **Labour:** For gearing a labour policy it is essential firstly to promote (*i*) training to labourers and (*ii*) to increase the mobility of workers. Further providing education and making them literate should be extensively be practised. The government can also raise the quality of

the labour force through apprentice training, scholarships and stipends to its trainers. All this would afford good human capital formation. **F.H. Harbinson** said that "Human capital formation refers to the process of acquiring and increasing the number of persons, who have skills, education, experience which are critical for the economic and political developments of the country Human capital formation is thus associated with investment in man and his development as a creative and productive resources[16]". The government therefore needs to establish more institutes to train the labour force in order to promote human capital formation.

### 1.4.3 Improving the Production Technique

The process of industrialisation can be accelerated by establishing optimum size concerns this involves the problems of adaptation since differences in the size of market entails the differences in the scale of operation. The improvement in the technique of production can resolve the hurdles. Along with inventions and innovations, control of drainage of people to abroad can remove the obstacles.

### 1.4.4 Change in Governmental Policy

Government policy have played an important role in promoting and encouraging economic activity. No country has made progress without positive stimulus from intelligent government"[17]. The policies comprise of 1. fiscal policy, 2. credit policy, 3. balance of payment policy, 4. tariff policy, 5. industrial planning.

1. **Fiscal Policy:** (*i*) The formulation of a sound fiscal policy is to bring about an investment in both old and new industries, (*ii*) to discourage speculative activities in unproductive activities, (*iii*) to increase the productivity of various factors of production engaged in secondary industry. Industrial development can be stimulated by means of tax concession to industries.
2. **Credit Policy:** The credit policy need to be regulated carefully by the state inorder to avoid inflationary tendencies. Expansionary Credit Policy acts as a stimulus to better utilisation of resources in under developed countries. The government while granting credit should regulate budgetary and balance of payment consideration so that any undue price rising tendencies generated by industrial programme may be restrained or countered. The monetary policy must regulate unproductive expenditures and regulate the money supply in the right direction.
3. **Balance of Payment Policy:** The initial strain on the balance of payment imposed by an industrialisation growth programme may be

16. F.H. Harbinsons, *Human Resources* in *Development Planning* in *Modernising Economics.*
17. Prof. W.A. Lewis, *Theory of Economic Growth.*

eased by foreign borrowings. The capital must be *invested* in industries contributing to *export promotion.*

4. **Tariff Policy:** A proper tariff export and import policy would also promote industrialisation. Promotion of export industries and import substitution would initate industrialisation.
5. **Industrial Planning:** Industrialisation has played a larger part in the policies of centrally planned economic of under-developed countries Industrial planning means (*i*) balanced development of various sectors of the economy, (*ii*) reasonable rate of industrial growth, (*iii*) order of priority in which industries are established, and (*iv*) extent of industrialisation aimed at.

## 1.5 INTERNATIONAL MEASURES/EXTERNAL FORCES

External forces helping to shape the course and influence the speed of the industrialisation process may be grouped into two classes :

(*i*) The role of international organisations

(*ii*) Industrial countries role to promote industrialisation in less developed countries.

### 1.5.1 Role of Industrial Countries

The industrial countries can influence industrialisation in under developed countries. Through (*a*) International trade, (*b*) International immigration, (*c*) International flow of capital and (*d*) Technical assistance. *Foreign trade* is one of the chief instruments of industrialisation in the hands of under developed countries. Its value for this objective depends directly on the nature of the commodities exported. The volume of export earnings, the currency in which export earnings are realised, the stability of these export earnings the terms of trade, the nature of goods imported. The value therefore depends upon the degree of monetary stability industrialisation was promoted through.

**International immigration, flow of capital and technical assistance:** In the industrial sector most of the assistance scheme has been designed to increase productivity in the existing occupation and industries by helping to improve method, raise quality and lower cost and prices. The international organisation play an important role in the industrialisation of the under-developed countries by producing the direct financial or technical aid , by facilitating the exchange of ideas, by disseminating the lessons learnt by the individual countries in the course of their industrialisation programmes and by engaging in comparative research. The establishment of the World Bank (I.B.R.D.), the International Finance Corporation, the International Development Association, the I.M.F and a special united nations fund for economic development deserves special attention in this connection. The bank advanced loans for basic facilities so that industrialisation may begin on a sound base.

## 1.6 PLANT, FIRM, INDUSTRY

### 1.6.1 Concept of Plant, Firm and Industry

In the present era of time, the size of industrial unit results in determining the *scale of production*. In the economic terminology *size* may be defined as *scale*. it is the scale which determines the cost of production, volume of production efficiency, choice of technique etc. The size is *dynamic* and not static. Generally, at its beginning stage the size is small which later expands to maximum size where it achieves the advantage of large size units. As such to understand the size it is essential to understand firstly various terms *.i.e.,* plant, firm, industry.

**Plant:** According to Sargent Florence the term plant refers of a congregation or body of persons assembling together at a certain time and place. The word 'plant' is synonymous with a factory, a mill, a workshop a mine, a warehouse, retail shop or an establishment. Plant, therefore, refers to a place where goods are produced or services are provided. It is also called as an establishment where utilities are created with the help of land, labour and capital.

**Firm:** A 'firm' is the unit which owns, controls and manages a plant or plants. If an individual or partnership organisation or the company owns one or more mills or factories or in other words plants, the individual or partnership organisation or the company whichever may be the case should from the financial and administrative point of view be regarded as a firm, *a single industrial unit.*

Thus, a firm is an *owner, organiser* and *manager of a plant* or *plants*. It is broad in scope as compared to plant. When a firm owns only one plant the firm and the plants are considered the same thing. Infact, a plant is a producing unit while a firm is an *organising and controlling unit.*

**Industry:** A group of firm either producing similar products or using similar raw material is called industry *e.g.*, cement, sugar industry etc. Sugar Industry means all firms producing sugar and all firms, using sugar cane as raw material. Hence, firm having common bond or using single raw material, or the use of the same process of manufacture. The units which manufacture tyres may form part of the automobile industry as their products are parts of the motor car and at the same time on the basis of the raw matarials they used may form part of the rubber industry. Industries as such have no identities they are simply classification of firms. Industry is therefore, termed as a *group of sellers or* close *substitute output who supply to* a common *group of buyers*". In other words, it is taken in a simpler term as a group of firm producing close substitutes good for a common group of buyers.

### 1.6.2 What is Industry?

Industry means a place where goods are manufactured. Industry includes all those firms or units which are engaged in the manufacture of goods or components of similar nature or which uses the similar raw materials. Industry thus covers such activities which are connected with rasing or producing or processing goods. 'Industry' is a part of business, which is concerned with the production or manufacture of those goods which are used either as finished products by consumers or used as raw material by other enterprises in the furtherance of production.

The **New Encyclopedia Brittanica defines** "Industry as a group of productive enterprises or organisation that produces or supplies goods services or sources of income".

**Sir Dennis Robertson and S. Dennison** defined industry as that which covers the whole series of processes by which desirable things are extracted from the earth, fashioned and transformed by man carried from place to place to place and stored through time and placed in the hands of those who are ready to pay for them."

According to a judgement made by Chief Justice **Shri Krishna Ayyar** in Supreme Court on a judgement on *Bangalore Water Supply* and Sewage Board case given on February 21, 1978". Industry was defined as such a unit where (*i*) Systemative Activity (*ii*) Organised by cooperation between employee and employer (*iii*) For the production/distribution of goods and services calculated to satisfy human wants and wishes (not spiritual or religious but inclusive of material things of services geared to celestial bliss making large scale of prasad or food)".

### 1.5.4 Classification of Industry

On the basis of the nature of industrial activity industry can be classified into various categories (*see* chart 3)

**CHART 3**

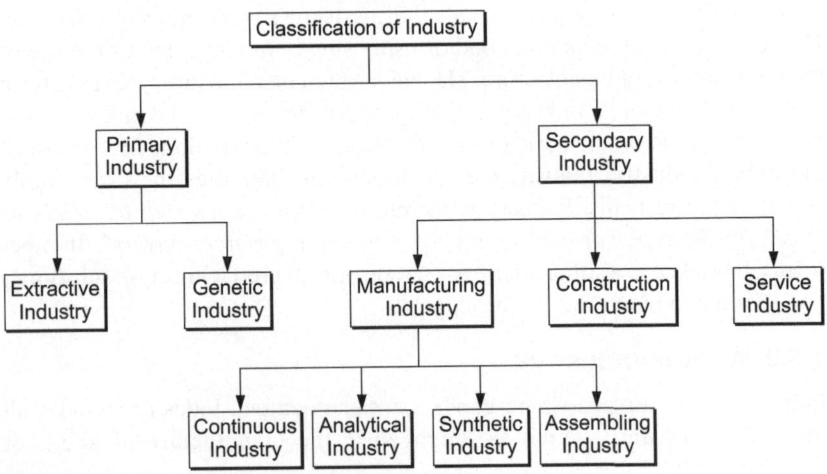

## 1. Primary Industry

Under *primary industry* goods are obtained from the earth, sea and nature. Primary industry comprises of extractive industry and genetic industries. *Extractive industries* are those which are primarily engaged in obtaining commodities either from inside the earth or from the bottom of the sea. Mining of coals, iron ore, crude oil etc and cutting of trees, hunting of animals, catching of fishes etc are included in *Extractive Industries.*

In case of *genetic Industry* it refers to such activities which are basically dependent on nature. In such industries greater amount of manual work is required, land, water, air are the main sources of genetic industry. Production and productivity depend on the application of human skill and knowledge. Forestry, cattle rearing, poultry, dairy farming belong to the group of industry.

## 2. Secondary Industry

Under *secondary industries* goods are manufactured with the help of resources available in nature by changing their form. Manufacturing, construction and service industry belong to this category.

Under *manufacturing* industry, raw material and semi-finished materials are the base of manufacturing industries. Examples include iron and steel plants, flour millsetc. The industry consists of four categories:

(*a*) **Continuous Industry:** In continuous industry, raw materials are turned into *finished goods through one or more processes*. For example, sugar is obtained by processing sugarcane and cotton clothe through processing cotton.

(*b*) **Analytical Industries:** Analytical industries are those in which the basic material is analysed and separated into several parts in order to obtain different finished products. For example, crude oil is analysed, seperated into petrol, diesel oil, kerosene oil, lubricating oil etc. To get different products from one raw material, different processes are undertaken.

(*c*) **Synthetic Industries:** Those industries under which various components or materials are brought together and are combined in the process of manufacture and thereafter quite different finished products are obtained. Thus, for one finished products more than one materials are used. Cement manufacturing, soap making etc are examples of such industries.

(*d*) **Assembling Industries:** Those industries under which different materials or components are brought together and after proper assembling finished products are obtained. Automobiles industry, bicycle industry, fan industry etc are examples of assembling industry.

*Secondary industry* also consists of construction and service industry. Under *construction industry* work is done at one place, Construction products are not taken away to market for sale. Construction of buildings, roads, bridges etc are examples of this industry while in *service industry* it does not produce physical products, its products are non-physical in nature and are intangible, inseperable, perishable, and variable in nature. For *e.g.*, Services provided by hotels, hospitals, banks, insurance companies etc are the examples of services industry.

❑❑❑

CHAPTER 2

# Market Structure

## 2.1 MEANING OF MARKET

Originally, says **Jevons**, a market was a public place in a town where provison and other objects were exposed for sale but the word has been generalised so as to mean any body of persons who are in intimate relations and carry an extensive transactions in any commodity. A great city may contain as many markets, as they are important branches of trade and these markets may or may not be localised. But the idea of locality is not necessary. The traders may be spread over a whole town, or region or a country and yet form a market if they are, by means of fairs, meetings, published price list, the post office or otherwise in close communication with each other[1]. **Cournot**, a French Economist, said, "Economist understand by the term market not any particular market place in which things are bought and sold but the whole of any region in which buyers and sellers are in such free intercourse with one another that the price of the same goods tends to equality easily and quickly". **Sidwick** said that "A market is a body of person in such commercial relation that each can easily acquaint himself with the rates at which certain kind of exchange of goods and services are from time to time made by the other". Market is defined thus as a closely interrelated group of sellers and buyers for a commodity.

Thus, the essentials of a market are:

(*a*) commodity which is dealt with

(*b*) the existence of buyers and sellers

(*c*) a place, be it a certain region, a country or the entire world

(*d*) such intercourse between buyer and sellers that only one price should prevail for the same commodity at the same time

(*e*) equilibrium at a particular price.

1. Quoted by Marshall – *Economics of Industry* pp 134-135

The market may be classified :

(*a*) on the basis of area as local, national, regional, world market.

(*b*) on the basis of time as market price on any particular day or moment, short period price, long period price.

(*c*) on the basis of process of sale via grading, trade marking, and inspection.

(*d*) on the basis of specialization.

(*e*) on the basis of sale as retail or whole sale.

(*f*) on the legal basis as legal market or theft/chor market.

(*g*) on the basis of competition as perfect and imperfect.

## 2.2 MARKET STRUCTURE

By structure of any complex body we mean the pattern or form or manner in which the constituent parts of that body are arranged together. This we can specify in terms of the organisational characteristics which determine the relations:

(*a*) of sellers in the market to each other

(*b*) of buyers in the market to each other

(*c*) of the sellers to the buyers

(*d*) of sellers established in the market to the new potential firms which might enter the market. According to **J.S. Bain**, it means those characteristics of the organisation of a market that seems to exercise a strategic influence on the nature of competition and pricing within the market[2]. The following *main features of the market* structure have even suggested by Bain which are important to understand the concept precisely and to measure it:

1. **The Degree of Seller Concentration:** This is the number and size distribution of firms producing a particular commodity or types of commodities in the market.
2. **The Degree of Buyer Concentration:** This shows the number and size distribution of buyers for the commodities in the market.
3. **The Degree of Product Differentiation:** This shows the difference in the product of different firms in the market.
4. **The Condition of Entry to the Market:** This shows the relative ease with which new firms can join the category of sellers (*i.e.*, firms) in the market.

Apart, from these aspects of the market structure mentioned there will be other characteristics coexisting side by side. They relate to the psychological

2. J.S. Bain, *Industrial Organization*, Hohn Wiley and Sons N.Y., 1968.p 6,7,

technological, geographical or institutional factors present in the market and conditioning the behaviour and performances of the firm. All such characteristics together constitute a set of "the economically significant features of market which affects the behaviour of the firms .... supplying that market[3]. Infact the different dimensions of the market structures will be important as such in determining the behaviour of the firms which in turn will be affecting their performance of the industry as a whole.

Market structure is a multidimensional concept and therefore a set of variables are required to measure it .For instance, if we try to measure market structure with the help of number of sellers we say that it is monopoly market, if two sellers then duopoly, if few than oligopoly and if many then we encounter it with the atomistic market. In each case the process of output and price determination will be different. Similarly, the buyers concentration in the market will have considerable impact on the action of the sellers and their performance. Product differentiation, entry condition in the market play their own roles in the life situation. Thus, in practice a set of variables related to different aspects of it are used simultaneously to measure the market structure.

**The Extent of the Market:** The size of the market depends upon several factors:

1. **The Characteristics of the Commodity:** In order to have a wide market a commodity must be:
   (*i*) portable
   (*ii*) durable
   (*iii*) suitable for sampling, grading and exact description
   (*iv*) such as its supply can be increased such commodities are wheat gold, government-security etc. Bulky articles like bricks and perishable articles like fresh fruit and vegetable have a narrow market.
2. **The Nature of the Demand for the Commodities:** A commodity which is in universal demand will have a wide market. A commodity of general consumption is found to have a wide market.
3. **Development of the Means of Communication:** Transport has enabled things to be carried long distance and has widened the market. Extension of transport system has necessarily led to the extension of the market.
4. **Peace and Security:** The extent of the market depends upon the peace prevailing in the region.

3. R. *Caves American Industry: Structure, Conduct and Performance*, Prentice-hall, Englewood cliffs, 1967.p 16.(2nd *edn*)

5. **Currency and Credit System:** If the currency and credit system are well-developed, marketing can be conveniently and profitably be carried on over extensive areas.
6. **The Policy of the State:** Prohibited duties and quotas restrict the market. The government policy can affect the extent of the market.
7. **The Degree of the Division of Labour:** The greater divison of labour the cheaper the articles and wider the market.
8. **Market Form:** The type of market depends upon the degree of competition prevailing in the market. Broadly speaking there are two possibilities :
   (*a*) Perfect competition
   (*b*) Imperfect competition.

## 2.3 MARKET POWER

This is a term which is used to give the firm or a group of firms a degree of discretion in controlling the prices, the output and the nature of product that it sells. With a high degree of market power the firms will be a wholesole authority in the business, while if competitions is great it would imply less of market power and in case prices moves down to the cost the firms will be a passive entity in the market.

## 2.4 MARKET CONDUCT

The entire process of reacting to the market situation in the pursuit of the desired goal is called *market conduct.* In this the firms follow a pattern in adopting or adjusting to the market in which they operate to achieve the well defined goal or goals. Given the market conditions and the target to be achieved the firm will be acting alone or jointly to decide about the price levels for the products the type of product and their quantities, produced design and quality standards, advertisement etc. The firm has to thus devise the ways for interaction, cross adaption and coordination among the competing group of sellers in the market. All these are elements of market conduct. The choice of the tactics or strategies reflects the behaviour of the firm in the given market situation. Take *e.g.*, duopoly market. Both the firms intended to maximise profit. Now the crucial work is how should they conduct their business? That is how to determine price/output in the market they may either join together/ ignore each other to determine objectives. As such how such strategies need to be chalked out and how to implement them is the task of the management. The entire process of reacting to the market situation in pursuit of the desired goal is called 'Market Conduct'.

The buyers of the industry also reacts to the market situation and adopts a behavioural pattern. Consumerism, a social movement meant to protect the interest of the consumers may be cited as the simple example of the market conduct from the buyers side. Monopoly and its behaviour in the market is another one.

## 2.5 MARKET PERFORMANCES

The index to measure market performances are high profit, high growth rate, increase in sale, capital turnover, rise in employment, rise in social welfare of the people. These variables can help to judge the market performances of the individual firm depending on their respected goals. For the society as whole, the performance of an industry may be judged on the basis of its contribution in increasing the welfare of the masses we may also look at the performances of the industry through its ability to generate employment in the economy.

## 2.6 STANDARD FORMS OF MARKET STRUCTURE

The following chart shows at a glance for different types of market forms.

| S.No. | Type of Market | No. of firms | Nature of Power |
|---|---|---|---|
| 1. | Perfect or Pure Competition | Infinite | Homogeneous |
| 2. | Imperfect Competition | No. of firms | Nature of power |
| | (*a*) Monopolistic<br>(*b*) Oligopoly<br><br>(*c*) Monopoly<br>(*d*) Duopoly | Many<br>Few<br><br>One<br>Two | Differentiated<br>Differentiated<br>Homogeneous<br>Homogeneous<br>Homogeneous |
| 3. | Pure/Absolute Monopoly | No. of firms<br>One | Nature of power<br>Homogeneous |

For each forms we will describe their characteristics and their reliance in the context of the structure conduct-performance relationship.

### 2.6.1 Perfect Competition

Although perfect competition is a rare and non-existant situation yet we study it, **Leftwich** defines it as "the study which furnishes us with a single and logical starting point for economic analysis".

1. **Characteristic:** We speak of a market as being perfectly competitive of the individual firm in that industry *which have no control* over the *price of the commodity, i.e.*, a firm has to take the *prevailing* price as given, which it cannot influence either way by its own action. What a firm does under perfect competition is to adjust its output to the prevailing price. There are infact a *large number of buyers and sellers.*

2. The product of any one seller (*i.e.*, firm) is identical to the product of every other seller in the market. The buyers therefore are indifferent to the sellers. They can buy the product from any one. That is *homogeneity* in products is another characteristic feature of perfect competition.
3. There are no *barriers to entry in the market or to exit from the market.* Sellers and buyers are free to join or leave the market whenever they want.
4. Each seller and buyer must have complete *information about the prices prevailing* in the market nature of product, cost, demand etc. There is absence of advertisment and selling expenses.
5. There are no *artificial restraints* in the market the factors of production are perfectly mobile. No middleman such as wholesalers, brokers, retailers etc. exist under such system the transactions are supposed to be costless.
6. The sellers and buyers are *independent in decision making* there is no collusion of any kind among the sellers or buyers.
7. Since in a perfectly competitive market there is only one single price therefore *no transport* cost is *included* .

The characteristic of perfect competition are quite exhaustive and many of them in reality are not satisfied hence quite hypothetical in nature. Yet it is studied in economic theory since it provides a simple framework to understand a more complex one it gives best norms for the functioning of the economic system.

Now, let us examine how a firm will behave in the situation of perfect competition in the market. Since the market power of the firm is negligible and is not able to influence the prices of the product and its market quantity significantly, the firm will be just "*Price Taker*" in the market and not *Price Maker*". The price of the product will be determined by the interaction of the market demand and market supply curve. The individual firm will accept the price as given and adjust their level of output to the maximum profit situation shown by the equality of price with its marginal cost and average cost. It is for this reason that the individual firm under perfect competition has a price line or demand curve which is perfectly elastic at the ruling price. The average revenue of the individual firm in the competition industry is a horizontal straight line parallel to OX axis as shown in Fig. 2.1. Since a perfectly competitive firm can sell as much as it wants without affecting the prices, addition made to total revenue by an extra unit of output, *i.e.*, marginal revenue is equal to the price (AR) average revenue of the commodity therefore the AR and MR would coincide with each other for a firm under perfect competition. In the Fig. 2.1, if price prevailing in the market is OP, then PL is both the average and marginal revenue curve, MC is the Marginal cost curve. Given at the price OP the firm will fix its output where its profits are maximum. Profits are maximum at that point at which Marginal cost is equal to Marginal revenue (MR), *i.e,.* MC = MR and *MC cuts MR from below.* Therefore, T cannot be the position of equilibrium, at point R or output OM, MC = MR and MC cuts MR from below. Therefore, at point R profits would be maximum and the firm would be in equilibrium position. Therefore, the firm will adjust its output at that point.

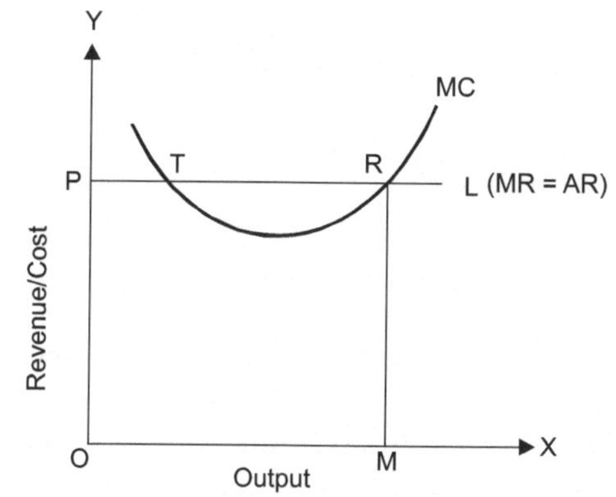


**Fig. 2.1** Market under perfect competition.

Under perfectly competitive market *time element* plays a vital role which thereby limits the conduct of firm. The market behaves in such a way that excepting short run there will be no profit in any other periods and even the existence of profit in short run would be temporary. Infact there will be just *normal profit* which means that both cost and revenue shall equalise with each other and as result there will be only *zero profit* situation in the *long run* and in case if even this is not achieved then the firm will quit away from the market since it never undergoes losses. Thus, if prices happen to be so low that the firm cannot cover even the *variable cost* it should shut *down.* The Fig. 2.2 shows the equilibriums position for the firms having positive profit in the short run under perfect competition $P_1$ is the equilibriums market price determined by the interaction of the market demand and supply curves at $E_1$ point. The individual firm takes this price as given which implies a straight line demand curve parallel to the X axis for the firm. The optimum profit position by point X where price $P_1$ = MC. So corresponding output $OQ_1$ will be the optimum for the firm. The firm will be content with this and earn optimum profit given by the area $P_1$. X. Y. AC, that is, $OQ_1$. XY.

The Segment XY on $Q_1X$ line shows the profit margin over the Average Cost (AC). If AC curve is above $P_1X$ line then there will be negative profit at Price = MC situation.

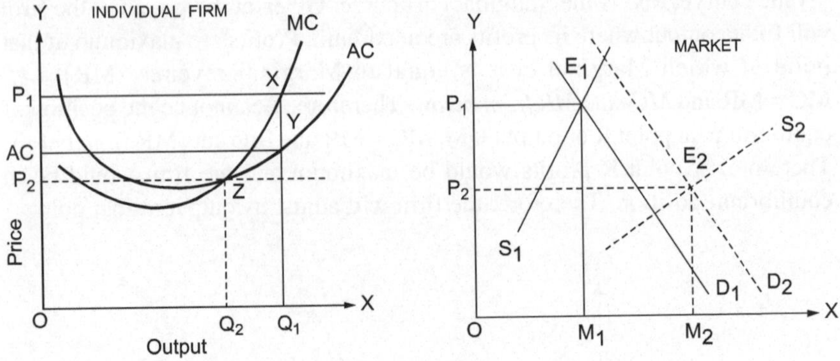


**Fig. 2.2** Equilibrium of the market and individual firms under perfect competition.

The existence of positive profit in the short run situation will attract new firms towards the market (industry) there is no restriction on their joining. By assumptions there are no barriers to entry here. If the number of suppliers goes up, then market supply increases. The supply curve for the commodity shift towards right showing a decline in the prices of the product with the fixed demand curve. The reduction in price reflects reduction in profit margins. However, the process of entry of firm disappears. This is the long run equilibrium situation under perfect competition. In the figure $P_2$ is the long equilibrium price which is given by the interaction of long run demand curve ($D_2$) and supply curve ($S_2$). The supply curve due to presence of a number of firm is flatter. The long run equilibrium for the firm is at lowest point of the AC curve. There is first normal profit The AC curve may shift in the long run showing either increasing cost, decreasing cost or constant cost but the equilibrium will always be at the lowest point of it this point shows the optimum economic efficiency as well as optimum technical efficiency for the firm. There will be just normal profit in the business. If there is negative profit in the short run the process of equilibrium will act in reverse direction that is some firm will leave the market making the supply curve to shift towards left and so an increase in market price. This will again come to a halt at the lowest point of the AC curve.

There will be no profit at all except in the short run but that too will be a temporary situation the zero profit situation implies that the firm will implies only on the basis of normal profit which constitutes a part of the cost production. It will try to maintain its normal profit in the long run if there is no normal profit firm cannot exist in the market. Hence, in the short run MC = MR = Price, while in the long run

$$\text{Price} = \text{MC}$$

$$\text{Price} = \text{MR}$$

$$\text{Price} = \text{MC} = \text{AC}$$

*i.e.,*

$$\text{Price} = \text{MC} = \text{Minimum A.C}$$

## 2.7 MONOPOLY

Monopoly is 'one firm industry' which supplies the goods in the market producing single or differentiated goods which has no close substitutes in the market and above all there is barrier to entry existing in the market. The demand curve is a downward sloping curve. The MR curve lies below AR curve. However, given the AR curve and the AC curve a monopoly firm maximises profits when MR = MC and the MC curve is rising from below. If the monopolist lowers price of his product the quantity demanded of the product rises. In other words, if the monopolist wants to sell a greater output he has to reduce the prices of his product. In that way it is not only the price of the additional unit that falls but the price of his total output goes down. Since his output affects price at which he can sell, price is not a given factor for him as it is under perfect competition. Thus, a monopolist is not free of market forces in establishing price. The monopolist cannot set his prices upward without losing sales and nor he can gain sales without charging a lower price. The monopolist chooses the price quantity combination on the basis of demand and cost situation. The aim of the monopolist like every other producer is to maximise his total profits. In other words he will go on producing so long as additional units add more to revenue than to cost. He will stop at that point at which additional units of production add more to cost than to revenue *i.e.* he will be in equilibrium position at that point at which MR = MC. He will continue producing so long as MR > MC. If this is done profits will increase. At that point where MR = MC, profits will be maximum. If production is carried beyond this point profits will decrease this can be understood through Fig. 2.3.

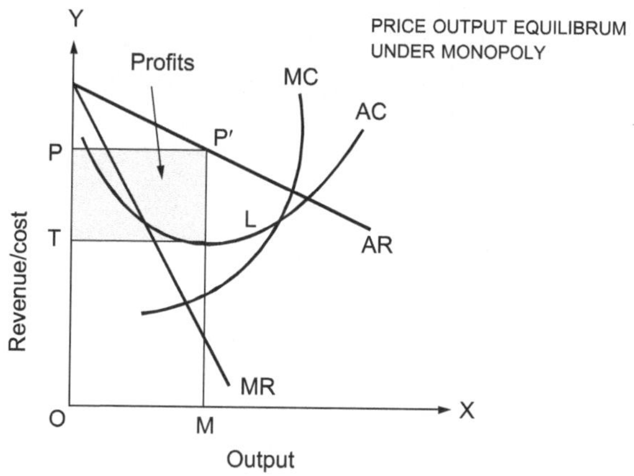


**Fig. 2.3** Equilibrium under monopoly.

### 2.7.1 Price Output Equilibrium Under Monopoly

In the Fig. 2.3 AR is average revenue curve facing the monopolist MR is marginal revenue curve, MC is marginal cost and AC is average cost curve until OM output MR is > than MC but beyond OM, MR < MC (MR is less than MC) therefore, the monopolist will be in equilibrium at output OM where MR = MC and profits are greatest. The price at which OM is sold in the market can be known from looking at demand or AR, corresponding to equilibrium output, *d* or AR curve is MP′ or OP. Thus, the monopolist firm will be in equilibrium at OM and will be charging price equal to MP (= OP).

At output OM while MP′ is the AR curve, ML the average cost. Therefore, P′L is the profit per unit. Now total profits = profit per unit × total output sold

= P′L × OM

= P′L × TL

= P′L TP

Thus, total profit P′LTP is earned by the monopolist.

In a monopoly market the equilibrium of the monopolist will always be at that level of output where the elasticity *or demand for the product is greater than one* provided that his cost are positive. A monopolist never fixes his output at any level where the elasticity of demand is less than one, since total revenue decreases then when output is increased. It is here that MR becomes negative. Since MC cannot be negative therefore monopolist cannot be in equilibrium at these output levels where elasticity of demand is less than one when MC is zero, the equilibrium of the monopolist is established at that output where elasticity of demand is unity, (see Fig. 2.4).

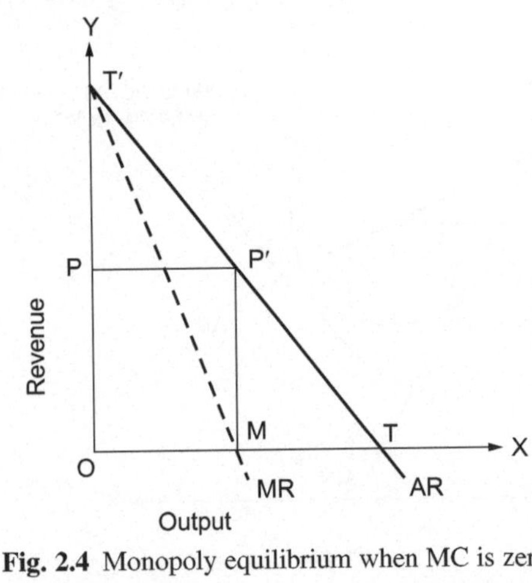


**Fig. 2.4** Monopoly equilibrium when MC is zero.

In this Fig. 2.4 the equilibrium position of the monopolist will be at OM output and price OP (= MP′), at OM output MR = zero. The equilibrium condition is satisfied at *OM*, as in this case we are assuming that MC = 0. P′ is the midpoint of the line TT′ where elasticity of demand is *Unity*, therefore, when MC is zero the equilibrium of the monopolist is established at that output where elasticity of demand is unity. Thus, the analysis so far made was in general and applies both to short and long run. In the *short run* it would be carefully noted that the monopolist has to keep an eye on the variable cost this price must not go below his average variable cost otherwise the production will stop. In the *long run* the monopolist can change the size of the plant in response to changes in demand. In the long run he will make adjustment in the amount of factors fixed and variable so that MR is equal not only in short run but also in long run. In the short run he equities MR with MC but in the long run he seeks to bring equality between MR with long run MC. Which reflects that the scale of the whole firm has been adjusted for misnaming of profits.

Another fact that needs emphasis is that in a monopoly market the entry of the firm is barred basically through permits, license, legal or institutional rights, economies of scale etc.

Whatsoever it needs to be emphasized that from the point of view of society monopoly is an inefficient market where the consumers remain unsatisfied.

## 2.8 MONOPOLISTIC COMPETITION

There is keen competition though not perfect among many firms producing very similar products. It refers therefore to a situation where there are many firms selling a *differentiated product.* E.H. Chamberlin was the first to analyse this type of market structure in detail. The *basic features* of this market are :

### 2.8.1 Basic Features

1. Existence of large number of firms supplying or selling the product.
2. Their is product differentiation.
3. Ease of entry/exit.
4. Each firm acts independently and formulates its own price output policy.
5. Elastic '*d*' curve due to the presence of close substitutes.

The revenue or demand curve of the firm under monopolistic competition is neither perfectly elastic nor rigidly inelastic. The demand for the product of the firm under monopolistic competition is much more sensitive to a relatively small change in price than that of the monopoly firm. A small fall in the price of the firm under monopolistic competition, prices of other firms being

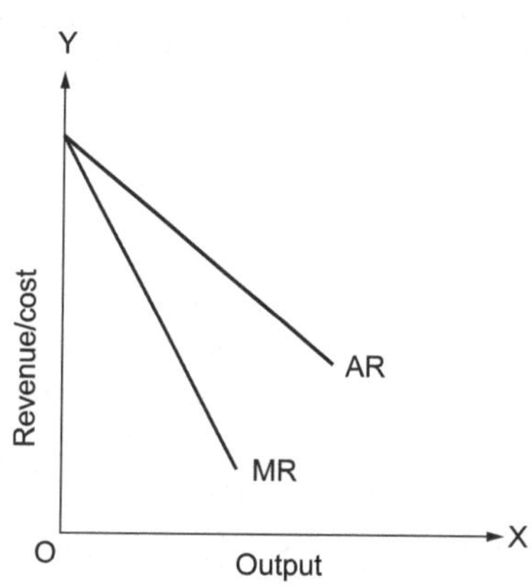


**Fig. 2.5** AR, MR Curve under monopolistic market.

given will result in large increase in the sales of that firm thus the AR curve of a firm under monopolistic competition tends to be quite elastic, further, if the number of firms is large the AR curve of firm will be more elastic. In the figure 2.5, we see that AR does not coincide with MR nor is it parallel to each other. In the monopolist market it is difficult to draw the revenue and cost curve of the industry as a whole since there is no single price ruling in the market what is possible, is to draw the cost and revenue curve of individual firm only. In a monopolistic market product differentiation prevails and as such the movement a firm charges high price, the buyers will leave and move to other firms. The fear of loosing customers restricts the power` of the firm to increase price of its product beyond a certain range.

*Equilibrium of Firm and Indstry under Monopolistic Market* reveals the fact that different firms produce different varieties of product. Therefore, different prices for them will be determined in the market depending upon their respective demand and cost conditions each firm will set price and output of his product. Now the question arises at which price-output level the monopolist competitive firm will be in equilibrium position? The profits in a monopolistic market will be maximised when MR = MC. So long as MR > MC the seller will find it profitable to expand his output and if MR < than MC, obviously it is to his advantage to reduce his output to the point where MR = MC. In the short run therefore, the firm will be in equilibrium when it is maximizing its profit, *i.e.*, when marginal revenue = marginal cost. In the Fig. 2.6, AR is the average revenue curve MC is marginal cost and MR is marginal revenue curve. In the figure MR and MC interest each other at the output OM at which price is [OP′ = MP]. Average revenue is MP and Average cost is MT.

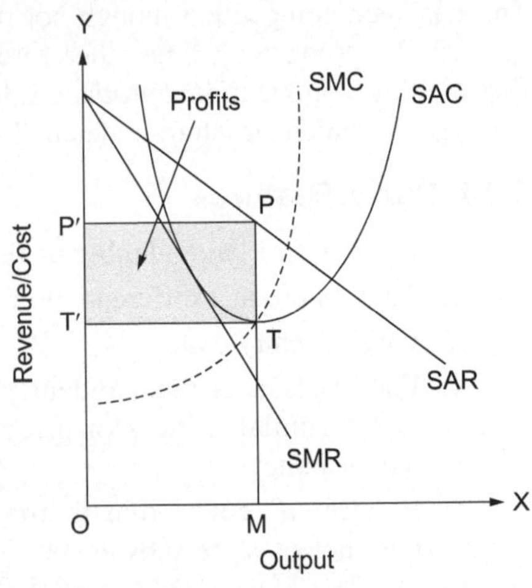


**Fig. 2.6** Short run equilibrium with profits.

Therefore, PT is the abnormal profit point per unit of output. Total abnormal profit will be measured by the area of the rectangle PTT′ P′, *i.e.*, output multiplied by abnormal profit per unit of output.

But if the demand and cost situations are less favourable, then the monopolistically competitive firm will be realising losses in the short run as illustrated in Fig. 2.7. Thus, in the short run the monopolistically competitive firm may either release economic profit or be faced with losses. In Fig. 2.7, we see that AC is MT while AR is MP at output OM. Therefore, the total loss is

P′PTT′. We have seen thus that a firm under monopolists market can earn abnormal profits in the short run. But in the long run such profits disappear. This is because we assume that entry is free and new firms will enter the industry if the existing firms are making abnormal profits. As we see new firms enter and start production the *d* curve or AR curve faced by the firm will fall and therefore the supernormal profits will be competed away and the firms will be earning only normal profits. If in the short run firms are realising losses, then in the long run some firms will leave the industry so that remaining firms are earning only normal profits. Further AR curve in the long run will be more elastic since large number of substitutes will be available in the long run. Therefore, equilibrium is restored in the long run when firms are earning only normal profit. Profits are normal when AR = AC. In Fig. 2.8, AC is tangent to AR curve at point P. Therefore, the equilibrium output in the long run is OM and the corresponding price is MP(= OP). AT this point AC is also MP and so is AR. Therefore, there are no abnormal profits there is only normal profits which form part of the cost of production. In the long run therefore the firm is in equilibrium when output is OM and price is MP(= OP′). Thus in short run only one condition, *i.e.*, MR = MC is prevalent but in long run MR = MC and AR = AC is prevalent.

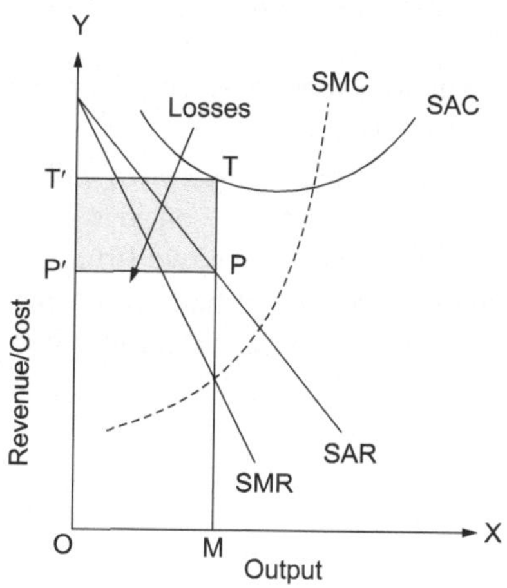


**Fig. 2.7** Short run equilibrium with losses.

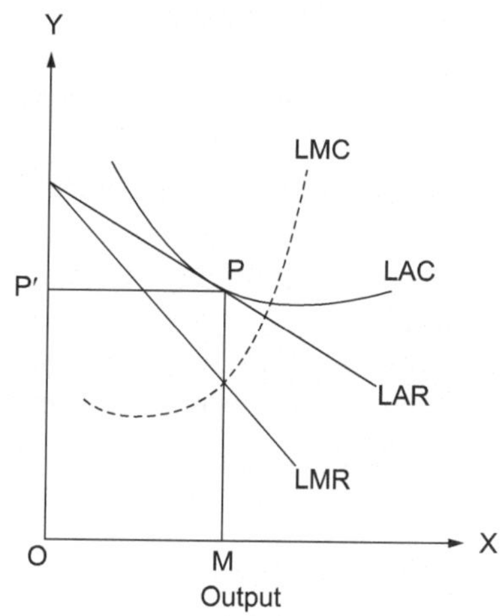


**Fig. 2.8.** Long run equilibrum with normal profit.

One fact that needs emphasis is that in a monopolistic market through product diversification advertisement, arrangements, economies of being established, patents etc. The entry in such industry may be restricted for potential rules and play a vital role under such market situation since every time the firms have to make their produces different from what they were having earlier.

## 2.9 OLIGOPOLY AND OTHER MARKET FORMS

There is another important market structure which is known as *oligopoly*. In an oligopoly market there are more than two or few sellers found in monopolistic competition. The basic characteristics of an oligopolist structure is the fact that every seller can exercise an important influence on the *price output policies of his rivals.* Every seller therefore is so influential that his rivals cannot ignore the likely adverse effect on them of a given change in the price output policy of any single manufacture. The rival consciousness or the recognition on the part of the seller of the fact of interdependence is the most important feature of the oligopolistic situation. The limiting case of the *oligopoly* is called *duopoly* when only two sellers operate in the market. When the product of the sellers under such situation is homogeneous we call it *Pure Oligopoly* but when it is different for different sellers, then it is called *Differentiated Oligopoly.* The essential characteristics which distinguishes oligopoly from others is the recognition of the mutual inter dependence of the sellers decisions. Under *duopoly* the simplest case will be those where the monopolist are supposed to be selling an identical commodity and there is no differentiation of product. Very likely there will be *collusion* between the two. They may agree on a *price or assign quota* or divide the territory in which each is to market his good. This will specially be the case if their respective cost curves are identical or nearly early so and if the demand is stable and less elastic obviously this collusion creates conditions almost analogous to a monopoly and the price determination will be similar to that under monopoly.

In case there is no agreement between the two a constant *war price* will be the cost probable consequences. The important factors to be considered are cost and gain in driving out the rivals, the relative sizes of the two firms, the demand elasticity and the mobility of purchasers, the promptitude with which the rivals react to the changes in the others policy and the extent to which price concessions can be kept secret and so on.

If there is no product differentiation and goods are identical the consumers are indifferent between two producers and the same price must be charged by both in the long run otherwise the one charging more will not be able to sell any. They must fix a price so that they are able to earn profit. In the short run duopoly price may be lower than the competitive price, none of the producers earning normal profit. In the long run this price may be somewhere between monopoly price and competitive price, then there is product differentiation each producer is his own clientele and goodwill. There is no fear of immediate retaliatory measures by rivals if one producer changes his price output policy There is less danger of price-war there will be no agreement between them. Since products are not similar the firm with better products can earn supernormal profit.

Under oligopoly the pricing theory is fundamentally the same with the difference that the larger the number of firms the greater will be the difference in the marginal cost and more remote will be the possibility of collusion or agreement whether tacit or explicit. "The price which will be fixed in oligopoly with out product differentiation is thus indeterminate, but is likely in general to be lower, the larger the number of producers until in the end there are enough for a perfectly competitive equilibrium to be reached".

Price under oligopoly is often stable, it is neither responsive to changes in demand nor to changes in supply. For instance, if demand increases no firm will venture to raise the price for fear that other firms may not raise the price and it may loose the market. Nor will it lower the price for the fear that the other firms may also lower their prices and deprive it of any initial advantage.

Similarly changes in costs, too do not much affect price and output under oligopoly. For instance, if wages have gone down each firm may like to reduce the price but it is not sure if other too will not lower theirs. Under oligopoly the number of firms is very small and any step taken by any one firm is likely to produce some reaction on the others.

Thus, the existence of oligopoly accounts for some of the price inflexibility that characterises our economy. The oligopolist knows that if he raises, the prices, he will loose his customers and if he lowers the price he will offend his rivals. He is content to leave the price and output as they are. As such **Henderson** and **Quandt** in his 'Micro Economic Theory' said that "analytical models based on different behavioural assumption regarding oligopoly and duopoly markets have been developed but none of them has yet taken the form of standard theory of oligopoly"[4].

The most popular solutions for the oligopolist is known *"Kinked Demand Curve Solution"*. There is one particular shape of the demand curve under oligopoly which has become very popular, *i.e.*, the 'kinky demand curve'. This curve is drawn on the assumption that kink in the curve is always at the *'Ruling Price'*. Taking the ruling price as given it assumes that a rise in price beyond the ruling price on the part of a given firm under oligopoly will not *invite retaliation from rivals* who wish to protect their own sales. The result will be if a firm under oligopoly lowers its price it cannot push up its sales very much because the rival firms also follows the suit with a *price cut so that there are no customers to be drawn from the* rivals. Hence, the lower part of the demand curve is less elastic than the upper.

Having drawn the demand curve we can draw the corresponding MR curve just below the point corresponding to the *Kink*. The equilibrium of the

---

4. J.M. Henderson and R.E. Quandt, *Microeconomic Theory* Mc grow Hill Book Co. Tokyo, 1971 pp 222–235
5. Paul. M. Sweezyn '*Demand under Conditions of Oligopoly Journal of Political Economy* , 47, 1938 pp. 568–573 and R.L. Hall and C.J. Hitch, *Price Theory and Business Behaviour in Oxford Economics In His is Paper,* Vol 2,1939, pp12–45.

firm will be at the point where MR = MC since, there is discontinuity in the point where MR = MC Since, there is discontinuity in the MR curve, shifts in the MC curve between point T and S as seen in Fig. 2.9 will not alter the equilibrium position as regards output and prices. This helps to explain an often observed phenomena under oligopoly that despite considerable variation in cost and demand the price under oligopoly often remains unchanged.

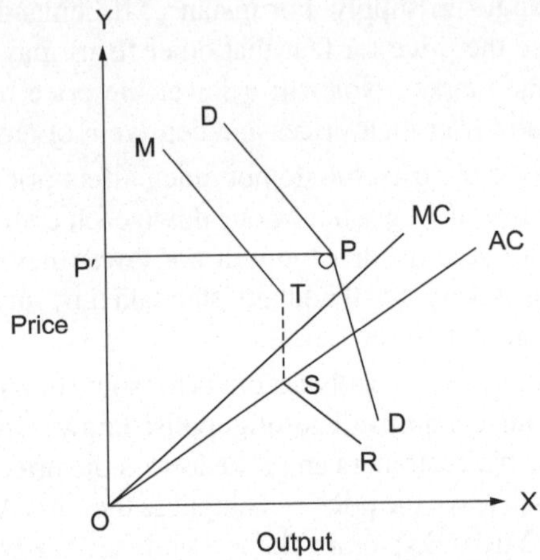


**Fig. 2.9** Oligopoly kinked equilibrium.

The kinky solution as given above is only one of the possible solution of oligopoly pricing and a number of variation are possible. The solution cannot therefore be accepted as a generalised solution since it offers an explanation of *sticky prices* under oligopoly. Here we start with the assumption that the *KINK* is always at the ruling price which is supposed to be therefore already known. But if the price is already known what is there to be investigated? It is thereof a challenge before the economist to study the behaviour of a seller in a meaningful way particularly when there is standard comprehensive theory to support them.

So far, we are looking at sellers behaviour as suppliers of goods and services in the market but they also require input such as labour and capital. How they behave in the market as buyers of input is another side of the market structure of which they are a part. In such case there is Monopsony, Duospony, Oligopsony and Bilateral Monopoly. Under Monopsony the buyer has got the bargaining skill and the sellers who aims at maximising profit as in monopoly while in *monopsony* it is the buyer who aims at maximising consumer surplus and firms the prices on the basis of marginal utility. Thus, *in studying market structure we deal with behaviour of both buyer and seller.*

❑❑❑

CHAPTER 3

# Industrial Location

## 3.1 INTRODUCTION

Planning requires deliberate manipulation of economic and natural resources. In setting up of a factory also a manufacturer has to take three major decisions. They are:

(*i*) the scale of operation, (*ii*) the technique to be adopted which involves the selection of the appropriate combination of the factors of production and (*iii*) the location of an industry.

The choice of location infact is an important factor since it affects the efficiency of production management in general and cost of production, cost of distribution, profitability and productivity of the enterprise in particular. **J. Laundy** said that "Total cost of manufacturing and distribution may vary as much as 10% simply by virtue of the choice of location". According to **Kimball** and **Kimball**, "The most advantageous location is that at which the cost of gathering material and fabricating it plus the cost of distributing the finished product to the customers will be a minimum".

However, a distinction need to be essentially made between three synonymous terms: *Location, Localisation and Planned Location of Industries.*

Entrepreneurs locate their industries in those place where the cost of production is the lowest at the time of their establishment. This is known as *Location* of industries.

The concentration of a particular industry mainly in one area is known as *Localisation* of industry and such localisation may be due to economic reasons and prevalence of external economics. **Prof. Robertson** said that "Localisation is the propensity of particular industries to cling breed and cluster around particular localities."

Planned Location of industry is a term used by **Lord Beveridge** for a policy where by the location of industry is planned to give each industrial area a variety of industry, large industries being dispersed and not localised. Planned location of industry precedes as a first step to develop the country on regional considerations in order to check expansion of industrial cities and areas only in certain regions.

## 3.2 FACTORS AFFECTING LOCALISATION

Location of industries substantially plays a crucial role in influencing the profitability of any industry. Profit maximisation implies cost mininmisation. An enterpreneur therefore has to take a careful decision regarding where the industry needs to be located. In the words of **Shubin**, "In selecting a general location management must investigate the present and future adequacy of markets for the product, sources of raw material , labour, transportation power and fuel supply and proximity both to allied and to necessary services industry. In addition it must consider the climate of the locality the character of the community, local and state tax rates and the advantages of decentralisation".

Thus, there are several factors which pull the industry to a particular place. Some of the major factors influencing location are:

### 1. Availability of Raw Material

In determining the location of an industry neareness to source of raw material is a vital consideration. The cost of raw material forms the bulk of the total cost. The pull towards the source of raw material would be greater in case of industries requiring localised gross material. (*i.e.,* weight losing). It is seen that most of the agricultural forest based industries are located in the vicinity of the sources of raw material supply. For instance, sugar industry is established at the places where sugarcane is available in abundance. Similarly, iron and steel industry is also localised near to the source of raw material.

### 2. Availability of Labour

Availability of labour also influences plant location decision. Every industry requires adequate amount of cheap and skilled labour force the attraction of an industry towards the labour center depends on the ratio of the labour cost to the total cost of production. For instance, since labour with good skill in carpet weaving is available in abundance in eastern belt of Uttar Pradesh, therefore carpet weaving industry is established in Bhadoi in U.P. Availabilty of skilled labour in the interior part of Mumbai region was an important factor responsible for the concentration of Cotton-textile industry in the region. Therefore, low labour cost was a potent factor responsible for locating the industry from centres of high wage cost.

### 3. Availability of Capital

The availability of capital at cheap rate of interest and in adequate amount plays a dominant role in influencing location of industry. Finance, plays a potent role in the establishment and expansion of an industry for instance, in case of jute industry the capital provided by the Scottish enterprise played a dominating role in the establishment of near jute units and in the expansion of the existing jute units in and around Kolkata. Capital is mobile factor of production, it is equally available for use in any part of the country. Capital can be raised both nationally and internationally. Therefore, in location of industrial unit financial consideration do not exercise much influence. However, what needs to be emphasised is that under certain circumstances financial factor may play vital role. For example, the government might influence the banks to withhold financial assistance in case the industries locate their industrial units in congested areas with a view to safeguard nations interest.

### 4. Availability of Power

Power has a vital decisive influence on the location of industries each industry requires cheap power. Water, wind, coal, gas, oil, and electricity are the chief sources of power. Recent development of hydro-electric power to industrial centres is likely to minimise the importance of power as an significant factor in industrial location. After the completion of the Pykara hydro-electric power to be located mainly in the district of Coimbatore, Madurae took the advantage of the new source of power. The pattern of locational distribution of most of the industries has considerably changed with the development of hydro-electricity. In other words, electric power is helping in the dispersal and decentralisation of industries. But an exception to the common rule is iron and steel industry where coal is still one of the chief ingredient. In case of cement industry besides raw material power and fuel also exercises a dominant pull on the location of the industry for they represent around 40% of the total work cost.

### 5. Availability of Proper Transport and Communication Facilities

Transport and communication facilities also affect location of industry. Transport cost influences the cost of production and distribution. Transport in used to bring raw material and components to the plant and is finally used to send finished products to the market. Industry, therefore tends to be established where communication facilities are easily available at a reasonable rate. For example, since Mumbai enjoyed cheap and excellent transport network both in regard to raw material and markets (internal and external) this led to heavy concentration of cotton-textile industry in Mumbai. Similarly transports played a vital role in the establishment of Vishakapatnam steel plant. The existence of a good sea port, the new (Dandarkarnya-Bolinghir-Kirbura) railway line and the proposed rail line from Vishakapatnam to Kothagudem influenced the location of steel plant in Vishakapatnam.

### 6. Proximity to Market

Access to market is another important factor influencing the entrepreneurial ability to plant location. Industries producing perishable goods which cannot be transported over a long distance and industries producing bulky commodities involving heavy transport cost are located in close proximity to markets. Industry producing for local markets are also drawn towards market. Industries located near the market could be able to reduce the cost of transport in distributing the finished products as in the case of bread, bakery, ice industry etc. Accessibility of market is more important in the case of industries manufacturing consumer goods rather than producers goods since they require adjustments constantly with the changes in the habits of the consumers. Industries using pure raw material *i.e.*, raw materials not losing much of their weights if converted into finished products are located near the market such as Brick-making industry, pottery industry etc.

### 7. Soil, Climate and Topography

All these are geographical factors influencing industrial location. Soil and climate has a direct impact on the type of industrial activities. Climate influences the ability and power to work of workers. It raises and detoriates the efficiency to work. For instance, warm climate reduces the efficiency of workers as compared to those who inhabited in cool climatic condition. In cotton textile industry, the humid climate of Mumbai provided an added advantage to the establishment of cotton-textile industry. Further those industries which require adequate and steady supply of water are located near the place of availability of water.

### 8. Sites and Services

Existence of public utility, cheapness of the value of the site, amenities attached to particular site level influences the location of industry to a certain extent. In view of the above, government of India has launched the scheme of developing 'industrial estate' to accelerate area in the country. The main aim of providing industrial estate is to encourage backward region which are not industrially developed. The government therefore tried to provide incentives to entrepreneurs like subsidies, finance at cheap rate of interest, power at cheaper rate, education etc to ensure that new industries will in future be located in order to boost up development of backward area.

### 9. Political Stability

Political stability boosts up growth and prosperity. Political stability ensures a sense of confidence in the heart of entrepreneur to establish and invest money in new industries since investment requires a peaceful state condition.

### 10. Personell Factor

**E.A.G. Robinson** quoted that Mr. Ford started manufacturing motor cars in Detroit because it was his home town. Lord Nuffield selected Cowley because the school in which his father was educated happened to be for sale.

Therefore, it is seen that personnel factors motivate an entrepreneur to establish plants in specific areas. The personal liking and dislikings mainly influences plant location decisions.

### 11. Strategic Consideration

Strategic consideration influences the role of determining industrial location. For instance, during war time a safe location is assuming significance. Industries meant mainly for manufacturing war weapons, explosives should be dispersed to places, far off from the borders so as to see that the enemy fails to do air attack on these industries of key and strategic importance.

### 12. Religious and Social Consideration

A few industries stand to be established near the place of pilgrimage and the centre for social activities *e.g.*, in Varanasi, Haridwar, Rishikesh, Mathura idol making, necklace, shang industries are established. Apart from this other products of religious use are made since they are pilgrimage centres.

### 13. External Economics

External economics also influence locations of industries. External economics arises due to the growth of specialised subsidiary activities when a particular industry is mainly localised at a particular center with port and shipping facilities. External economics could also be enjoyed when a large number of industrial units in the same industry were located in close proximity to one another.

## 3.2.1 Miscellaneous Factors

Historical forces also influences location of industries many times. Development of cotton textile industry provides an example "The cotton textile industry first settled in Lancashire for no particular reason except perhaps that wollen industry was already there and that foreigners were kindly received and Manchester was not a corporation. "Further, the size of an industrial unit also affects the choice of location. Governmental policy also acts as a potent factor in influencing industrial location. Government provides incentives in the form of Tax-Holiday, Tax concession/loans at low rate of interest. In certain specific areas in order to attract the entrepreneurs to establish industries in those backward areas. This is done to ensure balanced regional development.

It may thus be evidently said that the factors governing location are many and complex. Different set of factors are to be taken into account for industries of different nature. **Spreigel and Lansburgh** had remarked that plant location is often the result of a compromise among conflicting social economic, governmental and geographical consideration". What so ever may be the forces governing location decision, the decisions ought to be an ideal one as claimed by **Shubin** when he said that ideal location is one that permits the lowest unit cost in the production and distribution of a product or services".

## 3.2.2 Advantages of Localisation

Localisation thus implies clinging, breeding, clustering propensity of particular industries at a particular place. Localisation is beneficial for various reasons:

### 1. Reputation of the People

When industries concentrate at a particular place it becomes famous for that industry. Aligarh is famous for lock making, Muradabad is famous for utensil while Ferozabad is famous for bangle making industry. So to purchase these goods people flock to these places.

### 2. Availability of Adequate Capital

Localisation leads to concentrations of banks, financial units, insurance companies at specific place. The enterprise working there get easily adequate quantity of capital at a reasonable rate of interest.

### 3. Regular Supply Skilled Worker

Localisation of industries creates huge amount of employment opportunities. People come to these places in search of jobs.

### 4. Use of Modern Technology

Localisation creates congenial atmosphere. It enables the industries to make use of modern machines.

### 5. Better Research and Development Facilities

Research and development activities are promoted by industrial localisation. All the enterprises producing the similar products may set up research and development department collectively and secondly the big enterprises may have a separate facility for research and development.

### 6. Growth of Complementary Industries

Localisation of sugar industry led to the establishment of jaggery industry. Thus, Localisation enables the establishment of complementary industries.

### 7. Development of Transport and Communication

Tertiary sectors also develop and are enhanced due to localisation of industries.

### 8. Full Utilisation of Bye-Products

When several industries are concentrated at one place, waste material would be available which could be utilised properly. Industries based on those waste raw material could be established.

## 3.2.3 Disadvantages of Localisation

Localisation of industry has a number of disadvantages:

### 1. Dependence

When an industry is located in a particular locality, it makes the economy dependent for its requirements of the products manufactured. Such dependence is dangerous in the events of war, depression or natural calamities since the supply of products will be disrupted worsening the state of condition of the whole economy.

## 2. Fear of Depression

When several enterprises concentrates at one place the quantity of production increases. It is not always possible to sell the entire quantity of goods produced. This may create a fear of depression in the minds of the manufacturers.

## 3. Social Problem

Localisation of industries in a particular locality creates many social problems such as congestion, emergence of slum areas accidents, strikes etc. All this adversely affects the efficiency of labour and the productive capacity of the industry.

## 4. Restricted Type of Employment

Where an industry is localised, employment opportunities are limited to a particular type of labour. In the event of a recession in that industry specialised labour fails to get alternative employment elsewhere. Further formations of trade union may force the employers to pay higher wages which may raise the cost of production and adversely affect the industry.

## 5. Diseconomies

Economies of scale may at times due to localisation give way to diseconomies of scale. For Example, There may lie occurrence of power break down, financial stringency demand for high wages leading to rise in cost of productions. All this reduces production.

## 6. Regional Imbalance

Concentration of industries in one region leads to lop sided development of the economy. When one industry is localised in a region it attracts more entrepreneurs who establish other industries there due to proper infrastructural facilities available there. Thus, such regions develop more while the other regions remain backward this results in unbalanced economic growth in the country.

## 7. Lack of Mobility of Workers

When workers get jobs at one place, their willingness to move to another place is restricted, since they are skilled in only one type of job which may not be available at other places.

## 8. Danger of Attack

War attacks are generally made at those places which are industrially rich. This leads to economic loss.

# 3.3 DECENTRALISATION OF INDUSTRIES

In order to overcome the disadvantages of localisation decentralisation is recommended. Decentralisation means dispersal of industries where by an industry is scattered in different regions of the country. Decentralisation not only removes the disadvantages of localisation but is also recommended from strategic and defence point of view. The decentralisation of industry leads to balanced regional development. It leads to development of infrastructural facilities in all parts of the country.

### 3.3.1 Advantages of Decentralisation

There are certain basic advantages of decentralisation they are:

1. **Balanced Economic Development To Remove Regional Imbalances:** When industries are dispersed in various regions of the country it leads to balanced development of all the regions.
2. **Removes Social Degradation:** Since industries get dispersed therefore problems related to development of slum dwellings, congestion, get minimised leading thereby to reduction of social degradation.
3. **Mobility of Workers:** Workers get mobile and not restricted to a particular locality or region.
4. **Strategic View:** From strategic point of view decentralisation is beneficial to the economy. Since industries are not concentrated in a particular belt therefore, attacks when made during war does not disturb the whole economic set up at a time.

### 3.3.2 Dynamics of Industrial Location

It may be noted that the importance of different factors changes with time, place ideally suited for an industry under particular circumstances ceases to be so with changes in the technique of production, means of transport etc.[1] There is correlation between expansion, and dynamics of industrial location. Industrial location in a particular region in a particular period is closely bound up with the particular stage of economic development reached at that particular time. Changes in different factors may bring about a shift in the location of industrial activity. The basic causes of locational change have been classified by **E.M. Hoover**[2] as seasonal, cyclical, secular, structural according to their character and duration.

1. **Seasonal Changes:** Within the limitation of their mobility, producers shift their location to meet changing seasonal condition.
2. **Cyclical Changes:** Such changes are less predictable. They are due to vagaries of business cycle. Cyclical fluctuatiom affect investment, income distribution, relative prices and factor utilisation.
3. **Secular Changes:** Secular changes involve gradual alteration. Growth of population, for instance, affects location of industries.
4. **Structural Changes:** The development of new resources and technique brings changes.

---

1. E.A.G. Robinson, *The Structure of Competitive Industry*, p. 152.
2. E.M. Hoover, *The Location of Economic Activity*, p.145.

## 3.4 WEBER'S THEORY OF LOCATION

**Alfred Weber** was a German Economist who developed a systematic theory on industrial location in 1909 in German language ; which was later translated into English language by **Carl. J. Friedrich**[3] in 1929. It was only after 1929 that the modern and rational thinking on ideal location of industries and later approaches to the theories were taken up when his pure theory became approachable to the people.

His analysis was based on Deductive Method and therefore began with certain general principles and arrived at some individual facts. **Weber**, tried to identify the elements which influences the location of an industry, through a *Cost Analysis*. He tried to classify all these causes which influence the location into broad division.

**Table 3.1:** Factors Determining Industrial Location

| |
|---|
| **1.** Primary causes of regional distribution of industry (Regional Factors). |
| **2.** Secondary causes of distribution of industry (Agglomerative and Deglomerative Tendencies) |

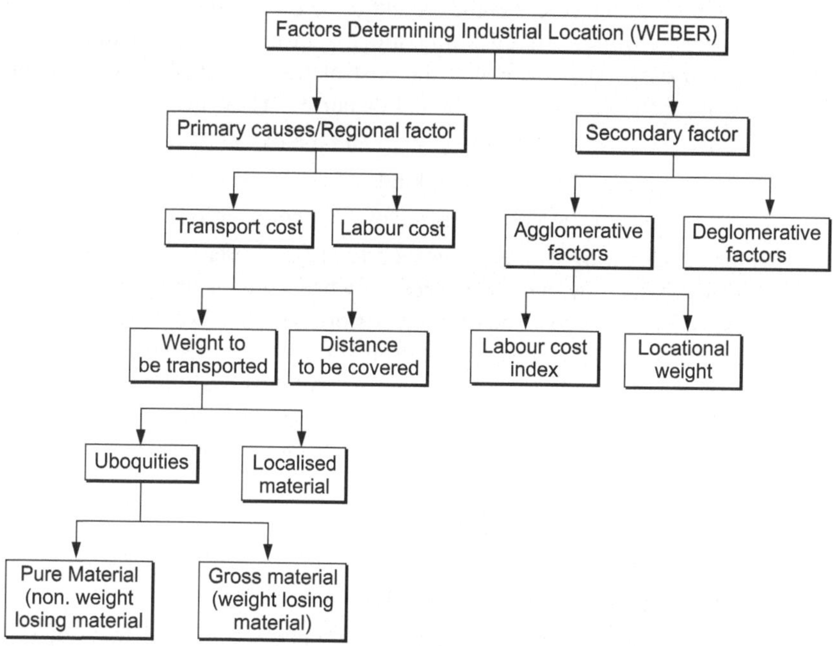


3. Carl. J. Friedrich; *Introduction to A. Weber's Theory of Location of Industries*; University of Chicago Press, Chicago, 1965, p.16.

**Weber** analyses the cost on following grounds:

(*a*) The cost of grounds, (*b*) cost of building machines and other fixed cost, (*c*) the cost of securing material, power, and fuel, (*d*) the cost of labour, (*e*) the cost of transportation, (*f*) the interest rates, (*g*) the rate of depreciation of fixed capital".

**Webers's** *theory* uses both transport and labour cost (regional factors) to locate an industry along with certain agglomerative and deglomerative factors.

This can be seen in Table 3.1.

### 3.4.1 Primary Causes (Regional Factors)

According to **Weber** the two key potent factors influencing location of an industrial unit are:

1. The cost of transportation
2. The cost of labour

#### 1. The Cost of Transportation

Location of an industry will be pulled towards those places which has the lowest transportation cost having regard both for the place of consumption and place of deposit of raw materials. In order to determine transportation cost two factors play a vital role: (*a*) the weight to be transported, (*b*) the distance to be covered. Weber, listed some more factors which influence the transportation cost. "It is clear that the cost of transportation depends upon the following factors besides weight and distance". They are:

(*i*) The type of transportation system and the extent of its use.

(*ii*) The nature of the region and kinds of roads.

(*iii*) The nature of the good themselves *i.e.,* the quantities.

Which besides weight determines facility of transportation"[4] By no means will all the deposits (raw material) necessarily be located nearer to the place of consumption. In such a case the optimal position will be chosen. The location of the place of production must be determined however in some relationship to the place of consumption and to the most advantageously located material deposits. The locational figure, therefore, represents the first and the most important basis for formulating the theory. The locational figure depends upon:

(*a*) The type of material deposit

(*b*) The nature of transformation into products.

Weber further classifies and calls those.

Raw materials as (*i*) *Ubiquities* (*ii*) *Localised Material.*

Ubiquities for example are water, brick , clay etc. These form of raw materials are easily available everywhere while localised example iron ore,

4. *Ibid*- p. 42.

minerals, woods etc. are those form of raw material which are found only in certain region.

Further Weber *categorised the raw material as* (*i*) *Pure* (non-weight losing) and (*ii*) *Gross* (weight-losing) materials. This depended on the nature of transformation of material into products. *Pure materials* impart their total weight to the products (cotton, wool etc) and the materials are said to be weight losing if only a part enters into the product (wood, coal etc). Therefore, those industries using weight *losing material* are drawn towards their place of *deposit* and those industries using pure material *i.e., non-weight losing materials* are drawn towards the place of *consumption*.

Weber, is therefore of the view that the extent to which localised material imparts their weight to the final product is the governing factor on location of industry. The proportion of the weight of the localised material to the weight of the product is known as the *Material Index of an Industry*. The "material index" measures the total weight to be moved. The total weight to be moved in a location figure per unit of the product is termed as "Location Weight" of the respective industry. All industries whose material index is not greater than one and whose locational weight therefore is not greater than two lie at the place of consumption[5], pure materials can never bind production to their deposits.

$$\text{Material Index} = \frac{\text{Weight of the Localised Material}}{\text{Weight of the Finshed Products}}$$

## 2. Cost of Labour

The second potent factor to determine location of an industry is the cost of labour. "The existence of difference in labour cost leads an industry to deviate from the optional point of transport orientation. Labour cost of an industry may differ due to (*i*) differing level of efficiency and of wages of labour (subjective reasons), (*ii*) due to differing levels of efficiency in the organisation and the technical equipment with which the labouring force is set to work *i.e.*, for more or less objective reasoning[6]. The first reason comes within the ambit of regional and geographical factor. Since the rate of wages are determined by the geographical distribution of population such migration of an industry from the point of minimum transport cost to a cheaper labour centre may be likely to occur only where the saving in the cost of labour are larger than the additional cost of transport which it ought to incur.

Thus, a particular place may be the best one for a specific industry on the basis of transportation cost, but the same location may not be suitable on the basis of factor-cost or labour cost because at that location the labour cost may

---

5. *Ibid* p.61
6. *Ibid* p. 96.

lie higher than transport cost Thus, it is seen that cheap labour may also attract the industries location. Weber provided theoretical solutions for this purpose. These are called *'Isodapanes'*. [Isodapanes, is a technical term introduced in analogy to the geographical term 'I sotherm'. 'Isodapanes' means expense or cost] If the actual labour centers lie within the area of such an 'Isodapenes', then migration of the industry takes place because it will result in economy more than to compensate. The extra transport cost involved. The labour location to attract the location of an industry is dependent on two important factors:

(*i*) Locational Weight, (*ii*) Labour Cost Index.

### 3.4.2 Locational Weight and Labour Cost Index

Locational weight depends on total weight per unit to be transported during the stages of production while index of labour cost depends on amount of labour cost per ton of product. This can be revealed as:

$$\text{Labour Cost Index} = \frac{\text{Labour Cost}}{\text{Weight of the Product}}$$

Labour cost index shows the average cost of labour required to produce one unit weight of output. In other words, it reveals the per unit or per ton labour cost and the weight of the product. Higher the labour cost index the greater the possibility of industry to move from the location of the least transport cost.

Locational weight refers to the weight to be transported in the whole process of production or manufacture. The proportion of labour cost and locational weight is expressed as "*Labour Coefficient*".

$$\text{Labour Coefficient} = \frac{\text{Labour Cost (Perunit)}}{\text{Locational Weight}}$$

Weber, thus said that for any industrial unit labour coefficient acts as a determining factor of location the higher the labour coefficient the greater would lie the tendency of an industrial unit to locate near the labour centres.

### 3.4.3 Secondary Factors (Agglomerative and Deglomerative Factor)

According to **Weber** location of an industry also depends upon certain secondary factors that is agglomerative and deglomerative factors. "An agglomerative factor is an advantage or a cheapening of production or marketing which results from the fact that production is carried on to some considerable extent at one place while deglomerative factors is a cheapening of production

7. A. Weber op.cit p.126.

which results from the decentralisation of production (production in more than one place)[7]. Agglomerative factors cause concentration of industries at one place. When there is concentration of industries it leads to prevalence of external economies *i.e.*, is it relates to:

(*i*) Prevalence of machines and other technical components.

(*ii*) Availability of repair and replacement facilities.

(*iii*) Availability of necessary skilled labour for specific industries.

(*iv*) Availability of organised markets both for procuring raw materials and distributing finished products.

(*v*) Availability of better banking facility etc.

Deglomerative factors lead to 'dispersal of industries'. These factors are also known as external diseconomies'. External Diseconomies relate to:

(*i*) Increase in local taxes.

(*ii*) High cost of land.

(*iii*) High wage rates.

(*iv*) Rise in rent.

(*v*) Problem of housing.

Infact, due to diseconomies cost of production rises and therefore in order to reduce cost of production a process of dispersal of industries to less developed area begins. This is Deglomeration.

Thus, it can be seen that *Agglomeration promotes concentration while Deglomeration promotes decentralisation* of industries.

Thus *Agglomeration factors further* depends on

1. *Index of manufacture* (*i.e.,* proportion of manufacturing cost to the total weight of the product).
2. *On Locational weight* (the total weight to be transported during all the stages of production).

To deduce a general principle Weber uses the concept of coefficient of manufacture which is the ratio of manufacturing cost to the locational weight Agglomeration is encouraged with high coefficient of manufacture and Deglomeration with low coefficient of manufacture.

### 3.4.4 Split in Location

Productive activities could be divided depending upon the nature of raw material, industry and market. Weber considers the location of an industry at more than one place. "Single location of production will be the exception and a split of production into several locations will be the rule for productive process which can technically be split. Hence, split in location is only possible if different stages of production can be technically carried on at different places independently. For instance, the first stage of production is near the raw material deposit and subsequent stage would be near the place of final consumption.

Paper industry represents split in location where the manufacture of pulp is carried on near the supplies of raw material and the second stage of paper manufacturing near the consumption outlet.

## 3.5 LOCATIONAL COUPLING

**Weber** conceives for several reasons that different types of industries in the same locality is feasible. The production of quite different articles may be combined in one plant because several raw material may diverge from a common source. For instance, chemical industry, garment industry manufacturers of overcoats, shawls etc. Locational coupling arises due to connections through materials. If the bye-product of an industry happens to be the raw material of another industry then two industries may select a single place of location. For instance, to utilise molasses which is a 'By-product' of sugar production the distilleries are invariably located near sugar factories. It is seen that market connections between two industries will bring about 'Locational Coupling'. In other words, product of an industry may enter into another industry without being used as material or half finished product. For *e.g.*, the main product and the wrapping material are brought together only for packing the main product. To put in a nutshell, there is no organic connection between the two except that connection to link the market of the one with the other.

## 3.6 CRITICISM OF THE WEBER'S THEORY OF LOCATION

Alfred Weber's theory received criticism at the hands of **Sargent Florence, Andreas Predohl, S.R. Dennison,** and A. Robinson on various grounds:

1. **Unrealistic Approach:** According to Sargent Florence Weber's analysis is based on unrealistic approach and deductive reasoning. According to *Florence vague* generalisation cannot provide solutions to the theory of location of industry as non-economic consideration also influences location, which are not mentioned in 'pure theory' Weber's analysis lacks explanation regarding location both from historical and social forces.
2. **Illogical Theory: Andreas Predohl** criticised Weber analysis as a selective theory. He said that the distinction made between primary and secondary factors in itself is artificial, illogical and arbitrary.
3. **Transport Cost Basis an Unrealistic Criterion:** Weber's analysis concentrated on only two elements of cost of transportation that is weight to be transported and the distance to be covered. In reality, several other factors also influence the cost of transportation such as the mode of transportation. Weber made use of 'Tons-Miles' to express transport cost.

4. **Artificial Notion:** Austin Robinson said that Weber's analysis makes a distinction between raw material as ubiquities and localised material. This is however an artificial analysis
5. **Labour Concept Unrealistic:** Weber assumes in his analysis regarding labour orientation two things-*firstly*, fixed labour centres and *secondly*, unlimited supplies of labour. The assumption regarding unlimited labour supply is irrelevant, further rise of industry would create new labour centers.
6. **Concept of Consumption Wrong:** In a dynamic economy enhancing competitive market structure to assume that there are fixed points of consumption does not seem correct. **Austin Robinson** is of the view that the consumption centres provided cause as well as the effect for the location changes.
7. **Lacks Price Consideration:** According to **Dennison**, the analysis of Weber's analysis is overburdened with technical consideration and coefficients. He said that any investigation of this type should infact be based on cost and price considerations that is it should measure the labour cost in monetary terms rather in terms of 'tons miles'
8. **Ignores Dynamic Factor:** Weber's analysis in based on a given condition ignoring the fact that location depends also on a set of dynamic conditions

## 3.7 CONCLUSION

Alfred Weber's deductive theory on location inspite of the shortcoming is the only theory which has been enjoying the universal acceptance and application as all the other alternative suggestions are neither complete nor comprehensive. The contribution of **Andreas Predohl** is perhaps the best on the subject.

Thus, although Weber's theory has been criticised yet it is an important land-mark in the history of economic studies. **R. Balakrishna** remarked that "It would be more profitable to give up some of the unreal assumptions of the Weber's deductive theory rather than to discard it altogether".

## 3.8 MODIFICATION TO THE PURE THEORY

The assumption of transportation cost which is considered unreal as only distance to be covered and weight to be transported are taken requires modification. The actual rate schedules must be consulted relating to different transport media to make the concept of transport orientations more appropriate. Further transport cost should be better expressed in 'actual cost instead of 'ton-miles'.

Labour centres being fixed should receive modification since labour is mobile. Existence of unstable wage levels in the labour centres should be taken into consideration.

The contention that Weber's technique are full of technical coefficient and can never be eliminated if calculations are introduced in terms of cost and prices wherever practicable.

## 3.9 SARGENT FLORENCE'S INDUCTIVE ANALYSIS

**Sargent Florence** offers a mode of inductive analysis. He did not accept the popular meaning of localisation that is "a relation of an industry to an area is not so important as the relation of the industry to the distribution of the occupied population as a whole"[6]. Sargent Florence has introduced two new concepts in the terminology of the theory of location namely:

" *Location Factor*" and *"Coefficient of Localisation"*

### 3.9.1 Location Factor

It is an index of the degree of concentration of an industry in a particular place. This index is arrived at by taking the percentage of all workers in a particular industry found in a certain region and diverting it by the proportion in that particular region of the total industrial workers in the country. The region chosen would be the political division of a county since a division into industrial zones is not feasible even though it might be more scientific. The underlying idea of such an index is that location should be explained as the degree of dissimilarity between the geographical distribution of the industry and the population of the country. If an industry is evenly distributed over the whole country the location factor for each region would be unity because the proportion of the total industrial workers of the region would be equal to the proportion of workers in a particular industry. In case industry is not evenly distributed the location factor will be either above or below unity. When it is above unity the region is supposed to have a higher share of the industry than what is legitimately due to it. On the other hand if it is below unity the region is not supposed to have a sufficient share of the industry.

**Coefficient of localisation:** It indicates the propensity of an industry to concentrate. Though it refers to a particular industry it is not in relation to a region. On the other hand it is in relation to an industry's tendency for localisation any where in the country. It can be worked out for an industry from the census of production by the following formula :

When workers are divided up region by region as percentages of the total in all regions, the coefficients is the sum (divided by 100) of the plus deviation of the regional percentage of workers in the particular industry from the corresponding regional percentages of workers in all industry. Complete coincidence region by region of the particular industry with all industries gives a coefficient of zero, extreme differentiation (*e.g.*, workers in the particular industry being all concentrated in one region) gives a figure approaching 1 (one).

---

6. Sargent Florence, *Investment, Location and Size of Plant*, p.34

The object of arriving at such an index is to classify industries according to their qualities of dispersion or concentration. On the basis of the coefficient of localisation all industries of a country can be divided into three categories of high, low and medium coefficient of industries. Thus, the locational significance of industries is shown and the problem of investigation becomes easier. Industries having low-coefficient of localisation like coal mining and other mineral industries are centralised in particular regions.

It is interesting to note that industries with high/low coefficient of localisation show little tendency to deviate particularly the former as they are predominantly localised near the sources of raw material. The latter, though greatly influenced by shifts in centres of population and consumption are usually evenly distributed over the whole region.

## 3.10 CRITICAL ASSESSMENT

1. The indices given by Florence only reveal the existing state of distribution of industries in a particular country. They are incapable of explaining the reasons for a particular form of concentration. Besides they cannot throw any light on the question of a correct allocation of industries among different regions. Thus, they fail to act as a guide in framing any policy for the future location of industries in a country.
2. The coefficient of localisation is based essentially on the pattern of distribution in each country. So that it would vary from country to country according to local conditions. It is merely difficult to determine on the basis of the coefficient whether an industry has a tendency for concentration or not. At best it can have only verification value. Therefore, inherent tendencies of an industry for concentration should also be examined.
3. The location factor is not always a sure guide of the degree of concentriation since it is based on the number of industrial workers employed in each area. A better basis of comparison may be the output in each area since differences in the efficiency of production may exist among the various industrial centres involving varying properties of labour employed by them. In terms of industrial concentration the output basis is more scientific than the employment basis.

The indices prepared by Florence are of immense significance for studying the locational dynamics in any country. The studying of coefficient of location help in deciding the types of industries that may be dispersed under a scheme of regionalism. Industries with a medium coefficient of localisation can be diversified over a wide area according to factor equipment in each region.

## 3.11 BALANCED APPROACH

During recent years industrial location has received closer attention. Interest has been taken in the study of locational dynamics not only for analysing the present framework of industrial orientation but also for formulating a realistic policy of locational coupling. There is a need for some kind of regional planning of industry which should aim not only at maximum efficiency of an industrial unit but also at an optimum distribution of industrial activity based on broader economic, social and strategical consideration. The reconciliation of the two apparently incompatible objectives is essentially due to the changing position and functions of the state in relation to economic system the growing disposition to look beyond narrow profit and loss consideration to the broader welfare aspect and the consequent demand for more conscious economic planning at the highest national level. In the past what was in the interest of each entrepreneur was considered to be in the best interest of the community as a whole. But now-a-days no such assumptions are made.

❑❑❑

CHAPTER 4

# Dispersion and Problem of Regional Imbalance in India

## 4.1 INTRODUCTION

The main problem faced by most of the countries is of regional imbalances and of the regional inequalities. Both developed and under-developed countries are victimised by a process of regional imbalances. In our country regional variations are present, we see that there are some states which are economically advanced while some are backward and even within each state some regions are more developed while some are undeveloped. As such the coexistence of this form is *termed as Regional Imbalance. Regional imbalances may therefore be inter-state or intra-state, total or sectoral.*

Regional imbalances may be natural when due to unequal natural endowments or man made in the sense of neglect of some regions and preference of other for investment and development effort *Economic backwardness of a region is indicated by symptoms like high pressure of population on land excessive dependence on agriculture leading to high incidence of rural employment, absence of large-scale urbanisation, low productivity in agriculture and cottage industries.*

## 4.2 BALANCED REGIONAL DEVELOPMENT—ITS OBJECTIVE IN TERMS OF INDUSTRIALISATIONS

Sound economic policy is very important for the harmonious development of a country. It is only by assessing the needs of the country that a development plan could be worked, but in a planned economy location of industry is an important factor in the creation of a climate for speedy development and acceleration of economic growth. At the same time it is also necessary to highlight the need for dispersal of industries On strategic grounds a parallel factor to meet the requirement of decentralised development[1] or on social and

1. J.R. Khurana, *Location of Industries and National Security*. The Economic Times 29th March, 1970.

economic grounds. Regional development as a matter of fact becomes a vital part of the Indian Economic planning. In other words this is the *sine-qua non* of planned economy on rational lines. Excessive concentration of industries in certain regions is a serious malady of the Indian Economy. In order to avoid this the device of Regional planning is resorted. "The extremely localised character of industrial activity presents a serious stumbling block to the smooth performance of a National plan .... super imposed on the national plan and becoming part of it there must be a regional plan in each area for dealing specially with the large local residue of unemployment". *Regional development may therefore lead to the distribution of employment opportunities in an equitable basis.* And they are not let to confine only to a handful of states which are creating gaps in the per-capita income among different regions. *National integrity may be affected with the regional disparities in their prosperity.*

Planned utilisation and conservation of scarce resources and exhaustible resources in the good interest of the nation is of prime importance in any type of economy. All efforts should be made through regional development to secure maximum efficiency in the utilisation of available resource rather than the adjustment of rival claims of different areas to achieve their own aim and ambitions. Hence, inter-provincial jealousies are detrimental to the execution of regional plan[3]. Any conflict that may arise in the sectional plans which are complementary to the national plan, should be reduced in the interest of the progress of the nation.

As such regional development aims to bring *even development of the economy there by curbing lop-sided development.* Certain social objectives may therefore be attained through sectional or regional planning. They may include the levelling of inequity in the per-capita income, the avoidance of emigration of labour and upliftment of backward regions. The very idea behind regional planning is the arresting of growth of agglomeration which will create a few industrial centres or towns which in their turn give rise to housing problem, insanitary climate, moral degradations etc. So there is a persuasive case for 'Balanced Growth' for diversification but within carefully considered limits.

Briefly speaking we may pinpoint the fact that Balanced regional development is essential for harmonious development of under-developed country due to the following reasons:

1. To maintain political stability.
2. To overcome social evils.
3. To develop and conserve resources.
4. To accelerate economic growth.
5. To reduce inequality in income.
6. To promote employment opportunity.

---

2. J.R. Bellerly, *Economic Reconstruction,* p. 287.
3. R. Balakrishana, *Regional Planning in India,* p. 73.

## 4.3 INDICATORS OF REGIONAL IMBALANCE

1. **Per Capita Income:** It is commonly used in assuming the economic position of states. Inter-state disparities in levels of agriculture growth and industrial development have contributed to difference in the growth of per-capita income. States like Punjab and Harayana have achieved high rate of agriculture productivity due to high proportion of area irrigated and high level of fertiliser used. The per-capita income of Bihar is at bottom and that of Punjab at the top. The regional disparities instead of being reduced are widening.
2. **Population Below Poverty Line:** The population below poverty line also creates regional imbalance. Due to strong production base the percentage of poverty in states of Haryana and Punjab is low.
3. **Electrification:** Power is a necessary pre-requisite for development and the states in which the power development process is not proper, they find obstacles in growing rapidly. Some states even today do not have cent per cent electrification, for example states like Assam, Bihar, Rajasthan and Arunachal Pradesh are lagging behind in this field.
4. **Agriculture Output Per Capita:** The agriculture production yield and techniques also differ widely from regions to region. States like Punjab and Haryana have progressed in agriculture production while states like Assam, Orissa, and Nagaland still use primitive methods of production.
5. **Urbanisation:** It is an important indicator of economic development. Percentage of Urban population was higher in states like Maharashtra, Tamil Nadu, Gujarat and Karnatka but lower in states like Orissa Assam, Nagland and Himachal Pradesh.
6. **Transport and Communication:** Another important indicator of regional imbalances is disparity found in availability of facilities relating to transport and communications, banking, insurance, public health and education. States like Punjab, Haryana, Maharashtra are well endowed with these facilities whereas regions like Assam, Bihar, Orissa are deficient in the same.
7. **Industrialisation:** The level of industrialisation attained by different states is also different. In Bihar, Orissa, M.P., Rajasthan share of industries in total income is low, *i.e.*, (between 10 to 12%) whereas it is high in Maharashtra, Bengal, Punjab. The heavy dependence on agriculture has opposed the industrialisation.
8. **Lack of Finance:** Lack of finance is another hindrance in the smooth development of any region. Financial institutions feel shy to finance various development activities schemes on account of non-recovery of their fund. As a result these regions remain backward.

9. **Political Pressures:** It has been correctly observed that political parties interfere in the process of development. Infact they want to bring catchy projects in their area only to influence the vote bank. This type of interference hinders the needy development of an area.

## 4.4 CAUSES OF ECONOMIC BACKWARDENESS AND REGIONAL IMBALANCES

There are certain deterrent factors which come in the way of rapid development of region most important of these are geographical isolation, inadequacy of economic overheads like transport, labour, technology etc. Let us now analyse some of these factors:

1. **Historical Causes:** It has been assumed that regional imbalance started occurring even since the British Rule. Britishers settled first in Mumbai, Kolkata, Chennai and therefore these states developed first. Maharashtra and West Bangal which also possessed potential form of manufacturing and trading activities required generous attention from British Industrialist and Businessman and made progress in this field.
2. **Encouragement by Government:** Government encouraged in the form of incentives, credit and other facilities to the entrepreneurs to attract maximum investment such that those regions go ahead leaving other states behind which lacked the special governmental attention. Therefore, encouragement by the government was responsible for regional planning of a region.
3. **Natural Causes:** Some regions owe their progress to nature. Punjab has rich fertile land while Rajasthan lacks this. Cities like Mumbai, Chennai and Kolkata basically developed due to their geographical location, on the other hand hilly areas remained backward owing to their topographic features.
4. **New Technology of Agriculture:** The use of new agriculture technology is very much responsible for widening inter-regional disparities. Those states like Punjab, Haryana, U.P and some parts of Tamil Nadu adopted new technology which led the states to progress.
5. **Attitude and Qualities of People:** Wherever people are skillful, and hardworking; states become progressive as compared to those states in which people lack these qualities For example, Punjab, Haryana, Maharashtra are more proficient in business than that of Bihar and Orissa.
6. **Infrastructure:** The regions in which infrastructure is sound has developed fast, as against those states which lacks good infrastructures.

## 4.5 ESTIMATES OF REGIONAL DISPARITIES

The Economic and *Scientific Research Foundation* showed that over the decade 1960–67 agricultural income from crop production registered a very high growth rate in case of already developed states. The national average agricultural income showed an increase of *142.6%, Punjab topped with growth of 224.2%, followed by Haryana 223.5%, Gujarat 203% and Rajasthan 200%.* The rate of increase in Mysore, Orissa, Jammu and Kashmir and Kerala was also more than the national average while all other states were below the national growth rate.

Another estimate was made by *Economic Times* regarding *poverty* in different states. It revealed that nine states had more than 48.13% of their population below the poverty line in 1977–78. These states were Orissa, Tripura, M. P., Bihar, West Bengal, Tamil Nadu, Assam, U.P. and Karnataka. The richest state Punjab with per-capita Net, State Domestic product of Rs. 2,278 had the lowest 15.13% of its population below poverty line followed by Haryana which had 24.84%.

"**Prof Raj Krishna** *made six categories of state disparities as such:*

(*i*) Indices of Income, Poverty and Unemployment.

(*ii*) Agricultural Indicators.

(*iii*) Industrial Indicators.

(*iv*) Infrastructure Indicators.

(*v*) Social Service Indicators.

(*vi*) Resource allocation indicators.

There is gross imbalance in the regional location of Industries in the country. The major industrial states of India are Maharashtra, Tamil Nadu, Gujarat, West Bengal and Andhra Pradesh. They jointly accounted for 40% of total location of large industries, 55% of total industrial employment, 59% of total industrial output and 57% value-Added. On the contrary of all other states and Unions territories jointly accounted the remaining 60% of total location of large industries 45% of employment, 41% of output and 42% of value. Added. Therefore, the present trends showed that *industrial rich state* achieved *higher rate of progress* while others remained backward and there is uneven spatial distribution of industries. However the states like Punjab, Haryana, Kerala and Karnataka have recorded remarkable progress in small scale sector (*see* Tables 4.1, 4.2, 4.3). These tables reveal disparities.

**Table 4.1.** Concentration of large scale industries in a few large cities

| **Industries** | **Main metropolitan centres around which development took place.** |
|---|---|
| (*i*) Textile machinery | Ahmedabad<br>Baroda<br>Mumbai<br>Kolkata |
| (*ii*) Machine tools | Bangalore and Pune |
| (*iii*) Telecommunication and electronics | Bangalore and Hyderabad |
| (*iv*) Railway coaches | Chennai and Bangalore |
| (*v*) Automobiles companies, jeep | Mumbai<br>Kolkata<br>Chennai<br>Pune |
| (*vi*) Precious Instrument | Mumbai and Kolkata |
| (*vii*) Electrical goods | Chennai<br>Pune<br>Mumbai<br>Kolkata<br>Delhi |
| Small machineries | Mumbai<br>Delhi<br>Chennai |
| Locomotive | Chittaranjan and Jamshedpur |
| Defence equipment scooters etc | Kanpur<br>Pune<br>Chennai<br>Mumbai |
| Diesel engines | Pune |
| Pharmaceuticals | Baroda and Mumbai |
| Basic industries | Kota and Rourkela |
| Fertiliser and antibiotics | Delhi<br>Pune<br>Mumbai<br>Ahmedabad. |

**SOURCE:** K.V. Sivayya and V.B. M. Das, *Indian Industrial Economy*, p.155

**Table 4.2.** Net State Domestic Product at Current Prices

| Sl.No. | State/UT | 1999-2000 | 2002-2003 | 2003-2004 | 2004-2005 | 2005-2006 | 2006-2007 | 2007-2008 | 2002-2003 | 2003-2004 | 2004-2005 | 2005-2006 | 2006-2007 | 2007-2008 |
|---|---|---|---|---|---|---|---|---|---|---|---|---|---|---|
| | | (Rs. Crore) | | | | | | | (% Growth) | | | | | |
| (1) | (2) | (3) | (4) | (5) | (6) | (7) | (8) | (9) | (10) | (11) | (12) | (13) | (14) | (15) |
| 1. | Andhra Pradesh | 116966 | 152066 | 173275 | 188855 | 210772 | 240261 | 279483 | 6.64 | 13.95 | 8.99 | 11.61 | 13.99 | 16.32 |
| 2. | Arunachal Pradesh | 1497 | 1920 | 2193 | 2549 | 2598 | 3020 | 3266 | –2.09 | 14.22 | 16.23 | 1.92 | 16.24 | 8.15 |
| 3. | Assam | 32011 | 39394 | 42927 | 47513 | 52390 | 57378 | 62852 | 12.25 | 8.97 | 10.68 | 10.26 | 9.52 | 9.54 |
| 4. | Bihar | 46097 | 59337 | 59742 | 66085 | 70966 | 86424 | 98373 | 13.34 | 0.68 | 10.62 | 7.39 | 21.78 | 13.83 |
| 5. | Jharkhand | 30229 | 32827 | 36528 | 44588 | 47538 | 54472 | 60548 | 9.09 | 11.27 | 22.07 | 6.62 | 14.59 | 11.15 |
| 6. | Goa | 5570 | 7008 | 8050 | 10039 | 11703 | 13284 | 15065 | 13.80 | 14.87 | 24.71 | 16.58 | 13.51 | 13.41 |
| 7. | Gujarat | 92541 | 118130 | 142534 | 155184 | 180271 | 208211 | na | 16.05 | 20.66 | 8.88 | 16.17 | 15.50 | na |
| 8. | Haryana | 47345 | 66414 | 75949 | 85832 | 97180 | 118995 | 140457 | 10.50 | 14.36 | 13.01 | 13.22 | 22.45 | 18.04 |
| 9. | Himachal Pradesh | 12467 | 16751 | 18127 | 20300 | 22488 | 24797 | 27542 | 10.10 | 8.21 | 11.99 | 10.78 | 10.27 | 11.07 |
| 10. | J & K | 13533 | 17400 | 18992 | 20724 | 22623 | 24747 | 27100 | 12.58 | 9.15 | 9.12 | 9.16 | 9.39 | 9.51 |
| 11. | Karnataka | 90532 | 105895 | 114230 | 136733 | 163412 | 174742 | 203703 | 7.08 | 7.87 | 19.70 | 19.51 | 6.93 | 16.57 |
| 12. | Kerala | 61359 | 75853 | 84720 | 95552 | 107583 | 123366 | 140889 | 11.61 | 11.69 | 12.79 | 12.59 | 14.67 | 14.20 |
| 13. | Madhya Pradesh | 72655 | 76661 | 90871 | 93654 | 101939 | 113221 | 123230 | –1.11 | 18.54 | 3.06 | 8.85 | 11.07 | 8.84 |
| 14. | Chattisgarh | 23840 | 27825 | 33823 | 39055 | 48328 | 56934 | 68045 | 9.40 | 21.56 | 15.47 | 23.74 | 17.81 | 19.52 |
| 15. | Maharashtra | 217198 | 258987 | 294471 | 333147 | 375915 | 437035 | na | 9.85 | 13.70 | 13.13 | 12.84 | 16.26 | na |

| (1) | (2) | (3) | (4) | (5) | (6) | (7) | (8) | (9) | (10) | (11) | (12) | (13) | (14) | (15) |
|---|---|---|---|---|---|---|---|---|---|---|---|---|---|---|
| **16.** | Manipur | 2954 | 3142 | 3564 | 4058 | 4477 | 4726 | 5044 | 4.25 | 13.43 | 13.86 | 10.33 | 5.56 | 6.73 |
| **17.** | Meghalaya | 3211 | 4310 | 4723 | 5138 | 5617 | 6162 | 6707 | 6.24 | 9.58 | 8.79 | 9.32 | 9.70 | 8.84 |
| **18.** | Mizoram | 1410 | 1933 | 2083 | 2181 | 2398 | 2629 | 2887 | 10.33 | 7.76 | 4.70 | 9.95 | 9.63 | 9.81 |
| **19.** | Nagaland | 2556 | 4382 | 4699 | 4980 | 5255 | na | na | 13.11 | 7.23 | 5.98 | 5.52 | na | na |
| **20.** | Orissa | 38200 | 44208 | 54047 | 62497 | 68576 | 81392 | 92603 | 7.65 | 22.26 | 15.63 | 9.73 | 18.69 | 13.77 |
| **21.** | Punjab | 61094 | 73513 | 79640 | 86250 | 97386 | 109459 | 122049 | 3.14 | 8.33 | 8.30 | 12.91 | 12.40 | 11.50 |
| **22.** | Rajasthan | 74174 | 76605 | 98236 | 102376 | 112145 | 128997 | 145125 | –5.29 | 28.24 | 4.21 | 9.54 | 15.03 | 12.50 |
| **23.** | Sikkim | 765 | 1078 | 1209 | 1356 | 1539 | 1746 | 1990 | 12.76 | 12.15 | 12.16 | 13.50 | 13.45 | 13.97 |
| **24.** | Tamil Nadu | 119704 | 138242 | 153858 | 177201 | 200302 | 229896 | 254268 | 5.22 | 11.30 | 15.17 | 13.04 | 14.77 | 10.60 |
| **25.** | Tripura | 4496 | 6223 | 6990 | 7648 | 8712 | 9533 | na | 5.67 | 12.33 | 9.41 | 13.91 | 9.42 | na |
| **26.** | Uttar Pradesh | 156809 | 182652 | 200463 | 217577 | 242156 | 271750 | 303228 | 8.48 | 9.75 | 8.54 | 11.30 | 12.22 | 11.58 |
| **27.** | Uttarakhand | 11187 | 16248 | 18009 | 20794 | 22781 | 25868 | na | 16.69 | 10.84 | 15.46 | 9.56 | 13.55 | na |
| **28.** | West Bengal | 125299 | 153831 | 173106 | 190245 | 208145 | 240775 | 274897 | 6.68 | 12.53 | 9.90 | 9.41 | 15.68 | 14.17 |
| **29.** | A & N islands | 838 | 1110 | 1258 | 1382 | 1527 | na | na | 14.91 | 13.33 | 9.86 | 10.49 | na | na |
| **30.** | Chandigarh | 3792 | 5969 | 6881 | 8163 | 9616 | 11266 | 13248 | 18.20 | 15.28 | 18.63 | 17.80 | 17.16 | 17.59 |
| **31.** | Delhi | 50930 | 65546 | 72709 | 82529 | 94282 | 109238 | 125700 | 10.19 | 10.93 | 13.51 | 14.24 | 15.86 | 15.07 |
| **32.** | Pondicherry | 2929 | 4450 | 4886 | 4512 | 5404 | 6231 | 7002 | 16.74 | 9.80 | –7.65 | 19.77 | 15.30 | 12.37 |
| **All-India GDP(99-00 base)** | | **1605104** | **2010938** | **2258122** | **2548660** | **2902074** | **3342347** | **3811441** | **7.57** | **12.29** | **12.87** | **13.87** | **15.17** | **14.03** |

Source: For Sl. No. 1-32 — Directorate of Economics and Statistics of respective State Governments (as on May/0/2009) and for All-India — Central Statistical Organisation. Economic Soruey, 2008-09, P.A–12.

**Table 4.3.** Per Capita Net State Domestic product at Current Prices

| Sl.No. | State/UT | 1999-2000 | 2002-2003 | 2003-2004 | 2004-2005 | 2005-2006 | 2006-2007 | 2007-2008 | 2002-2003 | 2003-2004 | 2004-2005 | 2005-2006 | 2006-2007 | 2007-2008 |
|---|---|---|---|---|---|---|---|---|---|---|---|---|---|---|
| | | (Rupees) | | | | | | | (% Growth) | | | | | |
| (1) | (2) | (3) | (4) | (5) | (6) | (7) | (8) | (9) | (10) | (11) | (12) | (13) | (14) | (15) |
| 1. | Andhra Pradesh | 15507 | 19568 | 22041 | 23755 | 26226 | 29582 | 34063 | 5.04 | 12.63 | 7.78 | 10.40 | 12.80 | 15.15 |
| 2. | Arunachal Pradesh | 13990 | 17124 | 19322 | 22185 | 22335 | 25639 | 27398 | –3.06 | 12.84 | 14.82 | 0.68 | 14.79 | 6.86 |
| 3. | Assam | 12282 | 14421 | 15487 | 16900 | 18378 | 19857 | 21464 | 10.43 | 7.39 | 9.12 | 8.75 | 8.05 | 8.09 |
| 4. | Bihar | 5789 | 6934 | 6857 | 7454 | 7871 | 9432 | 10570 | 11.77 | –1.12 | 8.71 | 5.60 | 19.83 | 12.07 |
| 5. | Jharkhand | 11549 | 11835 | 12951 | 15555 | 16327 | 18423 | 20177 | 7.26 | 9.43 | 20.11 | 4.96 | 12.84 | 9.52 |
| 6. | Goa | 42296 | 48839 | 54577 | 66135 | 74925 | 87570 | 96076 | 10.72 | 11.75 | 21.18 | 13.29 | 16.88 | 9.71 |
| 7. | Gujarat | 18864 | 22683 | 26922 | 28846 | 32991 | 37532 | na | 14.43 | 18.69 | 7.15 | 14.37 | 13.76 | na |
| 8. | Haryana | 23229 | 30413 | 34099 | 37800 | 41997 | 50488 | 58531 | 8.63 | 12.12 | 10.85 | 11.10 | 20.22 | 15.93 |
| 9. | Himachal Pradesh | 20806 | 26627 | 28333 | 31198 | 33954 | 36781 | 40134 | 8.21 | 6.40 | 10.11 | 8.83 | 8.33 | 9.12 |
| 10. | J & k | 13816 | 16739 | 17991 | 19337 | 20799 | 22426 | 24214 | 11.45 | 7.48 | 7.48 | 7.56 | 7.82 | 7.97 |
| 11. | Karnataka | 17502 | 19621 | 20901 | 24714 | 29185 | 30847 | 35555 | 5.79 | 6.52 | 18.24 | 18.09 | 5.69 | 15.26 |
| 12. | Kerala | 19461 | 23482 | 25995 | 29065 | 32450 | 36907 | 41814 | 10.47 | 10.70 | 11.81 | 11.65 | 13.73 | 13.30 |
| 13. | Madhya Pradesh | 12384 | 12303 | 14306 | 14471 | 15466 | 16875 | 18051 | –3.10 | 16.28 | 1.15 | 6.88 | 9.11 | 6.97 |
| 14. | Chattisgarh | 11629 | 13002 | 15515 | 17513 | 21290 | 24647 | 28955 | 6.84 | 19.33 | 12.88 | 21.57 | 15.77 | 17.48 |
| 15. | Maharashtra | 23011 | 26063 | 29165 | 32481 | 36090 | 41331 | na | 8.25 | 11.90 | 11.37 | 11.11 | 14.52 | na |

| (1) | (2) | (3) | (4) | (5) | (6) | (7) | (8) | (9) | (10) | (11) | (12) | (13) | (14) | (15) |
|---|---|---|---|---|---|---|---|---|---|---|---|---|---|---|
| **16.** | Manipur | 13260 | 13250 | 14728 | 16433 | 17770 | 18393 | 19258 | 2.16 | 11.15 | 11.58 | 8.14 | 3.51 | 4.70 |
| **17.** | Meghalaya | 14355 | 18208 | 19702 | 21170 | 22852 | 24766 | 26636 | 5.60 | 8.21 | 7.45 | 7.95 | 8.38 | 7.55 |
| **18.** | Mizoram | 16443 | 20896 | 21963 | 22417 | 24029 | 25682 | 27501 | 7.55 | 5.11 | 2.07 | 7.19 | 6.88 | 7.08 |
| **19.** | Nagaland | 13819 | 20407 | 20821 | 20998 | 21083 | na | na | 7.63 | 2.03 | 0.85 | 0.40 | na | na |
| **20.** | Orissa | 10567 | 11788 | 14252 | 16306 | 17707 | 20805 | 23403 | 6.44 | 20.90 | 14.41 | 8.59 | 17.50 | 12.49 |
| **21.** | Punjab | 25611 | 29316 | 31182 | 33158 | 36759 | 40566 | 44411 | 1.27 | 6.37 | 6.34 | 10.86 | 10.36 | 9.48 |
| **22.** | Rajasthan | 13619 | 13128 | 16507 | 16874 | 18141 | 20492 | 22649 | –6.88 | 25.74 | 2.22 | 7.51 | 12.96 | 10.53 |
| **23.** | Sikkim | 14890 | 19428 | 21476 | 23791 | 26628 | 29788 | 33553 | 12.15 | 10.54 | 10.78 | 11.92 | 11.87 | 12.64 |
| **24.** | Tamil Nadu | 19432 | 21828 | 24084 | 27509 | 30847 | 35134 | 38573 | 4.24 | 10.34 | 14.22 | 12.13 | 13.90 | 9.79 |
| **25.** | Tripura | 14119 | 19059 | 21138 | 22836 | 25700 | 27777 | na | 3.76 | 10.91 | 8.03 | 12.54 | 8.08 | na |
| **26.** | Uttar Pradesh | 9749 | 10648 | 11458 | 12196 | 13315 | 14663 | 16060 | 6.53 | 7.60 | 6.44 | 9.18 | 10.12 | 9.53 |
| **27.** | Uttaranchal | 13516 | 18636 | 20312 | 23069 | 24870 | 27800 | na | 14.81 | 8.99 | 13.57 | 7.81 | 11.78 | na |
| **28.** | West Bengal | 15888 | 18776 | 20872 | 22675 | 24533 | 28073 | 31722 | 5.12 | 11.16 | 8.63 | 8.20 | 14.43 | 13.00 |
| **29.** | A & B islands | 24005 | 29830 | 32670 | 34640 | 36984 | na | na | 10.85 | 9.52 | 6.03 | 6.77 | na | na |
| **30.** | Chandigarh | 44502 | 63840 | 70434 | 79562 | 89034 | 99262 | 110676 | 16.42 | 10.33 | 12.96 | 11.91 | 11.49 | 11.50 |
| **31.** | Delhi | 38727 | 45123 | 48628 | 53639 | 59555 | 67054 | 75000 | 7.34 | 7.77 | 10.30 | 11.03 | 12.59 | 11.85 |
| **32.** | Pondicherry | 30865 | 44331 | 47778 | 43303 | 50900 | 57596 | 63524 | 14.54 | 7.78 | –9.37 | 17.54 | 13.16 | 10.29 |
| **All-India Per Capital NNP** | | **15881** | **18885** | **20871** | **23198** | **26003** | **29524** | **33283** | **6.20** | **10.52** | **11.15** | **12.09** | **13.54** | **12.73** |

**Source:** For Sl. No. 1-32— Directorate of Economics and Statistics of respective State Governments (as on May/01/2009) and for All-India — Central statistical Organisation Economic Soruey, 2008-09, P.A–13.

## 4.6 REGIONAL DISPARAITY AND ECONOMIC PLANS

Balanced development of all regions and state is necessary to draw available human and material resource throughout the country into the development process and to enable people in all regions to share the benefits of development. It was seen that though in the *First-plan* problem of regional disparities got *no attention* it was the *Second plan* and *Third plan* which gave importance to see that industries should be located in less developed area.

*In 1968, National Development Council* considering the problem of Regional Imbalances recommended the following criteria for the identification of industrially backward states and union territories:

1. Total per capita Income together with the contribution of Industry and mining.
2. Number of workers in factories per lakh of population.
3. Per capita Annual consumption of electricity.
4. Length of surfaced roads in relation to population and area of the state.
5. Railway mileage in relation to the population and the area of the state.

*The National Development Council appointed two working groups (a) The Pandey working grouping to identify industrially Backward states and (b) The Wanchoo working group to recommend fiscal and financial incentives for starting an industry in Backward area. Let us analyse their reports.*

### 4.6.1 Pande Committee Report

The Pande Committee has laid down the following criteria for the identification of industrially backward states as well as backward district:

(*i*) Total per capita income.

(*ii*) The per capita income from industry and mining.

(*iii*) Number of workers in registered factories.

(*iv*) Per Capita annual Consumption of electricity.

(*v*) Length of surfaced roads in relation to the population and area of the state.

(*vi*) Railway mileage in relation to the population and the area of the state On the basis of the above criteria the committee has identified the states of *A. P. Bihar, M. P., Orissa, Rajasthan, U. P., Assam, Jammu and Kashmir, Nagaland, as backward. Coming to the district level the committee recommended the following criteria for the identification of backward districts.*

1. District beyond a radius of about 80 km to large cities or large industrial projects.
2. Poverty as indicated by low *P. C. I.*
3. High density of population in relation to utilisation of productive resources and employment opportunities.

4. Low percentage of population engaged in secondary and tertiary activities.
5. Low percentage of factory employment.
6. Low utilisation of economic and natural resources like minerals and forest and
7. Adequate availability of electric power, transport, and communication and water.

The Pande committee further desired that these criteria be made applicable only to backward districts in Backward states. The distinction by this committee between backward state and backward areas in developing states was not accepted by the planning commission though it was agreed for the purpose of grant of incentives that backward states should select two districts for development whereas a developed state should select only one. The limitation of available fund was obviously the deciding factor.

### 4.6.2 Wanchoo Committee

The Wanchoo committee recommended the following *fiscal incentives for industries set up in backward areas.*

1. Grant of higher development rebate.
2. Exemption from income tax including corporate tax for five years after providing the development rebate.
3. Exemption from import duties on plant, machinery and components.
4. Exemption from excise duties for five years.
5. Exemption from sales tax both on raw material and finished products for five years from the data of going into production.
6. Grants of transport subsidy for the dispatch of finished products for five years. (No subsidy has been recommended upto a distance of the 640 km) and the subsidy has been recommended only in areas of difficult communication.

*The Central government after considering the recommendation of the Pande and Wanchoo committee announced two schemes in 1971 for providing financial assistance and transport subsidy to the Entrepreneurs intending to establish industries in the selected backward areas*. Simultaneously, the national financial institution also decided to offer finances at concessional terms for units establishing industries in backward regions.

The industrial policy 1956, stated thus that 'The lack of industries in different parts of the country is very often determined by factors such as the availability of the necessary raw material or other natural resources. A concentration of industries in certain areas has also been due to the ready availability of power water supply, transport which have been developed there. Since then development of backward areas and regional disparities has continued to be one of the principal objectives of industrial policy of the Government of India.

Eighth five years plans documents stated that some sign of improvement in certain less advanced states have been observed. Regional, disparities continue to exist even in eighties. Development institutions and organisational capabilities in the backward regions of the country and the delivery system for development programs would need to be strengthened to deal effectively with the problem of development and redistributive justice.

To take the problem of regional imbalances and backwardness a *three fold strategy* was adopted by the Indian planning commission. They were:

1. The recognition of backwardness as a factor to be taken into account in the transfer of financial resources from the centre to the states.
2. *Special area development programme formulated* for the *development of backward* areas.
3. Measure to promote private investment in backward areas. Let us discuss the three-fold strategy in detail.

## 1. Transfer of Resources to Backward Areas

The resource transfer relates to central assistance for state plans-transfers effected under the recommendation of the finance commission, adhoc transfers from the centre to the states the distribution of long-term and, short-term credit from financial institution. The share of backward states in plan outlay and in central assistance steadily rose from 48% in the first plan to 57% in the third plan since then share of backward states in central plan assistance has been declining to 50% in the fifth plan, 46% in the sixth 37% in the eighth plan. The tenth plan has further projected a decline to 36% Refer to Table 4.4. Many states demanded that the proportion of central assistance should be raised to 25% from 10%.

**Table 4.4.** Central assistance to state plans (1980–2007)

| Plans | Total assistance in in all states (Rs crores) | Total Assistance to backward states (Rs. crores) | Percentage of assistance to backward states |
|---|---|---|---|
| Sixth plan (1980–85) | 16,560 | 7,590 | 46 |
| Seventh plan (1985–90) | 31,420 | 13,200 | 42 |
| Eighth Plan (1992–97) | 93,830 | 35,160 | 37 |
| Ninth Plan (1997–02) | 185,260 | 69,990 | 38 |
| Tenth Plan (2002–07) | 2,54,100 | 91,080 | 36 |

Compiled from Tenth five year plan 2002–07

**Source:** Table – 6.1 p.118 of Volume III.

Infact, there are certain major lacuna to solve the problem of regional disparities through transference of resources. There is no guarantee that resource as transferred from the centre to the states would be automatically used for the development of the backward areas. Infact it may be diverted to development of forward areas.

### 2. Special Area Development Programme

*Special plan schemes* have been formulated with central assistance to develop hilly areas, drought- prone areas and tribal areas. Moreover schemes of rural development directed towards the improvement of specific groups like small farmers and agricultural labourers and for those were also located in backward areas. In course of time these special schemes for particular target groups became a part of the programme of block level planning for integrated rural development and employment. An area based approach of Tribal Sub Plan is now being implemented for the development of scheduled tribes located in the backward rural areas. The *tribal sub-plans are implemented through 194 Integrated tribal Development Projects. (ITDP) and 250 modified Area Development Projects.*

### 3. Incentives to Promote Investment in Backward Region

In order to promote private investments in backward regions various fiscal and other incentives have been given by the centre to the states and other financial institution under public sector. These incentives are:

### I. Central Government Incentives

(*a*) **Income Tax Commission:** New industrial units located in backward areas set up after January, 1971 are allowed a deduction of 20% of Profits for computation of assessable income. This concession was started in April, 1974 for ten years in industrial units.

(*b*) **Tax Holiday:** The 1993–94 budget introduced a system of Tax Holiday for new industrial units located in backward regions *i.e.* in all states in N.E. Region Jammu and Kashmir, H. P., Sikkim, Goa and the Union Territories of Andaman and Nicobar Islands, Dadar and Nagar Haveli Daman and Diu.

(*c*) **Central Investment Subsidy Scheme:** The Central Government announced the scheme of central investment subsidy in 1970. It made provisions for outright subsidy at the flat rate of 10% subject to a maximum limit of Rs. 5 lakhs on fixed capital investment like land, factory, building. The rate of subsidy was raised to 15% and then to 25% Since April, 1983 the following pattern of Investment subsidy is being followed.

(*i*) **Category A areas (No industry districts and special regions):** 25% investment subsidy be provided subject to a maximum limit of Rs 15 lakhs.

(*ii*) **Category B areas:** 15% investment subsidy be provided subject to a maximum limit of Rs. 15 lakhs.

(*iii*) **Category C areas:** 10% investment subsidy be provided to a maximum limit of Rs. 15 lakhs. By April, 1984 the maximum limit of investment subsidy was raised to Rs. 50 lakhs to be fixed at the rate of 25% for electronic industry settled in *hilly districts* in *Category A.*

(*d*) **Transport Subsidy Scheme:** In July, 1971 this subsidy was introduced for those industrial units established in hilly, inacessible, remote areas of the country. As per this scheme these aforesaid industrial units were entitled to 50% transport subsidy on the expenditure incurred particularly for movement of raw materials and finished goods in certain selected rail heads to the location of industrial units.

(*e*) **Promotion of New Financial Institutions in Backward Regions:** In order to bring industrialisation to backward areas the Government of India has promoted new financial institutions especially in backward regions. Government established Regional Rural Development Bank for the north -eastern region in 1995–1996.

More over, the Government of India also established a rural infrastructure development fund within NABARD from April 1995 for the infrastructure development of rural and backward areas.

## 4.7 MISCELLANEOUS MEASURES

The Central Government has been introducing some miscellaneous measures for promoting less developed regions. The Government has granted liberal concessions to MRTP/FERA Companies for setting up particular type of industries to be located in backward areas.

### 1. State Government Incentives

The Government has given incentive in various forms. These incentives include providing plots with electricity, water connection on a no profit, no loss basis exemption from payment of water charges for some years. Sales tax exemption, interest free loans, exemption from octroi duties, exemption from payment of property taxes for initial years providing subsidy on industrial housing scheme, establishing industrial estate for setting up small industries. The institutions like SFC, SIDCO and SIICS has sanctioned loans under concessional financial scheme, which had gone to backward districts.

### 2. Concessional Finance Available from Major Financial Institutions

Major Financial Institutions like IDBI, IFCI and ICICI. are giving loans at conessional rates of interest at longer period repayment facilities and they participate in the risk capital or debenture issues, waiving off commitment charges. Moreover these institutions are preparing feasibility study of industrial projects to be located in backward areas and they encourage the prospective entrepreneurs to implement such projects. Moreover these institutions are setting up technical consultancy organisation to give technical consultancy services to prospective industrial limits of backward areas at cheaper rates.

### 4.7.1 Tenth Five Year Plan and Regional Disparities

As States with better infrastructure generally attract private investment in much larger measure than other States. *The tenth plan adopted a multipronged strategy to accelerate the development of less developed states and backward regions within developed states. Accordingly, the tenth plan strategy was:*

(*a*) **High level of capital investment:** A high proportion of central assistance and states over resources would be devoted in improving infrastructure gap in less developed states.

(*b*) **Funds alone cannot address backwardness but development effort should be accompanied by:**

(*i*) Government and institutional reforms to make the targeted investment effective.

(*ii*) Decentralisation of powers and functions to local bodies to set a pattern of development more in tune with their aspirations.

(*iii*) Strengthening of people participation to make development efforts really meaningful.

The tenth plan formulated a new scheme called Rashtriya sam vikas Yojana. (National equal development plan) in 2002–2003 with the specific focus on development programmes for backward regions, which helped to reduce imbalances, speed up development and overcome poverty and unemployment in backward regions. RSVY is purely a grant based programme and acts as an incentive for states to take up reforms. These grants would be in addition to existing flow funds undergoing schemes. The release of funds was performance based.

### 4.7.2 Why Regional Planning Failed to Remove Regional Imbalances?

1. Refusal by rich state to transfer resources to poor state.
2. Lack of self-reliance on the part of poorer state and there by too much dependence on the transfer of resources from richer state.
3. Area development programmes for backwards areas are lacking an integrated approach.
4. Failure of large central projects to be called in the backward areas to improve their economies.
5. Non-approaching attitude of the entrepreneurs to seek concessional finance from the public sector financial institutions.

6. Too much concentration of central Government subsidy meant for specific backward areas into a few areas of some districts and too much of such investment subsidy on capital related investments leading to creation of lesser employment opportunities.
7. Inadequate fund provided by State Government for tackling the problem of Intra-state inbalances existing within a state.
8. Non-utilisation of plan outlays and loans and advances given to the state for the development of backward areas.

## 4.8 SUGGESTIONS

The planning commission in India has sought to tackle the problem of regional disparities and backwardness.

1. The procession of adequate fund should be available by the *Centre to states for the backward areas according to their needs and importance.* The responsibility of developing the areas should be entirely left to the state except in the case of very large project requiring huge investment.
2. *Separate development programme* for each region. In the backward regions of U. P., Bihar plains where the populate is large the development programme should follow from technical breakthrough in agriculture and water and improvement of transport and communication and of social and institutional reform. While in regions like Rajasthan, the programme should train local youth for emigration to adjoining regions of better economic opportunity where projects or development of natural resources can be started.

## 4.9 CONCLUSION

The steps taken to resolve the problem of regional imbalances have been largely in financial terms. Infact central assistance should be *linked with specific programmes* for the *development of the relatively backward* regions. Besides the *financial approach should be replaced by the planning approach under which the backward regions should be clearly identified along with their capabilities and potentialities so that separate agencies be adopted for each backward regions.* This is therefore the necessity to see that agricultural, industrial and infrastructure development all be coordinated. Only then development of backward area shall take place.

❑❑❑

CHAPTER 5

# Industrial Organisation and Ownership Structure

## 5.1 INTRODUCTION

Industrial organisation occupies a very significant place on the map of business organisation. It is the fundamental tool for growth and diversification of industrial economy. It is an index of industrial development.

Industrial organisation is a combination of two words industrial and organisation hence, to understand the term industrial organisation, we need to understand the meaning of industry and organisation. *Industry* is a group of productive enterprise or organisation that produces or supply, goods, services or sources of income. This concept was made by the *New Encyclopedia Britannica*.

Organisation was defined by **J.C. Denyer** as : "Organisation is concerned with the arrangement of work, with the division of activities and with the allocation of duties, authority and responsibilities". In this way *industrial organisation* is concerned with organising industrial activities in an *integrated* and *coordinated manner* to gain *industrial goals*. Industry organisation is thus a systematic assemblage of men, machine, material, market money, and management for the achievement of common goals. It may also be thought of as a complex of relationship among human factor and physical factors and work cemented together into a network of systems so that the pre-decided goals can be achieved effectively and efficiently.

## 5.2 ORGANISATIONAL FORMS

A business firm may be identified on the basis of certain characteristics like the type of ownership and so on. According to this we can classify the firms in categories like proprietorship partnership, and the corporation. The organisational pattern of firms or business is shown in chart below:

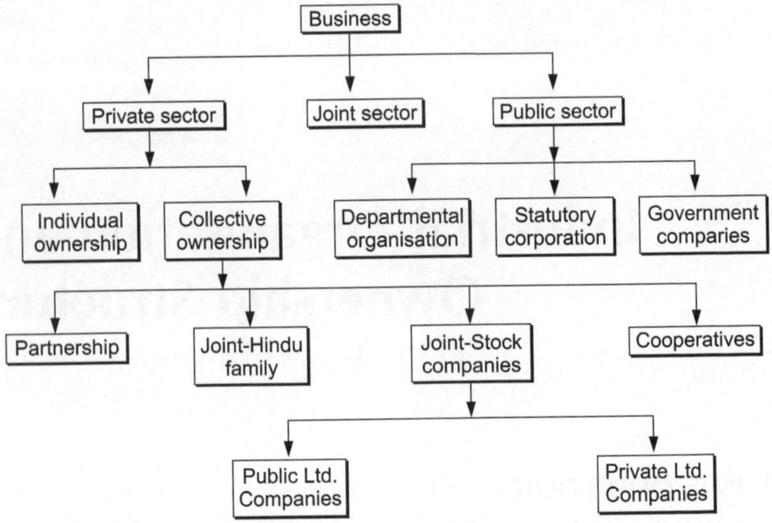


All firms doing business can be classified into these categories: (*i*) Private Sector, (*ii*) Public Sector, and (*iii*) Joint sector firms, (*iv*) Cooperative Sector. *In the private sector* the ownership is exclusively in the hands of the private individuals whereas in the *public sector* central or state government owns the firm. In the case of joint sector, the government, the private entrepreneur and *the public together share of the firm.* Similarly, in a cooperative sector people mark together with common economic objectives organising themselves on the basis of equality for the fulfillment of objectives. The *organisational forms of the* firms in each of *these three categories may be described briefly as follows.*

## 5.3 STATE/PUBLIC SECTOR ENTERPRISES

The state enterprises refer to those business enterprises whose ownership and management are directly in the hands of the government. Such enterprises are directly managed *by the government* **Prof. S.S. Khera** defines it as the industrial commercial and economic activities carried on by the central government or the state government and in each case either solely or in association with private enterprise so long as it is managed by a self-contained management"[1]. For example, Railways, post and telegraph department are the government enterprises. *Encyelopaedia Britannica* : *defined it as such;* "The term usually refers to government ownership and active operation of

1. Khera S.S., *Management and Control in Public Enterprises,* Asia Publishing House, Bombay 1964, p. 10.
2. *Encyclopaedia Britannica,* Vol. 18 Encyclopaedia Britannica Inc. Chichago 1965, p. 738.

agencies engaged in supplying the public, the goods and services which alternatively might be supplied by privately owned profit motivated firms[2]." The definition has laid emphasis on government ownership and absence of profit motive. V.K.R.V. Rao stated that " Sectors of economic activity which involves either monopoly conditions of strategic economic power or possession of large resources in private hands should be publicly owned and operated as public enterprises. It also means that it should make it self-available for the building of *economic overheads.* On the *external economics,* like transport, power fuel and basic capital goods without which increase in production of consumption goods and services either on the required scale or necessary economic basis will not be possible. *Without public* enterprises there can *be no private enterprises*. Infact it is in the former that allows full growth of the latter[3].

If we look into the *Evolution* of the *public sector in India,* we would say that prior to 1947 there was virtually no 'public sector' in the Indian economy. The expansion of public sector was undertaken as an integral part of the 1956, industrial policy, which gave the public sector a strategic role in the Indian economy. It was felt that only through government intervention in a big planned way the agricultural and industrial production could be accelerated in a big way, employment opportunities be expanded with reduction of poverty. In other words, the public sector was thought of as the engine for self-reliant economic growth to develop a *sound agricultural* and *industrial base, diversify the economy* and overcome economic and social backwardness.

### 5.3.1 Characteristic Features of State Enterprises

The characteristic features of state enterprises are as follows :

1. State enterprises are financed by the government.
2. State enterprises are managed by the government.
3. State enterprises are financially independent.
4. The primary objective of state enterprises are to provide services to the society.
5. State enterprises at times are monopoly enterprises such as water, electricity, military equipments etc.
6. State enterprises are helpful in implementing government policies and plans.
7. Autonomous functioning of public enterprises provided sufficient autonomy to manage their affairs.

Thus, public enterprises can be defined as an *activity of the government* whether *central, state or local* involving *manufacturing* or *production of goods including agriculture* or making *available the* services, it has a sound *blending of public*.

---

3. *India Economy,* Ruddar Datt and K.P.M Sundharam, p. 190.

### 5.3.2 Main characteristics

1. **Government Ownership:** The public enterprises should either be wholly owned by the central or state government or local authority or jointly owned by two or more of them. Government ownership means that more than 50% of the equity is held by a public authority. Section 617 of the Indian Company Act clearly specifies that government company means any company in which not less than 51% of the paid up share capital is held by the central government or by any state government or central government partly and partly by one or more state government". Further the public corporations and the departmental undertaking are fully owned by the government. The Government manages the enterprises.
2. **Public Accountability:** The enterprises are provided funds from the public exchequer. It becomes imperative that they should be accountable to the public through the Parliament whose funds are invested to carry on the activities of the enterprises. This goal is achieved through ministers, government, Parliament, audit bodies etc.
3. **Constituent of Political and Administrative Structure:** The establishment and constituent of public enterprises is a political decision and its operation are controlled at strategic points by a system where the politicians have the finals say.
4. **Public Purpose:** In public enterprises social aspects can well precede, supersede and even engulf business consideration. The public interest in various forms and shape provides an under current for all its strategic decisions.
5. **Wide Coverage of Activities:** Public enterprises are found operating in vast area *e.g.,* construction, marketing, agriculture, finance, development mining etc.
6. **Economic Enterprise:** In a public enterprise the price charged for the goods and services is expected to cover the cost.
7. **Autonomous Functioning:** Inspite of the huge investment made by the government, the public enterprises are provided sufficient autonomy to manage their affairs in their own fashion. The self-contained management has the right to manage the affairs on the basis of sound business consideration and prudent commercial practises. The government does not interfere in their day to day activities. *Purpose, public accountability, autonomous functioning and inherent* right to *manage and control* the enterprise *is done by the government*"[4].

### 5.3.3 Benefits from Public Sector Enterprises

The benefits derived from public sector enterprises are:

1. Economic Benefits
2. Social Benefits

---

4. *Narain. L., Principles and Practices of Public Enterprises Managements,* p.48.

## I. Economic Benefits

Public Enterprises strengthen the economy by providing the *following benefits*:

1. Public enterprises generate *revenue* for the *government* through various means. Dividends, interest on loans, excise duty, octroi; sales tax, corporation tax are paid to the government by the public enterprises. The revenues generated by the public enterprises has risen in the recent years.
2. Public enterprises *exploit* the *natural* and technological *resources* of the state. This maximizes the social welfare and development opportunities in the economy.
3. Public enterprises save *enormous* amount of scarce *foreign exchange* either by exporting *these surplus* goods and services of the country or by making in vigorous effort in substituting imported products.
4. The public enterprises help to reduce the regional disparities through a planned dispersal of industries. The claims of relatively backward areas are considered by the government in proper perspective.
5. Public enterprises provide infrastructure facilities for the development of the economy.
6. Development of *ancillary SSI units* by *public enterprises* is undertaken to meet the requirements of various supplies. This facilitates the development of subsidiary and incidental industries to the line of manufacture engaged by the public enterprises.
7. Public enterprises also help in reducing unfavourable balance of trade.

## II. Social Benefits

Social benefits of public enterprises are an follows:

1. Public enterprises act as model employers. They at a time provide *amenities* like housing, medical, conveyance and other statutory, benefits they show how labour, management, relation is maintained.
2. Public Enterprise protects the interest of the consumers. By adopting discriminatory *pricing policy* they provide goods and services to low income groups at cheaper price they provide goods and make effort to maintain the price line of the goods manufactured.
3. Public enterprises *change the environment* of the society.
4. Public enterprises *generate employment opportunities* directly and indirectly (*see* Table 5.1).
5. Public enterprises helps in reducing *disparities* of *income and wealth.*
6. For adoption of *socialistic pattern* of society the operation of public enterprises is the prime condition.
7. State enterprises are inspired not by profit motivation but by welfare motivation. The consumers therefore are greatly benefitted.

**Table 5.1:** Employment in organised sectors—public and private (Lakh Persons)

| | 1991 | 1994 | 1995 | 1996 | 1997 | 1998 | 1999 | 2000 | 2001 | 2002 | 2003 | 2004 | 2005 | 2006 |
|---|---|---|---|---|---|---|---|---|---|---|---|---|---|---|
| (1) | (2) | (3) | (4) | (5) | (6) | (7) | (8) | (9) | (10) | (11) | (12) | (13) | (14) | (15) |
| **Public sector** | | | | | | | | | | | | | | |
| **A. By branch** | | | | | | | | | | | | | | |
| **1.** Central Government | 34.11 | 33.92 | 33.95 | 33.66 | 32.95 | 32.53 | 33.13 | 32.73 | 31.61 | 31.95 | 31.33 | 30.27 | 29.38 | 28.60 |
| **2.** State Government | 71.12 | 73.37 | 73.55 | 74.14 | 7485 | 74.58 | 74.58 | 74.60 | 74.25 | 73.84 | 73.67 | 72.22 | 72.02 | 73.00 |
| **3.** Quasi-Governments | 62.22 | 65.14 | 65.20 | 64.58 | 65.35 | 64.61 | 63.85 | 63.26 | 61.92 | 60.20 | 59.01 | 58.22 | 57.48 | 59.09 |
| **4.** Local bodies | 23.13 | 22.02 | 21.97 | 21.92 | 22.44 | 22.46 | 22.59 | 22.55 | 22.61 | 21.75 | 21.79 | 21.26 | 21.18 | 21.18 |
| **Total** | **190.58** | **194.45** | **194.67** | **194.29** | **195.59** | **194.18** | **191.15** | **193.14** | **191.38** | **187.73** | **185.8** | **181.73** | **180.07** | **181.88** |
| **B. By industry** | | | | | | | | | | | | | | |
| **1.** Agriculture, hunting etc. | 5.56 | 5.45 | 5.39 | 5.40 | 5.33 | 5.30 | 5.15 | 5.14 | 5.02 | 4.83 | 5.06 | 4.93 | 4.96 | 4.69 |
| **2.** Mining and quarrying | 9.99 | 10.15 | 10.16 | 9.93 | 9.78 | 9.37 | 9.26 | 9.24 | 8.75 | 8.61 | 8.47 | 10.30 | 10.14 | 11.46 |
| **3.** Manufacturing | 18.52 | 17.84 | 17.56 | 17.38 | 16.61 | 16.16 | 15.69 | 15.31 | 14.30 | 13.50 | 12.60 | 11.89 | 11.30 | 10.92 |
| **4.** Electricity, gas and water | 9.05 | 9.38 | 9.35 | 9.46 | 9.56 | 9.54 | 9.62 | 9.46 | 9.35 | 9.23 | 9.13 | 8.74 | 8.60 | 8.49 |
| **5.** Construction | 11.49 | 11.67 | 11.64 | 11.59 | 11.34 | 11.09 | 11.07 | 10.92 | 10.81 | 10.26 | 9.48 | 9.32 | 9.11 | 8.94 |
| **6.** Wholesale and retail trade | 1.50 | 1.61 | 1.62 | 1.62 | 1.64 | 1.64 | 1.63 | 1.63 | 1.63 | 1.57 | 1.82 | 1.81 | 1.84 | 1.82 |
| **7.** Transport, storage and communications | 30.26 | 30.84 | 31.06 | 30.92 | 30.92 | 30.84 | 30.84 | 30.77 | 30.42 | 30.09 | 29.39 | 28.15 | 27.51 | 26.75 |
| **8.** Finance, insurance, real estate etc. | 11.94 | 12.73 | 12.83 | 12.80 | 12.94 | 12.88 | 12.95 | 12.96 | 12.81 | 12.30 | 13.77 | 14.08 | 14.08 | 13.90 |
| **9.** Community, Social and personal services | 92.27 | 94.78 | 95.04 | 95.20 | 97.47 | 97.37 | 97.94 | 97.71 | 98.30 | 97.35 | 96.09 | 92.76 | 92.52 | 91.76 |
| **Total** | **190.58** | **194.45** | **194.67** | **194.29** | **195.59** | **194.18** | **194.15** | **193.14** | **191.38** | **187.73** | **185.80** | **181.97** | **180.07** | **178.73** |

| (1) | (2) | (3) | (4) | (5) | (6) | (7) | (8) | (9) | (10) | (11) | (12) | (13) | (14) | (15) |
|---|---|---|---|---|---|---|---|---|---|---|---|---|---|---|
| **Private sector** | | | | | | | | | | | | | | |
| **1.** Agriculture, hunting etc. | 8.91 | 8.83 | 8.94 | 9.19 | 9.12 | 9.04 | 8.71 | 9.04 | 9.31 | 8.55 | 8.95 | 9.17 | 9.83 | 10.28 |
| **2.** Mining and quarrying | 1.00 | 1.01 | 1.03 | 1.07 | 0.92 | 0.91 | 0.87 | 0.81 | 0.79 | 0.68 | 0.66 | 0.65 | 0.79 | 0.95 |
| **3.** Manufacturing | 44.81 | 46.30 | 47.06 | 50.49 | 52.39 | 52.33 | 51.78 | 50.85 | 50.13 | 48.67 | 47.44 | 44.89 | 44.89 | 45.49 |
| **4.** Electricity, gas and water | 0.40 | 0.40 | 0.40 | 0.42 | 0.41 | 0.42 | 0.41 | 0.41 | 0.52 | 0.42 | 0.50 | 0.47 | 0.49 | 0.40 |
| **5.** Construction | 0.73 | 0.51 | 0.53 | 0.53 | 0.54 | 0.74 | 0.71 | 0.57 | 0.57 | 0.56 | 0.44 | 0.45 | 0.49 | 0.55 |
| **6.** Wholesale and retail trade | 3.00 | 3.02 | 3.08 | 3.17 | 3.17 | 3.21 | 3.23 | 3.30 | 3.39 | 3.35 | 3.60 | 3.51 | 3.75 | 3.87 |
| **7.** Transport, storage and communications | 0.53 | 0.56 | 0.58 | 0.60 | 0.63 | 0.65 | 0.69 | 0.70 | 0.76 | 0.76 | 0.79 | 0.81 | 0.85 | 0.87 |
| **8.** Finance, insurance, real estate etc. | 2.54 | 2.82 | 2.93 | 3.06 | 3.22 | 3.41 | 3.58 | 3.58 | 3.70 | 3.91 | 4.26 | 4.58 | 5.23 | 6.52 |
| **9.** Community, social and personal services | 14.85 | 15.85 | 16.03 | 16.58 | 16.44 | 16.77 | 17.00 | 17.23 | 17.34 | 17.42 | 17.56 | 17.92 | 18.20 | 18.78 |
| **Total** | **76.77** | **79.30** | **80.59** | **85.12** | **86.86** | **87.48** | **86.98** | **86.46** | **86.52** | **84.32** | **84.21** | **82.46** | **84.52** | **87.71** |
| **BY Sex** | | | | | | | | | | | | | | |
| **Public sector** | | | | | | | | | | | | | | |
| Male | 167.10 | 168.80 | 168.66 | 167.94 | 166.31 | 166.55 | 166.04 | 164.57 | 162.79 | 158.86 | 156.76 | 153.07 | 150.86 | 151.85 |
| Female | 23.47 | 25.65 | 26.00 | 26.35 | 27.28 | 27.63 | 28.11 | 28.57 | 28.59 | 28.87 | 29.05 | 28.90 | 29.21 | 30.03 |
| **Total** | **190.57** | **194.45** | **194.66** | **194.29** | **195.59** | **194.18** | **194.15** | **193.14** | **191.38** | **187.73** | **185.8** | **181.97** | **180.07** | **181.88** |
| **Private sector** | | | | | | | | | | | | | | |
| Male | 62.42 | 63.41 | 64.31 | 67.20 | 67.77 | 67.37 | 66.80 | 65.80 | 65.62 | 63.83 | 63.57 | 62.02 | 63.57 | 66.87 |
| Female | 14.34 | 15.89 | 16.28 | 17.92 | 19.09 | 20.11 | 20.18 | 20.66 | 20.90 | 20.49 | 20.64 | 20.44 | 20.95 | 21.18 |
| **Total** | **76.76** | **79.30** | **80.59** | **85.12** | **86.86** | **87.48** | **86.98** | **86.46** | **86.52** | **84.32** | **84.21** | **82.46** | **84.52** | **88.05** |
| **Public and Private sector** | | | | | | | | | | | | | | |
| Male | 229.52 | 232.21 | 232.97 | 235.14 | 236.08 | 233.92 | 232.84 | 230.37 | 228.40 | 222.71 | 220.32 | 215.09 | 214.42 | 218.72 |
| Female | 37.81 | 41.54 | 42.28 | 44.26 | 46.37 | 47.74 | 48.29 | 49.23 | 49.49 | 49.35 | 49.68 | 49.34 | 50.16 | 51.21 |
| **Total** | **267.33** | **273.75** | **275.25** | **279.41** | **282.45** | **281.66** | **281.13** | **279.60** | **277.89** | **272.06** | **270.00** | **264.43** | **264.58** | **269.93** |

**Source :** Ministry of Labour and Employment, Director general of Employments and Training, Economic Survey, 2008-09, P.A.-52

**Note:**
1. Coverage in construction, particularly on private account, is known to be inadequate.
2. Employment in private sector relates to non-agriculture establishments in private sector employing 10 or more person. Employment and public sector relate to all establishments irrespective size.
3. Excludes Sikkim, Arunachal Pradesh, Dadra and Nagar Havelli and Lakshadweep as these are not yet covered under the programme.
4. Due to non-availability of data as per NIC 1998, information in respect of J & K, Meghalaya, Mizoram, Daman & Diu not included in totals of 2006.

8. Public enterprises can provide *better work-force by employing* higher *salaries and perks.*
9. Public enterprises due to adequate financial resources can use latest techniques and machines.
10. Suitable only in certain enterprises which can be operated only by public enterprises since they do not generate immediate profits *e.g.*, transport, electricity.

## 5.4 LIMITATIONS OF PUBLIC ENTERPRISES

Limitation of public enterprises are given below :

1. There is a good deal of *Red Tapism* in government enterprises. The work proceeds slowly in government enterprises. Prompt decisions are not taken.
2. The workers have little or no incentive for hard work in government enterprises, therefore *efficiency* to *work is low.*
3. It is mostly seen that there is only *routine working in government* departments. There is little *spirit of new initiative* being displayed by any employee.
4. In a public enterprises it is often seen that there is lack *of economic motive.*
5. *Favouritism, nepotism reign* supreme in government enterprises. High officials generally appoint their own kith and kin in government departments.
6. Too much interference by ministers and politicians disrupts autonomy in the working of state enterprises.
7. Unnecessary burden on tax payers. Since, if there is any financial loss then the burden is borne by tax payers.
8. In the enterprises, there is lack of concern about cost control, avoidance of waste, improvement of efficiency or increasing the capacity utilisation. Even if they are incurring losses no *special concerted* efforts are made to reduce *that or improve* the *situation.*
9. Public enterprises have poor and weak *labour-employee relation.*
10. Public enterprises suffer *from inefficiency* and *poor profitability as compared* to their counterpart in private sector.
11. *Mounting losses* are seen in public enterprises.
12. *Political factors* influence decision about location
13. In many cases it was seen that inspite of rise in cost, prices may not be increased on non-economic ground. Often this may lead to back-door taxation of the consumers.
14. The public enterprises may perform poorly due to faulty controls exercised over them.

*Performance of Public Sector* in Indian economy can be viewed in Table 5.2.

**Table 5.2:** Percentage share of public sector [Rs. Crores]

| Item | 1999-2000 | 2000-01 | 2001-02 | 2002-03 | 2003-04 | 2004-05 | 2005-06 | 2006-07 |
|---|---|---|---|---|---|---|---|---|
| Gross domestic product | 25.6 Rs(178625) | 25.0 (1925017) | 25.0 (209726) | 25.5 (226145) | 24.2 (2538171) | 23.3 (287706) | 21.7 (3275670) | 21.4 (3790063) |
| Gross domestic saving | –3.2 (484256) | –7.4 (499033) | –8.6 (534885) | –2.5 (647970) | 3.6 (821027) | 6.9 (1000424) | 7.5 (1227348) | 9.3 (1441423) |
| Gross domestic formation | 29.3 (493999) | 29.9 (493285) | 29.2 (536854) | 24.7 (605533) | 24.5 (712900) | 22.7 (954889) | 22.8 (1195408) | 22.3 (1442604) |
| Final consumption expenditure | 16.7 (1510285) | 16.5 (1610671) | 16.1 (1752087) | 15.8 (1854596) | 15.4 (2013844) | 15.5 (2186542) | 15.3 (2435298) | 15.5 (2751116) |

**Source:** *India, 2009 P-131*

## 5.5 PRIVATE SECTOR

Private sectors or private enterprises refer to all types of individual or corporate enterprises domestic and foreign in any field of productive activity. Private sector enterprises are characterised by ownership and management in private hands, personal initiative and profit motive.

In the 18th centuries private sector units were of *laissez-faire* variety *i.e.*, private sector was completely *free* of *governmental interferences*. Private enterprises were normally small units owned and managed by sole proprietor. He bore the risk of the business According to **L.H. Haney** "The sole entrepreneurships in the form of business organisation on the head of which stands an individual is the one who is responsible who directs its operation, who also runs the risk of failure". Therefore, there is *one owner, who conducts the use of factors of production , and bears both profits and loss.* In sole proprietorship the business and his ownership exists together. There is complete secrecy. Their main motive was to earn profit.

But today, private sector is qualitatively different from corporate industrial units which are owned by the shareholder and managed by professional managers. The latter is not always interested in maximising profit but have other corporate objectives as well such as *expansion, consolidation social conciseness and social welfare.*

### 5.5.1 Characteristics of Private Enterprise

Following are the characteristics of private enterprise:

(*i*) *Low cost of production:* Since business is exclusively his own, the single entrepreneur works day and night for the success of his enterprise. He allows no wastage of material in his establishment.

(*ii*) Close contact with customers.

(*ii*) Close contact with workers.

(*iv*) Promptness in decision since it is one man's decision.

(*v*) Security of trade secrets.

### 5.5.2 Disadvantages

Disadvantages public enterprises are an follows:

1. Limited economic resources.
2. Inability to face competition from bigger units due to limited capital
3. No-large scale economics.

The *private sector and public sector* are *distinguished* in some way from each other. The public sector is entrusted with the responsibility of developing heavy and basic industries social and economic infrastructure

| Main points of differences | Public enterprise | Private enterprise |
|---|---|---|
| 1. Motive | Service motive | Profit motive |
| 2. Nature of Industry | Capital intensive and Risky Industries | Comparatively little requirement of capital and less risk |
| 3. Performance | Surplus generation, Cost of production, productivity and contribution to Exchequer | Profitability mainly |
| 4. Secrecy | Except in defence, inother sector, secrecy is not maintained | Secrecy is maintained |
| 5. Autonomy | Comparatively lesser autonomy is given to top officials | They are autonomous units |
| 6. Risk | Risk is not personal in nature | Risk is personal by nature |
| 7. Market | Monopolistic in majority of cases | Competitive in majority of cases |
| 8. Pricing | Administered pricing | Not so |
| 9. Public Accountability | Government and parliament facilitate public accountability | It is not so in this case |
| 10. Audit control | Audit is done | Audit is not a must |
| 11. Social overheads | They have to act as model employer | It is not so in this case |
| 12. Flexibility | Lack of flexibility | There is flexibility |
| 13. Role of industrial policy statement | Prime role | Secondary role |

The private sector is given the right to develop consumer good industries, while banks and financial institution, railways, civil aviation, power generation and distribution etc are in the public sector, The whole of agriculture and allied activities, plantation mining internal trade, both retail and wholesale are embraced by private sector. The private sector has indeed come to mean the *corporate industrial sector*. Private sector was suitable to consumer goods industries which involves *limited risk* and short *gestation period.* On the other hand the public sector investment being autonomous was considered more suitable to low profit yielding long gestation and heavy investment sectors. The infrastructure industries were thus reserved for *public sector*.

## 5.6 JOINT SECTOR

It is known as a *corporate form of business*. A joint stock *company is an association of individual as shareholders, who are authorised by the government to run a particular business*. According to **L.H.Haney,** "A joint-Stock company is a voluntary association of individuals for profit, having capital divided into transferable shares, the ownership of which is the condition of membership". Large scale commercial and industrial enterprises are run under the joint stock company system. This system exists in U.S.A., Japan, Western European countries.

### 5.6.1 Characteristic Features of Joint-Stock companies

There are an follows:

(*i*) The *capital of the firm is contributed by a large number of shareholders* who are the real owners of the business enterprises.

(*ii*) The *liability of the shareholder* is *limited to the value* of the shares held by him.

(*iii*) The *policy making* job of the firm *is entrusted to a board of directors* who are elected from amongst the shareholders.

(*iv*) The *actual management* of the company is carried on by the paid managers who work under the direct *supervision* of the *Managing Director.*

(*v*) The joint stock company has a separate and distinct legal entity from that of the shareholders.

### 5.6.2 How a Joint-stock Company is Organised?

An entrepreneur conceives of some new enterprise which in his view is likely to yield good profits, under the Indian companies act such an entrepreneur is required to gather around him six persons who are interested in the new project. These persons are known as *promoters of* these company. These promoters will *draft a memorandum of association* which would include name of the company, its headquarters, the aims and objects, the aggregate share capital to be raised from the public, the types of shares to be issued and the value of each share etc. Besides this another document known as *Article of Association* which contains internal rules and regulations of the company. *Both the documents are submitted to the Registrar of companies*. The Registrar after scrutinising these documents extends his approval in the form of a *certificate known as* the *certificate of incorporation*. With the using of this certificate the company comes into formal existence, the *promoters* sell shares *through newspaper advertisement* to raise the capital *from company.*

The joint stock company raises capital either *through shares* or *through debentures.* Those who purchase the shares become the shareholders or part owners of the company to the extent of the value of the shares. They will naturally bear the risk involved in the business of the company. They are not owners. They are merely entitled to a *fixed percentages of interest on the amount invested by* them *in debentures*. In case the company meets with failure a prior claim over its assets is enjoyed by debenture holder.

*There are two types of* joint-stock companies (*i*) private limited company (*ii*) public limited company. The former can have 2 to 50 shareholders. The liability of each shareholder is limited to the value of shares held by him. This type of company is debarred under the law from raising funds from the capital market through debentures. The capital contribution comes from the shareholders alone.

In a public limited company ceiling is *fixed on the number of shareholders. Any number of persons can become the shareholders by contributing* capital *to the funds of the company*. The liability of each shareholder is limited to the extent of shares held by him. The *public limited* company can *invite capital subscription* from the *public through newspaper, advertisement.* It can raise funds through issuing of bonds and debentures. The company has to follow rules of Indian Companies act.

### 5.6.3 Advantages

(*i*) **Adequacy of capital:** A joint-stock company raises capital on larger scale, through selling shares.

(*ii*) **Economies of large scale production:** Since production is done on a large scale therefore economies of large scale production exists.

(*iii*) **Limited liability:** Under this system the liability of a shareholder is limited to the value of shares held by him. The shareholder thus runs only a nominal risk in buying the shares of the company it is therefore seen that men of small means like to invest their surplus fund in the shares of joint-stock companies

(*iv*) **Specialised management:** Since it has large resources. A joint stock company can provide specialised management

(*v*) **Shares of small values:** It checks the concentration of economic control in the hands of a few rich person.

(*vi*) **Transferability of shares:** in stock exchanges

(*vii*) **Permanent identity of the company:** although directors may change.

(*ix*) **Model of economic democracy:** If the works of director is unfair he can be removed.

### 5.6.4 Disadvantages

(*i*) **Separation between ownership and control:** The ownership of the company vest in the hands of *shareholders*, while management is in the *hands of managers*, who are paid and do not share profit.

(*ii*) **Delay in decision:** The joint-stock company cannot take quick yielding decision. The manager has to place all important matters before the meeting of the board of director for decision making.

(*iii*) **Lack of interest on company affair:** Since the company is a joint affair there is lack of individual interest in company.

(*iv*) **Political correction:** enters the working of joint-stock company.

(*v*) **Danger of monopoly:** The fear of monopoly is present in this type of organisation. The joint-stock company drives away small forms and establishes its own monopoly. There by raising the 'prices' of its product to the detriment of the consumers.

## 5.7 CONCLUSION

Despite the disadvantageous of joint stock company it is still an important form of business organisation. Almost all the large scale business and industrial enterprises are run by joint-stock companies.

## 5.8 COOPERATIVE ENTERPRISES

Cooperation may be defined as that type of economic organisation in which a number of persons with common *economic* objectives organise themselves on a *basis* of equality for the fulfilment *of those objectives in practise.*

### 5.8.1 Characteristics

1. *To work together on an organised basis:* The first principle of cooperation is that the person concerned should work together on an organised basis for the promotion of their common interest.
2. *This organisation is purely voluntary.*
3. *It aims to achieve certain commons objectives:* The objective of cooperative society is to achieve certain common objective. It aims at providing cheap credit to the members, to sell agricultural produce at economic prices and to purchase for the members raw materials etc at fair prices.
4. *Nearness of members to each other:* To see that all members are close to each other all the members belong to a particular village or to same area.
5. *Equality:* All member have equal right. There is no distinction between poor class and rich class or between low and high caste.
6. *Self-dependence:* It should be dependent.
7. *Economy*: It should be economical in expenditure.
8. *"Each for all and all of each"* should be the basic principle of cooperation.
9. *One Man one Choice* should be the basis of the society.

### 5.8.2 Types of Cooperatives

Producer cooperatives, consumer cooperatives marketing, credit society, farming are some examples of this type of organisation. The motive of these societies is to provide maximum services to its members and not to make profit.

**1. Producer Cooperatives:** This type of cooperative organisation was initiated in *France*. Under this type of *cooperative organisation* the *workers make their* own *capital contributions* to *these fund* of *the concern* and are themselves the owners of *the business*. They elect the manager and other office bearers from amongst their own rank. The capitalist is thus displaced under producers cooperation. The worker not only own the business but also manages it themselves through their elected representatives. The profit accruing from business is distributed among the workers.

The cooperative society helps to eliminate class struggle, controls wastages, promotes educational value. The disadvantages it promotes are:

(*i*) Deteoriation in the standard of management.

(*ii*) Inadequacy of Capital and

(*iii*) Government Control.

**2. Consumers Cooperatives:** This type of organisation was first introduced in Britain. The consumers belonging to a particular locality get together to organise a cooperative society. They make their own capital contribution. The society buys essential consumer goods and directs them from the producers and sells them at market price to the members as well as to the non-members. The profits made after a year are then distributed among the member according to two criteria. They are:

(*i*) Capital contributed by the members.

(*ii*) Purchase made by members concerned.

Those persons who have made larger purchases will be entitled to large portion of the profit. This has two advantages:

(*i*) It induces the members to purchase from the cooperatives store and not from private trader.

(*ii*) It encourages more people to become member of the cooperative store.

**3. Credit Cooperatives:** This type of cooperatives was first started in Germany in the $19^{th}$ century. Thousands of Cooperative Credit Society have been started in India to meet the credit requirement of the farmers. A number of farmers may join together to form a Cooperative Credit Society. They may make small cash contribution by buying the shares of the society. This is the working capital of the society. The society gives loans to its members against approved security at reasonable rate of interest. The primary objective of this society is to protect the farmers from the money lender who charges high interest rate. The principle of cooperation can be applied to any field of economic activity to protect the weaker section of the society. Cooperative organisation is a Compromise between Capitalism and Socialism.

The Cooperative has its drawback. It cannot run large scale business enterprise which requires specialised management and large capital investment.

**Joint sector:** The joint sector implies the participation of both the government and the private sector in the business. Under this organisation, a firm is owned and run jointly by the government and a private entrepreneur. The public and the private sector work together under the same roof and put a mutual checks on each other. The best aspects of these two type of organisations are combined together in the interest of the public. Not more than 50% of equity can be owned by the government and financial institution together *A* single private investor is not allowed to hold more than 25% of the equity of the government of India. **The advantages of the joint-sector** are (*i*) helps to foster the industrial development with social justice, (*ii*) It checks the growth of monopoly and malpractices in the business, (*iii*) It provides scope for movement financial viability and strengthm, (*iv*) It combines the best of both the systems, (*v*) It makes nationalisations unnecessary.

There are some limitations:

1. There may be conflict between the two parties.
2. It may lead to managerial autonomy making the owner passive in business.

## 5.9 THE CHOICE OF THE ORGANISATIONAL FORM

The choice of the organisational form is closely related to the objective of the owners. It is very personal issue, the individual investor should be balancing the institutional requirements, economic opportunities and risk and uncertainty factors in his own perspective while making a choice of these organisational form so as to assess the prospects of his business.

❑❑❑

CHAPTER 6

# Size–Optimum Unit

## 6.1 INTRODUCTION

It has been argued that larger firms in an industry are more efficient than the smaller firms. In the process of discussion there are certain vital issues regarding the 'size' and 'scale' of production. Output or operation cost of production, volume of production, efficiency and competitiveness of the unit, arrangement of capital, choice of technology, strength of workforce and nature of risk depends to a great extent on the 'size' of the industrial unit. Hence, determination of the appropriate 'size' of the industrial unit is one of the crucial decision making function of an entrepreneur. When talking of the 'size' even the economist are not clear as to whether they meant 'plant', a group of plants or any manufacturing or productive group under one management, ownership or control. It is necessary therefore to define the terms used in connection with the 'size' of business unit that is plant, firm and industry.

**Plant:** Plant has been defined by **Sargant Florence** as "congregation or body of persons assembling together at a certain place and time. The word plant is synonymous with a factory, a mill, a workshop, a mine, a warehouse, a retail shop or an establishment"[1]. A plant is therefore a place where utilities are created with the help of physical unit, land, labour and capital.

## 6.2 FIRM

A firm refers to a unit which owns, controls and manages the plant. If an individual or a partnership organisation or a company owns one or more mills or factories or in other words plants, the individual or the partnership organisation or the company which ever may be the case should from the financial and administrative point of view be regarded as a 'firm' a single industrial unit. A 'plant' may be identical with the firm. When a firm owns and controls only one plant. Sometimes the firm may own more than one plant. In

1. Florence. P. Sargant quoted from *Statistical Method in Economics and Political science,* London, 1928.

such a case plant and firm are not identical. From the point of view of size, profits, productivity and cost the whole group of plants or factories under one owenership will have to be treated as one single firm *Plant* is a *producing technical unit* while a *Firm is an organising, controlling unit which administers* the *different functions of management relating to the plants owned by it.*

## 6.3 INDUSTRY

*Industry* is generally defined as a 'group of firms' producing the same product for the same market. Infact, in the absence of perfect competition this definition stands to be irrelevant. Different producers seldom produces the same good each one attempts to make slight variation in its product through advertisement thereby creating a separate market and separate demand for his goods. Hence, industry may be defined as a group of firms producing one type of product with slight differences, but with greater scope for stabilisation. *Firm* which have a common bond are also regarded as parties of a single industry'. The common bond may be the same type of product or the use of a single raw material or the use of the same process of manufacture. Industries, as such are classification of firms which may for the moment be convenient . A change of technique and of organisation may require[2] a new classification and a new industry *e.g.*, Sugar industry refers to all firms producing sugar, Iron and Steel industry refers to all firms using iron ore are as raw materials.

## 6.4 FACTORS FOR MEASURING THE SIZE OF AN INDUSTRIAL UNIT

The size of an industrial unit determines the performance of the unit. Hence, an enterpreneur needs to consider economic and non-economic factors which affects the size of any unit. The size of an industrial unit is determined by the following factors:

1. **Type of Product:** It is the type of the good which is to be produced which ultimately decides what shall be the size of an industrial unit. For example, A consumer good producing unit may be set up at small or medium level whereas an industrial or capital good industry is normally set upon a large scale basis. Iron and steel industry needs to be established on a large scale basis while a unit to produce leather goods may initially be established even on a small scale basis.
2. **Nature and Extent of Demand:** This influences the size of an industrial unit. It is seen whether the demand is drastic or inelastic. Whether the demand is seasonal or constant. If the demand is seasonal then normally the size of the unit would be small. On the other hand, if the demand is regular, then the size of the unit would be large.

---

2. E.A.G. Robinson, *Structure of Competitive industry*, James Nisbel Co. Ltd. Cambridge, 1964, p.8.

3. **Nature of the Product:** Product varies on the basis of perishability transferability, storability, divisibility. High perishable products are produced by small size units while non-perishable products mays be produced by big sized plants *e.g.*, Textile industry would be big sized units.
4. **Financial Consideration:** To set up big industrial unit huge amount of capital is required while to set up a small unit small amount of capital is invested. Therefore, when huge capital is invested then the size of the unit would be large and *vice-versa.*
5. **Extent of the Market:** If the size of the market is both national and international then the size of the industrial unit would be large enough to satisfy both national and international demand.
6. **Ability of the Entrepreneur:** The size of industrial unit depends upon the skillfulness of the entrepreneur. If skillful he expands the size of industrial unit to large one. It is thus dependent on the efficiency of the entrepreneur.
7. **Government Policy:** The government with the help of industrial policy regulates industrial activities of the country. In order to promote regional development and generate employment, the government provides certain incentives including low rates of taxes to set up small units. In such a situation initially small scale industrial units are set up so that the benefits allotted by the governments may be availed and further on units can be expanded to large size.
8. **Risk:** Risk , influences productivity and profitability which thus affects the size of an industrial unit. Where the risks are high profits can be earned after a long period. The size of the unit should be large enough so that till the unit earns profit, various cost and expenses could be met out comfortably.
9. **Availability of Labour and Raw material:** If there is lack of human resources and raw material then the size of the unit would be small or else large.
10. **Use of Technique:** The level of technology also governs the size of an industrial unit. If production requires the use of complicated technology the size of the unit should be large but if simple technology is used, then the size of the unit would be small (*e.g.*, making of furniture).
11. **Combination and Integration:** If two industrial units combine together, then the size of industrial unit would become large.
12. **Complexity in Management:** Managerial efficiency governs the size of an industrial unit. Lack of good managerial personnels leads to inefficient management. Hence, size becomes small and sickness may erupt.

13. **Cost of Transport:** Cost of carrying raw materials and components to the plant and cost of carrying finished goods may be big. If the cost are high size, will be small and if the cost are low the size would be large. Further, products involving high cost of transport are produced locally by small units and are sold locally (*e.g.*, Brick making industry).
14. **Other Factors:** Lack of proper infrastructure also affects the size of an industrial unit

## 6.5 MEASUREMENT OF THE SIZE OF INDUSTRIAL UNIT

The study of the size of firms it becomes difficult due to the problem of identifying the firms and of finding a proper measure of size. Several standards of measurement has been suggested. Infact the accuracy of each standard used depends upon the nature of industry and character of its output. A criteria suitable to one industry may not be applicable to other industry.

However some standard is to be adopted to measure the size of industrial units. These are as follows:

1. **Volume of Invested Capital:** The larger is the volume of capital investment, the larger is the size of an unit and *vice versa*. But to obtain accurate data concerning the size capitalisation is difficult. Although the figures regarding the paid-up-capital can be obtained with some effort, they do not afford a relevant basis to measure the size of an industrial unit since the method of financing the industry may be widely different in different centres or even within the centre between different units . Some other factors like location, time of flotation or promotion, the character of technical equipment etc. used may also set formidable problems and strictly speaking the value of the assets will vary with there profitability quite independently of physical changes in size **Kimball and Kimball** said that "Capital investment is one of measure of size that could be used to compare both like and unlike establishment but accurate data concerning capitalisation are difficult to obtain hence the measure is unreliable".
2. **Volume of Output:** Volume of output is a suitable criteria to measure the size of an industrial unit. According, to this criteria the greater the volume of output the larger is the size of a industrial unit and smaller the volume of output the smaller is the size of an industrial unit. This measure is useful where all unit produces the same variety of products (*e.g.*, cement industry and sugar industry) and is irrelevant where different varieties of products are produced like cotton textile unit which produces hetregeneous units of product.
3. **Value of Output:** The larger is the value of output the larger is the size and *vice versa*. To evaluate the value it is done in terms of rupees. If the value of output fluctuates the accuracy of measurement may be

doubtful. Further, if the size of an unit is measured over different periods this method would not be appropriate *e.g.*, during the trade cyclical fluctuation *i.e.,* booms/depression. During depression volume may be more but value less. In this way changes in the value of output may vitiate the result of measurement of the size of industrial unit.

4. **Volume of Sales and Value of Sales:** If large size then sale is large and *vice versa*. Higher is the volume of sales, the larger will be the size of industrial unit and low volume reflects small size similarly when sale value is high reflects large size of a unit and *vice versa.*

5. **Technical Equipment:** The size of technical equipment determines the size of an industrial unit irrespective of the area of land occupied, or the dimension of the factory buildings. It is true that this measure may serve as a reasonably suitable standard for the measurement of size in some industries like cement, sugar, coal where the unit of product is quite uniform or homogeneous and hence intercomparable; but in some industries like cotton textile which produces wide varieties of goods, some producing, fine, light and artistic wares, while others specialising in rough, coarse and standarised goods, physical capacities of plants or even the total volume of output may fail to reflect the differences in the size of industrial units[3]. There may be greater differences in the nature and character of technical equipment and degree of mechanisation. The plant and equipment may not be fully utilised. But generally in the case of cotton textiles and jute manufacturing units the number of spindles and looms installed are taken as the standard for measuring the size. In case of industries like paper, chemicals, glass iron and steel the number of plants or their productive capacity is considered to be a reasonable standard[4].

6. **Number of Workers Employed:** This is another process to measure the size of an industrial unit. This criteria is suitable for comparing the units producing similar type of goods passing through the same stage of development and using same technique of production. A unit employing more workers can be put into the category of larger units than those employing lesser number of workers. But when there exists differences in the type of goods, stages of development, working condition and technique of production the result obtained by applying the criterion would be defective and misleading.

7. **Consumption of Power and Electricity:** The amount of power used by industrial unit is also furnished as a standard to measure the size. The annual consumption of raw material by an establishment is also used as a standard for the measurement of the size of an industrial

3. M.M. Mehta, *Structure of Indian Industries*, Popular Book Depot Bombay 1961 p.13.
4. M.M. Mehta as cited above p.13

unit where the units are self-sufficing and the difference in the character of output is least. On the basis of this the greater is the consumption of power and raw material the larger is the size of the unit. But in this case the units if it uses different rawmaterial or different sources of power, the result wouldnot be reliable.

8. **Complexity of Management Structure:** If the structure of management is big, then it reveals that the size of the unit would be large and *vice versa*. The structure of management of MNC'S (Ford, proctor and Gamble) is large and complex the size is large.

It may be said that to lay down a uniform standard to measure the size of an unit is rather a complex issue. Size is relative to the industry and hence different classification of size may be needed for each industry for *e.g.,* the large size unit in one industry may just be smaller than the medium and even small sized units in some other industries. The basis of classification therefore depends on individual and cannot be uniform one for all industries.

## 6.6 OPTIMUM FIRM

Each firm must be of a certain minimum size to ensure production technically feasible and economically viable. Hence , "In every industry and for every method of production within each industry there is more or less a fixed minimum size of plants below which production is technically impossible or economically unprofitable"[5]. This is known as the 'minimum' 'technical' or 'economic' size. In reality firms are always willing to expand beyond their minimum size and thereby derive the advantages of large scale production. Infact after a certain expansion in size diseconomy emerges in the scale of production. This limits the size of the firm. This is the optimum limit. At this limit there will be an exact balance between the economies that can be derived by expansion. The firm operating in such a limit is called *'Optimum Firm'*[6]. By the optimum firm **E.A.G. Robinson** said that "we must mean that the firm which in the existing condition of technique and organising ability has the lowest average cost of production per unit, when all those cost which must be covered in the long run are included"[7].

**Bye and Hewett** said that the organisation of business enterprises which in given circumstances of technology and the market for its product can produce its good at the lowest average cost in long run is an optimum firm. By the optimum firm **A. Beacem** claimed that "In an ideal world all firms should expand until they are producing these outputs which they produce at the lower average cost of than any other output".

5. P.S. Lokanathan, *Industrial Organisation in India,* Allen and Unwin, London, 1935 p.132.
6. Douglas Needham, *Economic Analysis and Industrial Structure,* pp. 12-13
7. E.A.G. Robinson, *Structure of Competitive Industry,* James Nisber and Co. Ltd., Cambridge 1964. p. 21.

Thus, for determining *the optimum size of* a firm *some conditions are to be fulfilled* :

1. Conditions of technique and organising ability to be the same.
2. Period must be long run.
3. Existence of perfect competition firm must be there:

The concept of optimum firm can be illustrated diagrammatically:

## 6.7 EQUILIBRIUM FIRM

The size is measured along *OX* axis and the average cost along *OY* axis the curve shows the trend in cost. The cost falls per unit with rise in size until it touches at point *P* beyond this point the average cost per unit tends to increase. Hence, the firm attains 'optimum size' level at OM-where the average cost per unit remains at PM representing the lowest level.

Though some people think of the representative firm enunicated by **Marshall** while dealing with the size, of the firm. There is distinction between the *'representative firm'* and the *'optimum firm'*. **Marshall** put forth the concept of representative firm with a view to studying the cost of production as it would determine when the firm is working under the *Law of Increasing Returns*'. By *Representative firm*' he meant a firm which has had a fairly long life and fair success which is managed with normal ability and which has normal access to the economies, external and internal, which belong to the aggregate volume of production; account being taken of the class of goods produced, the condition of marketing them and the economic environment generally". The concept of representative firm is abstract and static to have much practical utility. Moreover, there are many firms which are from the very start of large size. Similarly many small firms may not find it profitable to expand even after a long time. Hence, a representative firm need not necessarily be an optimum firm that is, the firm which has the lowest average long period cost of production per unit of output in given conditions of technique, knowledge and organising ability. **Prof. Pigou**, conceived of another firm the *Equilibrium Firms* which in itself will be in equilibrium. The concept is of little practical utility since it gives rise to the problem of ascertaining the point of equilibrium. No producer can be expected to make experiments with size of his firm as is envisaged under the concept. On the other hand, optimum firm is a concrete possibility, it owes its existence both to the conscious direction of the entrepreneur and the forces of competition. The

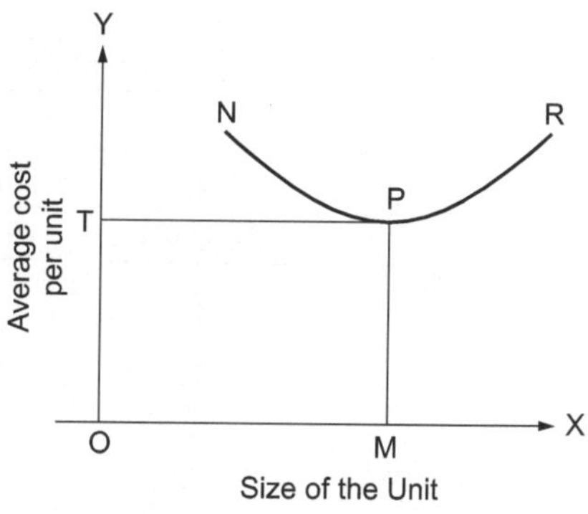


**Fig. 6.1**

optimum is thus not a rigid point but it tends to grow with the development of modern industrial method though the rate of increase varies very widely as between different countries. Thus, *optimum* is a *relative* and not an *absolute concept.*

## 6.8 FACTORS DETERMINING OPTIMUM SIZE

**E.A.G. Robinson** categorised the forces determining industrial units into five main categories:

1. Technical forces making for technical optimum unit
2. Managerial forces for making an optimum managerial unit.
3. Financial forces making for an optimum financial unit.
4. Marketing forces for making an optimum sale unit.
5. Risk and fluctuation forces making for a unit possessing the greatest power of survival in the face of industrial vicissitudes. This is illustrated in a tabular form:

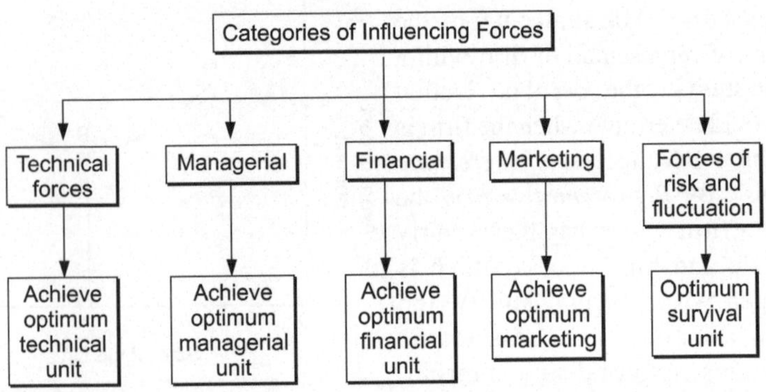


These five forces may in certain cases lead to an approximately similar optimum size. In other cases, the advantages of growth on the technical side may balance the losses from growth through the building of an industrial unit too large to be managed with the highest degree of efficiency. Conflict between the different forces can be resolved by different devices and methods of management. The optimum firm itself may be in equilibrium because of some devices. "The equilibrium may be similar either to that of the tug of war rope which is motionless because no one is yet pulling in either directions or to the tug-of war rope which is motionless because the two teams are for the moment equally matched"[8].

### 1. Technical Forces

Technical forces influences technical performances of the industrial unit. Technical forces in the main, include division of labour, specialisation,

8. Robinson op.cit . p. 17

standarisation and integration of process. These forces are related to production process and increases the production efficiency of the enterprises. Technical consideration operates mostly in favour of increasing the size of the firms.

### (*a*) Division of Labour

**Adam Smith** in his *Wealth of Nations* has made a strong case for specialisation or division of labour as a source of increased productivity. The entire production process which is composed a set of inter related activities is split into a number of simple operations and each one is assigned to a member of the working forces who being a specialist for doing that operation can increase the output or reduce the cost of production considerably. Adapting division of labour can (*i*) increase the dexterity of every worker, (*ii*) save time which is generally lost in moving from one job to another and also of tools and equipment, the workers can concentrate with speed in production without wasting time, (*iii*) invention of a greater number of specialised machines which facilitates labour and enables one man to do the work of many. The division of labour depends on the size of plants. Greater the scope for division of labour greater is the size.

**Adam Smith** took the example, of the manufacture of pins. It is found in a concern where in division of labour was not applied a workman with his utmost industry perhaps makes only a few pins in a day and under any circumstances could not make twenty. But in a concern in which the manufacturing process of the pins was divided into 18 distinct hands a workman could turn about 4800 pins of middle size in a day. It is evident from the above *e.g.*, that division of labour which increases the dexterity in every workman and saves the time which is commonly lost in passing from one stage to another leads to a higher level of productivity.

Technical economics may also be reaped by large units through the integration of process. The integration of process entails the designing of a large machine to take over what has hitherto been done by a series of manual or less completely mechanical, operation. The economies that arises from integration of process are reduction of fixed cost, transport cost and other internal economics. It is found that in many cases the large mechanical unit is both more efficient in operation and relatively cheaper to construct. But a point comes beyond which further growth is uneconomical because further economics of the division of labour or of integration of process cease to arise A double decker bus is much less than twice as costly to buy and run as a single decker bus and will carry almost double the number of passengers. But the addition of a third and fourth deck would make the bus dangerously top heavy and its use would involve the raising of the majority of bridges under which roads run.

Technical considerations usually place a premium on a large scale production. Optimum technical unit are large in two types of industries in which the product or the productive machinery is large as in steel making, ship building etc and in those in which the final products is highly complex and is built up of a great number of small parts like manufacture of type writers, motor cars etc. In such industries small firm may be completely excluded. But where the minimum technical unit is small the small firm may continue to flourish. Further small firms can operate efficiently by obtaining access to some of the technical economics of large scale through *vertical disintegration*. Vertical disintegration entails the splitting off of the major productive function into specialised operations which are carried on economically by separate firms. It may be noted that even where economies of large scale cease completely it is unlikely that certain countervailing diseconomies will begin to crop up. The technical cost of production are likely to fall as more and more is produced upto a certain limit and there after they are likely to remain constant. So the technical optimum though it provides a minimum scale of efficient operation does not fix a maximum scale beyond which growth will lead to progressively increasing cost per unit. The technical scale of production can be increased by mere multiplication if other considerations require a scale larger than the technical optimum.

### (*b*) *Indivisibility*

This is another technical factor which is frequently cited as a source of economies of large scale production in the theory of production, we assure that the factors of production like man and machines are perfectly divisible. However, in practice such factors are indivisible. A skilled worker has to be appointed in general for say full day even if there may be work for just few hands. A machine having larger production capacity has to be used to produce a much smaller quantity of output since smaller machines may not be existing Such factors of production will cause economies with increasing output particularly in the short run till they are fully utilised without any additional expenditure on them. If a firm is large enough it will be capable of using men and machines at their capacity levels.

The *indivisibility phenomena* need not be confined to the factors of production only. It may exist in the functional areas of the firm such as research and design unit repairs and machines unit marketing, finance processing etc. All of them will have considerable implications for determination of the optimum size of the firm.

### (*c*) *Economies of Big Machines*

If a firm is large enough it can profitably employ larger machines and equipment in production. This is so because of lower cost in operating larger machines than smaller one. The construction cost of big machines or plants increases less rapidly than their capacity of production.

### (*d*) *Economies in Operation*

The larger size of firm the lower will be the unit inventory cost of inputs as well as lower product inventory cost.

### (e) The Economies of Linked Process

This is another technical factor which causes economies of scale at plant level. When different heterogeneous processes are housed under the same roof a firm gains from this arrangement. For example, in a steel mill all stages of production such as extraction of iron ores in the blast furnance, conversion of iron ores into steel in the melting shop and making the finished products will be carried on at the same place, in order to save heating, cooking as well as transportation cost. All such proceses are technically linked together. The technical efficiency therefore requires that they must be carried at the same place under the same roof. The firm then saves certain vital cost like transportation, marketing, packaging cost etc.

Thus, we see that technical forces influence performances of the industrial unit. Technical forces thus include division of labour, specialisation standarisation, mechanisation and integration of processes. These *forces are thus related to the production processes* and *raise the enterprises efficiency.* Due to technical forces the firm achieves economies in production with the expansion of size. The optimum technical unit refers to a stage where the unit does not face diseconomies. The optimum technical unit determines a minimum scale of operation but not the maximum one.

## 2. Managerial Forces

Managerial optimum occurs due to economies and diseconomies associated with the division of labour and integration of processes in the managerial function. A large firm can divide the task of management into many parts so that skilled person can look into some work of management. The division of labour enables the large firm to select the man who is best fitted by aptitude and experience for performing each function. A large firm can select managers in a better way as "brains are cheap for any price". Efficient management promotes productivity of the worker as the production is well-planned and the worker will not face any interruption in his work. Further it also reduces the cost of actual productive departments due to the efficiency of the management.

One thing that needs to be emphasised is that further division of labour is either impossible or unprofitable. As the firm introduces more and more elaborate division of labour the problem of coordination arises. Infact the gains of increasing the size are negligible as the higher cost of coordination are likely to exceed them[8]. A big firm is in danger of becoming a series of wheels within wheels, an elaborate hierarchy, in which every decision requires consultation with this man , the reference to that man, permission of a third, agreement of a fourth, and as such decision becomes endlessly delayed[9]. Thus

8. Herold Koontz and Cyril 'o' Donnell, *Principles of Management*, Mc-Graw hill. 1955 PP. 352 - 353.
9. E.A.G. Robinson op cit p.44.

where an industry needs quick decision in that case a highly individualist small firm tends to survive and prosper. Thus, we see that beyond a point the cost of management per unit of output rises if further divison of labour is implemented which requires coordination. Therefore, managerial forces set the maximum limit to the growth of firms. If the size is expanded further diseconomy sets in.

### 3. Financial Forces

Financial forces favour the large sized unit. A large unit is in a position to raise capital easily at a low rate of interest. Owing to availability of capital easily the firm can easily expand in size. The financial institution and the banking concerns may also be inclined to finance large firms as they will be in a better position to offer an eligible security. The financial market is seen to be biased in favour of large firms. Industrial units of fairly large size find it easier to raise the working capital from the banks because size gives an idea of soundness solidity and security. Government also cannot remain indifferent to the possible failure of the large firm which contributes a major part to the national product. The financial institution and the banking concern may also be inclined to finance large firms. Although the larger firm is in an advantageous position with regard to finance it has some limitation, judging that greater investment would involve increasing risk or that resources invested in some quite different form of development would bring a greater "return in a world of imperfect market"[10]. Further it has to be understood that the financial forces do not prescribe either a minimum or maximum size of the firm"[11].

### 4. Marketing Forces

The success of the industrialisation unit depends upon the marketing efficiency. The economies associated with bulk buying of raw material and selling of output are known to everybody. A large firm which needs greater volume of raw materials gets price demand from suppliers. The cost of sales administration does not rise in the same proportion as their total value or volume which implies economies in the markerting favouring the larger plants. Further, a large firm will be able to have a better and forceful advertising campaign than a small firm. A large firm can have a better reputation and command over market through its efficient sales organisaton.

### 5. Forces of Risk and Fluctuation

A business is always full of risk and uncertainty. Larger the firm the stronger it will have to face such situations. Risk and uncertainties come in varieties of ways, for example, there may be an unforeseen change in demand, or change in production technology or product itself or change in governmental policy and the business environment. A large firm can devise ways and means to

10. *Ibid.* p. 58
11. Joel. Dean, *Managerial Economics,* p.564.

fight risk and to diversify its product, its market and its sources of supplies without losing much of the economies of large scale production. A large firm will be able to do so. But a small firm cannot.

Economist have further classified the changes in demand into four types permanent cyclical, seasonal, erratic. Where an industry is subject to considerable changes of demand due to either permanent changes in taste on the part of the consumer or to change in method of production caused by improvement in the technique. That firm will be the strongest which can face the problem or reorganisation and adoption. A large firm by virtue of its huge investment on fixed specialised plants and equipment, find it difficult to reorganise and adapt to changes. But a small firm by virtue of its size possess an advantage over a large firm in reorganisation. It can also adapt to the changes in the taste and fashion of the consumer by making its versatile machinery to manufacture suitable commodities .

Cyclical variations are caused by the maladjustment between the demand and supply. In times of cyclical fluctuation adjustment has to be made that is, during boom and depression demand rises or falls. At times demand behaves erratically or irregularly. Sometimes the demand for some commodities may be seasonal. In such cases it will be better for firm to manufacture the goods at or about the mean rate of consumption accumulating stocks in season of low consumption and reducing stocks in seasons of high consumption. If this is not possible than seasonal commodity can be produced in combination with another seasonal commodity whose period of maximum consumption corresponds to the minimum period of the first commodity *e.g.*, manufacturing of summer and winter clothes.

Another useful strategy to reduce uncertainties and risks is to resort to the instrument of massed reserve. In this situation a firm keeps the reserve of equipment, stocks, cash and perhaps labour to meet sudden or unforeseen demands or emergencies. A larger firm will be able to do but the smaller cannot. A bigger firm will have better chances to offset the random losses. It may be able to predict such losses on the basis of the law of averages and maintain the necessary mechanism to avoid them.

## 6.9 RECONCILIATION OF DIFFERENT OPTIMA

The above factors determines different optima although they are seldom same. It may happen that technical forces may favour X as the optimum size, while managerial forces may favour 2X as the economical size. Therefore the different optima with respect to the various factors have to he reconciled. When an industrial unit attains the optimum level in entirety the unit achieves the maximum efficiency with the minimum cost of production. If all the units have the same optimum level an enterpreneur would not face any problem. Therefore, reconcilation is essential. For example, in case if the technical optimum size is greater than the managerial optimum size, steps should be taken to increase the managerial efficiency by proper planning, and controls. Further if the technical optimum size is smaller than the managerial optimum size, then steps should be taken to increase technical productive facilities and arrangements. Number of factories may be increased.

In this way effective reconcile amongst various optima can be achieved.

In addition to the above discussed factors which influences the size of an industrial unit. There are some other consideration which affect the size. **External economies** which can be derived by the firms through their location may also influence the size of the firm. For example, the establishment of industrial units which are subsidiary to the main industry, the development of a pool of the appropriate kinds of skilled labour and the rise of the organised markets and special financial facilities etc. may help the firms to increase the size. In modern times the entrepreneur tries to get license to start units. The governmental policy as regards the size is generally viewed not purely from the point of view of costs and economies but also from various social and political considerations.

❑❑❑

CHAPTER 7

# Economies of Scale

## 7.1 INTRODUCTION

The scale of large scale production has been classified into *internal* and *external* economies of scale of production. 'Internal Economies' are internal to a firm when its cost of production are reduced and output rises. They are not the result of invention but are due to the use of known method of production which a small firm does not find worthwhile. 'External Economies' are external to a firm which are available to it when the output of the whole industry increases with the expansion of the industry itself. They are shared by a number of firms or industries when the scale of production in any industry or group of industry increases. They are not monopolised by single firm when it grows in size but are conferred on it when some other firms grow larger".

## 7.2 INTERNAL ECONOMIES

**Causes of Internal Economies:** Internal economies are caused by

(*i*) Indivisibility, (*ii*) Specialisation

**(*i*) Indivisibility:** Many fixed factors of production are indivisible in the sense that they must be used in a fixed minimum size. Such factors of production can be most efficiently employed at a fairly large output but work less efficiently at small output because they cannot be divided into smaller units"[1]. Thus, as output increases the indivisible factors which were being used below capacity can be utilised to their full capacity thereby reducing cost. Such indivisibility arises in the case of labour, machine, marketing, finance and research. Labour is not divisible in the sense that if a manager works half the time he may be paid half the salary, or as said by **Stonier** and **Hague** "he cannot be chopped into half and asked to produce half the current output". For example, a college will require the services of a Principal regardless of the number of students and lecturers. Similarly a factory may be managing the same with 200 workers

1. A.W Stonier and D.C. Hague p.113.

to start with. But when the factory expands in size and the number of worker increases gradually to 1000. The salary of the manager is spread over this number and thus there is saving on this count to the management.

A machine is also indivisible, suppose a hydroelectric plant is installed with the maximum capacity of producing 2 lakh KW of electricity, it may start producing 20,000 KW of electricity. The cost of producing a unit of power would be very high to the electricity board because of the high cost of installing and operating the plant. But as the plant starts producing more units and till it reaches its maximum capacity of 2 lakh KW the per unit cost of electricity will fall.

A firm may enjoy marketing indivisibilities with its expansion. The same representatives may be asked to sell the products in large areas and the per unit cost of advertising in a newspaper, on the radio, on the T.V. may be reduced.

It may also procure cheap and timely finance. People subscribe to the shares and debentures of a large firm readily. Again the larger the number of shares and debentures floated in the market the smaller will be the cost of managing such issue.

There is also research indivisibility. A large firm has the capacity to set up a research laboratory and benefit by the invention of new processes of production which helps in expanding production and reducing costs.

***(ii)* Specialisation:** Division of labour leads to specialisation this is another cause of internal economies. When a firm expands in size not only its production increases but the quantity of raw material and the number of workers also increases. This necessitates division of labour whereby each worker is assigned one particular job and the splitting up of processes into sub process for greater efficiency. These specialisation leads to splitting relating to manufacturing, assembling, packaging and marketing under the charge of separate managers who will work under the overall charge of general manager who coordinates the activities of four departments. Thus, specialisation leads to greater productive efficiency and reduction in cost.

### 7.2.1 Types of Internal Economies

### 1. Technical Economies

Technical economies are those which arise to a firm from the use of better machines and techniques of production. As a result production increases and the per unit cost of production falls. **Prof. Cairncross** divides technical economies into the following parts:

(*a*) **Economies of Superior Techniques:** The installation of large machines itself brings many advantages to a firm. The cost of operating large machine is less than that of operating small machines. The high cost of such machines can be spread over a larger output which they help to produce. The per unit cost of production falls in a large firm which employs costly and superior plant and equipment and thereby enjoys a technical superiority over a small firm.

(*b*) **Economies of Increased Dimensions:** The installation of large machine itself brings many advantages to a firm. The cost of operating large machine is less than that of small machine. Even the cost of construction is relatively lower for large machine than for small ones. The manufacture of a double decker bus is lower as compared to the manufacture of two single decker buses.

(*c*) **Economies of Linking Processes:** A large firm is able to reduce its per unit cost of production by linking the various processes of production. For instance a large sugar manufacturing firm may own its sugarcane farms, manufacture sugar, pack its gunny bags, transport and distribute sugar through its own transport and distribution departments. Thus, by linking the various processes of production and sale a large firm saves the expenses incurred on intermediaries thereby reducing unit cost of production.

(*d*) **Economies of the Use of By-products:** A large firm possesses greater resources than a small firm and is able to utilise its waste material as a by-product. For example, the molasses left over after manufacturing sugar from the sugarcane can be used for producing spirit by installing a plant for the purpose.

(*e*) **Economies of Increased Specialisation:** A large firm is able to reap economies by dividing its production process into sub-process thereby leading to greater division of labour and to increased specialisation. This increases the productive efficiency of the firm and reduces the unit cost of production.

(*f*) **Marketing Economies:** A large firm also reaps the economies of buying and selling. It buys its requirements of various inputs in bulk and is therefore able to secure them at favourable terms in the form of better transport concessions etc. Because of its larger organisation it produces quality products which are offered for sale in attractive packaging by its packing department. Thus a large firm is able to reap the economies of marketing through its superior bargaining power and efficient packing and sales organisation.

(*g*) **Managerial Economies:** A large firm can afford to put specialists to supervise and manage the variouse departments. This leads to functional specialisation which increases the productive efficiency of the firm. These managerial economies reduce per unit cost of management because with expansion of the firm the various departmental managers will manage large output as efficiently as they are managing smaller output at less salary.

(*h*) **Financial Economies:** A large firm can procure cheap finance both from the banks and the market because it possesses large assets and good reputation. It can raise fresh capital by floating shares and as debentures in the capital market thereby reaping financial economies.

(*i*) **Risk-bearing Economies:** A large firm is in a better position than a small firm in spreading risk. It can produce a variety of products and sell them in different areas. By the diversification of its produce then large firm is able to reduce risk by counter balancing the loss of one product by the gain from other products. By the diversification of market it can counter balance the fall in demand in one market by the increased demand in other market. Even if the demand in other market is constant the loss can be easily borne by it.

(*j*) **Economies of Research:** A large firm possesses larger resources than a small firm and can establish its own research laboratory and employ trained research workers. This reduces cost of production.

(*k*) **Economies of Welfare:** All firms have to provide welfare facilities to their workers. But a large firm with its large resources can provide better working condition in and outside the factory. It may run subsidised canteens provide creeches for the infants of women workers and recreation room for the workers within the factory premises. It may provide cheap house, educational and medical facilities for the families of workers and recreation clubs for the workers outside the factory premises. This would initate in raising the productive efficiency of workers and reducing cost.

## 2. External Economies

External economies benefit all firm within the industry as the size of the industry expands. Such economies accrue to firm when the industry is localised in a particular area makes inventions and evolves specialisation of production processes. These are:

(*a*) **Economies of Concentration:** When an industry is concentrated in a particular area, all the member firms reap some common economies. *Firstly,* skilled labour is available to all firm, *secondly*, means of transport and communication are improved. *Thirdly*, bank and other financial institution are set up in this concentrated area and the firm get easily cheap credit at cheap rates. *Lastly* subsidiary industry develop to supply the localised industries with tools, equipment and raw material. All this reduces the unit cost of production of all firm in the industry

(*b*) **Economies of Information:** An industry is in a better position to set up research laboratories than a large firm because it is able to pool large resources. It can employ highly paid and more experienced research personnel. The fruits of their research in the form of new inventions are passed on to the firm through a scientific journal. The industry can set up an information centre which may publish a journal and pass on information regarding the availability of raw materials, modern machines, export potentialities of the products of the industry in various countries and provide other information needed by the firm. All this helps in raising the productive efficiency of the firms and leads to reduction in cost.

(*c*) **Economies of Welfare:** As compared to large firms an industry is in a position to provide welfare facilities to the workers *e.g.*, educational, housing facilities etc encourage the workers efficiency, which helps to raise the quality and quantity of the products of the industry.

(*d*) **Economies of Specialisation:** The firms in an industry may also reap the economies of specialisation. When an industry expand in size firms start specialising in different processes and the industry benefits on the whole. The unit cost of production falls.

## 7.3 RELATION BETWEEN INTERNAL AND EXTERNAL ECONOMIES

The relation between the two is one of degree only. For example, firms may be enjoying external economies but if they combine together then all external economies become internal for them. Again an internal economy reaped by a firm becomes external for some other firm. If molasses are used by the sugar factory itself for manufacturing spirit it is an internal economy but if some other firm buys molasses for manufacturing spirit it is an external economy to the buying firm Often external economies leads to internal economies. **Mrs. Robinson says**, "Economies of large scale industry are likely to have the effect of altering the optimum size of the firm and the reorganisation of the firm to adapt itself to the new optimum size many lead to further economies **Mrs. Robinson** terms them *as internal external economies* they are internal economies since they depend on the size of the firm and external because they depend upon the size of the industry"[2].

## 7.4 DISECONOMIES OF LARGE SCALE PRODUCTION

The economies of scale does not continue indefinitely then diseconomy sets in. The diseconomies are:

1. **Financial Diseconomies:** An entrepreneur needs finance to expand his business. But finance may not be easily available in the required amount at the appropriate time. Lack of finance prevents the firm from expanding with appropriate direction and retards its production plan and raises cost of production.

---

2. Joan Robinson, *The Economies of Imperfect Competition* 1933

2. **Managerial Diseconomy:** There is a limit beyond which a firm becomes unmanageable and hence unamangeable. Supervision becomes lax, decision-making becomes difficult. Coordination between workers and management disappears and production cost increases.
3. **Marketing Diseconomies:** The expansion of a firm beyond a certain limit may involve marketing problems. Raw material may not be available in sufficent quantity due to their scarcities. The demand for the products of the firm may fall as a result of change in taste and the firm may not be in a position to change accordingly in the short period. The market organisation may fail to foresee changes in the market condition where by the sales might fall.
4. **Technical Diseconomies:** Due to diseconomy in finance, marketing or management the firm may fail to operate its plant to its maximum capacity. It may have *excess or idle capacity e.g.*, if the plant can manufacture 2000 units but only 1500 units are manufactured; operating below full capacity. As a result cost per unit rises.
5. **Diseconomies of Risk Taking:** As the scale of production rises risk also rises. An error of judgement by either sales/production manager may affect adversely sale of production which leads to loss.
6. **External Diseconomies:** If an industry expands its growing demand for the various factors of production like labour, raw material, capital etc. one part of the firms may eventually raise their prices. The localisation of industry may lead to shortage of transport, power, raw material. All such external diseconomies tends to raise cost per unit.

❑❑❑

CHAPTER 8

# Rationalisation in Industry Automation and Standarisation

## 8.1 INTRODUCTION

Rationalisation implies a revolutionary change in the structure and control of industrial activity in a well-coordinated and integrated manner to remove the wastages and inefficiency and reduce cost at all levels. Rationalisation, infact is one of the most controversial technique.

The origin of the concept of rationalisation dates back to the period immediately after the first world war. After the defeat in the war, Germany found her industries in a stage of nearing collapse. Her industrial degeneration was so threatening that she had a radical recourse to the most affective measures. The measures that was adopted by the German industrial entrepreneurs to revive the German economy came to be known as *rationalisation.*

Rationalisation is termed in the, German language as *rationalisierung* which meant a *new industrial phylosophy revolution* by Walter Meakin. After Germany, achieved industrial progress other countries of the world too adopted rationalisation to regenerate and strengthen their industrial economy.

## 8.2 CONCEPT AND DEFINITION

The scope of rationalisation is wide and it is not possible to compress the full implication and intricacies of the term within any rigid definition. *A few definition are given below.*

### According to the *National Board of Economy and Efficiency, Germany*

"Rationalisation consists in understanding and applying every means of improving the general economic situation through technical and systematic organisation".

### World Economic Conference, Geneva, 1927

"Rationalisation refers to the methods of techniques and of organisation designed to secure the minimum waste of either effort or material. Thus, it includes the scientific organisation of labour, standaraisation of both materials and products, simplification of processes and improvement in the system of transport and marketing. The objective of rationalisation therefore was categorised as (*i*) to secure maximum efficiency of labour with minimum effort, (*ii*) to facilitate standarisation by a reduction in variety of patterns, designs, manufacture, (*iii*) to avoid wastage of raw material and power, (*iv*) to simplify the distribution of goods, (*v*) to reduce unnecessary transport and burden some financial charges, (*vi*) to avoid dispensable middlemen.

**C.S. Meyers:** "He stated that the derivation and first use of the term rationalisation are wrapt in obscurity[1]".

**Prof. Sargent Florence:** "Rationalisation as a movement to eliminate waste and inefficiency scientifically and logically by some sort of joint action between all the firms within one industry[2]".

**Professor D.H. Macgregor:** "Rationalisation is the right organisation of industry considered as a type of government, the producers being so related as to enable such policies to be applied as works specialisation, non-destructive elimination of the weak and the control over the entrance of new establishments".

**L. Urwick:** "Rationalisation is both an attitude and a process, as an attitude it records the belief that a more rational control of world economic life through the application of scientific method is possible and desirable. As a process it implies the applications of the methods of science to all problems arising in the organisation and conduct of production distribution and consumption"[3].

**German Federation of Industries** meant by rationalisation rational employment of all technical and organisational means in order to increase to the highest degree possible the productivity of workers. It must be the effort of all who take part in the production of commodities through these means to improve, increase and cheaper production. It also aim to cover a general expansion of trade and consumption and an improvement in the standard of workers".

**The International Labour Office** in 1931 stated that rationalisation means that instead of traditional processes, established routine, empirical rules and improvisation, use is made of the methods that are the fruit of patient scientific study and aim at the optimum adjustment of means to ends, thus securing that efforts produces the maximum useful results".

---

1. C.S. Meyers, *Business Rationalisation,* Sir Issac Pitman Sons London, 1932 p.54
2. Sargent Florence, *Logic of Industrial Organisation,* Kegan Paul, London 1933 p.87
3. L. Urwick; *The Meaning of Rationalisation*

**The Advisory Committee on Management of the International Labour organisation in 1937** (*a*) Rationalisation in several, is any reform tending to replace habitual antiquated practices by means or methods based on systematic reasoning, (*b*) In the narrowest sense it is any reform of an undertaking, administrative or other services, public or private tending to replace habitual antiquated practises by means or methods based on systematic reasoning, (*c*) In a wider sense it is a reform which takes a group of business undertakings as a unit and tends to reduce waste and loss due to unbridled competition by concerted action based on systematic reasoning to collective activities of the large economic and social group"[4].

**Kanpur Textile Mills Rationalisation Enquiry Committee 1956:** "The reform on rational and scientific basis in all its facets—men, material management and money—with a view to having the optimum of output with the minimum of cost and effort, without intensification"[5].

**The National Commission on Labour** will **discussing** the concept of rationalisation defined "Rationalisation as rational use of inputs in a planned and rational distribution of its output to meet current market demands and simultaneously to bring about a reduction in costs. More recently it means a basic change in the structure and control of industrial activity with the word 'industry' used in its generic sense. Elimination of waste and promotion of efficiency by means of coordinated, well-integrated and all round view of industry will fall within the purview of rationalisation. In its application it is a process which brings together the advantages of planned production, pooling of research and scientific and technical know-how, centralised regulation of finance, modernisation of productive processes and sales and optimum utilisation of manpower. It is thus closely akin to a broad based productivity drive through every available technique"[6].

An analysis of the various definition given above indicates that there is no verbal agreement in them. *But there are certain common features in all the definitions they are:*

(*a*) Rationalisations implies a fundamental change in the purpose, structure and control of the industries.

(*b*) It aims at elimination of waste of all kinds through scientific study.

(*c*) It increases the efficiency of the workers.

(*d*) It maximises production with minimum of expenditure

(*e*) It strives to ensure increased gains to both the partners in industry (employers and employees) and also to consumers and the community at large.

---

4. *International Labour Review,* August 1937, p. 251
5. *Report of the Kanpur Textile Mills, Rationalisation Enquiry Committee,* 1956, p.233.
6. *Government of India, Report of the National Commission on Labour,* 1969s p. 257

In India too, the aims and objects of rationalisation were determined. The **Bombay Textile Labour Enquiry Committee** 1941 stated that the *aims of rationalisation* are:

1. Increase in production per man and its relation to wages.
2. Improvement in the efficiency of workers and in the working conditions.
3. Financial and industrial reorganisation, thus the *basic objectives of rationalisation are*:
   (*i*) **Elimination of Waste and Inefficiency:** Rationalisation leads to replacement of traditional and absolute and unsystematic methods of production by modern scientific methods of production.
   (*ii*) **Ensures maximum utilisation of resources:** The next important objective of rationalisation is to ensure optimum use of scarce resources such that it ensures maximum production at minimum cost.
   (*iii*) **Maximising efficiency.**
   (*iv*) **Simplification of marketing and distribution system.**
   (*v*) **Improving the Quality of the Product Through Use of Better Quality Rawmaterial:** *Standarisation and simplification* is another important objective of rationalisation
   (*vi*) **Establishment of Industrial Stability:** Changing and restructuring of the industrial structure promotes stability.

Thus, rationalisation tends to revive the whole economy. It encompasses all those activities which are undertaken to raise production and productivity

## 8.3 ASPECTS OF RATIONALISATION

A study of various aspects of rationalisation is essential in order to clearly understand it. The various aspects of rationalisation are:

1. Technological aspect
2. Organisational aspect
3. Financial aspect
4. Social aspect.

### I. Technological Aspect

Technologically rationalisation involves standarisation, simplification, mechanisation, intensification and specialisation:

(*a*) ***Standardisation*** is a process of careful and judicious selection of materials, size products etc. It entails the fixing of certain standards. The standard in any case is the best possible shape with specific description that clearly eliminates the unsuitable. Standarisation as such is necessary for efficient and economic production as it increases the productive capacity of existing plants as a result of decrease in the number of types and size. The standards should be flexible to enable the unit to be adaptable in accordance with the changes in the technology. However, standards remain constant as long as there is a possibility of technical obsolescence as they are borne out of scientific experimentation and industrial practise.

(*b*) ***Simplification*** is an act of rendering industrial process simple or making less complex or less difficult while standarisation is the act or process of conforming to any measure or extent, quantity or quality or value established by law, general usage or consent[7]. The producer, the distributor and the consumers all would be benefitted by such simplification. It would mean greater production, productivity, with less wastages due to an easy acquisition of proficiency by operatives, blocking up of lesser capital in materials and spare parts and a simpler costing system. To the retailer, it means the carrying of smaller stock. Further selling becomes less complicated. To the consumer it brings the advantages of the improved quality, reduced selling prices and enhanced purchasing power.

(*iii*) ***Mechanisation*** emphasises the use of machines as against manual labour in the process of manufacture. Machines helps to promote standarisation. Mechanisation permits the best advantages, provided right material of right type fed into the machines at the right time by the right operative. Thus, from the stage of feeding of raw material through various stages of manufacture to the stage of handing over of the product to the consumer. The coordinated process of mechanisation have given cooperative effort to instill life into standarisation technique. Thus, mechanisation helps to reduce the cost of production, brings about standarisation, raises the efficiency of labour, improves the quality of the products.

(*d*) ***Intensification*** aims to remove slackness and inefficiency. In the course of standarisation, the advanced stage will be reached where high speed of execution is to be achieved and this is known as intensification. At this stage, rationalisation movement simply depends upon the acceleration of the standarisation and would not introduce any further factors of production. The existing production and distributing machinery works with full speed. Intensification is opposed on the ground by the workers that they are burdened with more work loads.

(*e*) ***Specialisation:*** Mechanisation results in specialisation. When repetitive work on a massive scale is carried out the natural

7. R.M. Hudson, *Simplification and Standarisation,* p.689.

consequences in course of time is specialisation. To achieve the benefits of specialisation the ultimate interdependence is established with highest coordination and integration of layout, machines, process and method. Specialisation is also called *'simulation'* as simultaneous link between machine, labour, process and method would be established in it. Specialisation becomes so regular a routine and almost mechanised cooperation and internal adjustments of high degree is essential in such a situation as failure of an element at one point dislodges the entire programme, and it becomes costly to readjust the whole programme. Specialisation can be obtained in every field of production and distribution.

## 2. Organisational Aspect

Rationalisation stresses not only on technological aspects but also on destruction and revampining within an industry that is bringing about organisational changes. On the organisational aspect rationalisation claims some kind of agreement between the various producers with a view to adjust the total demand. It envisages a few large units with central control and management in place of a large number of uneconomic and inefficient independent units. The independent unit should work with full capacity with each unit producing a small range of products for which they are best suited. Thus, rationalisation leads to cooperative methods of action. As rationalisation suppresses competition among the units in an industry **Meakin Walter** calls it as "the tangled phrase to describe the old fashioned device of eliminating competition"[8]. *According to* **Mc. Groger.** Rationalisation has been built so as to imply the right organisation of an industry considered as a type of government, the producers being so retailed as to enable such policies to be applied as work specialisation, non-destructive elimination of the weak and the control over the entrance of new establishment".

*Thus, the organisational changes are brought about with the help of:*

(*a*) **Industrial Combination:** In order to make the industry vibrant and effective the tool of combination is adopted. Combination implies the integration or merger of various types of small and inefficient units with large and efficient units. This ensures in achieving planned utilisation of resources effectively.

(*b*) **Works Specialisation:** It entails that different enterprises within an industry produce specific components of a product not the entire product. This removes wastages of labour and capital and also wasteful competition.

(*c*) **Matching of Supply and Demand:** Rationalisation enables to regulate the behaviour of the market by suitably adjusting the overall production to the overall demand. Thus, production is controlled keeping in view

8. Meakin Walter, *The New Industrial Revolution,* V. Gollance, London, 1928, p. 13.

the total or aggregate demand. The enterprises within an industry for the purpose of exercising control over production come into agreement.

(*d*) **Control over the Entrance of New Units:** It is operated to regulate production in accordance to demand.

(*e*) **Nationalisation:** The government takes over the ownership and management of the industry. This is done with a view to making the enterprise within an industry more efficient more effective and more productive

### 3. Financial Aspect

Rationalisation is concerned with the capitalisation of the units of the rationalised industry in a fair manner. Adequacy of capital and financial strength are very much essential for maintaining the efficiency of manufacturing enterprises. The inadequacy of the financial resources may affects the units adversely as improvement in techniques and organisation cannot be made. Rationalisation also emphasises the need for modernisation of plant and equipment through self-financing. Self-financing needs a conservative attitude on the part of the management since it should not come into conflict with the payment of dividends and also adopt a liberal provision for maintenance and renewal of reserves.

### 4. Social Aspect

Rationalisation is not merely a mechanical process but it is also an art. According to **C.S. Myers** "Rationalisation demands the consideration of business not in its own purely selfish, technical and commercial aspect. But also in a wider economic, social and generally human aspects. With out all these aspects it will be pseudo rationalisation of business affairs".

Rationalisation though aims at the material prosperity of the community should also see that its benefits are conducive to hygienic, cultural ethical progress and the advancement to the physical mental and moral welfare of the community . Rationalisation to be more conducive should also entail various provisions and measures like adequate incentives, recognition of efficient worker organisation of satisfactory schemes of promotion etc to encourage the workers.

Thus, the main aspect of social rationalisation in industry is to build good industrial relations by facilitating proper utilisation of manpower resources, by providing welfare to its labour force. Rationalisation also promotes protects and preserves national interest.

## 8.4 BENEFITS OF RATIONALISATION

A number of benefits accrue from rationalisation. They are classified under the following heads:

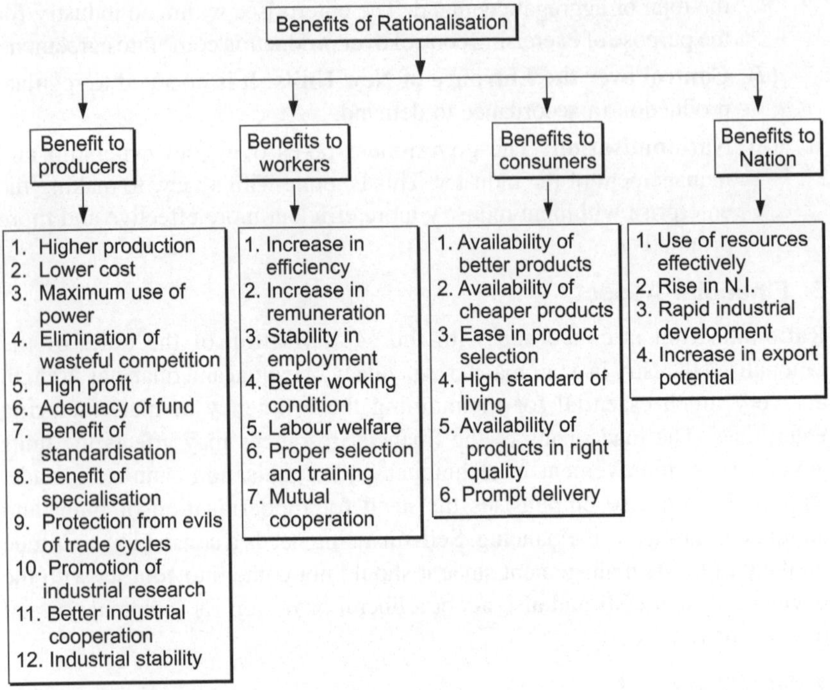


### 8.5.1 Benefits to Producers

Benefits to producers are as follows:

1. **Higher Production:** Rationalisation increases the quantum of production. Rationalisation stress on removal of worn out and obsolete plants, machinery and equipments and introduction of modern machine and equipment. Through the process of simplification and automation rationalisation promotes rise in production.
2. **Lowering of Cost:** Through elimination of waste and inefficiency Rationalisation reduces the cost of production.
3. **Maximum Use of Power and Materials.**
4. **Promotion of Highest Profits:** Higher production at reduced cost maximum use of power and material and other economies of large scale production raises the producers profit.
5. **Elimination of Wasteful Competition.**
6. **Adequacy of Fund.**
7. **Benefits of Standarisation.**
8. **Benefits of specialisation, mechanisation and scientific management** are reaped by the producers due to rationalisation. Specialisation helps in concentrating effort upon a limited field of endeavour. According to **Kimball and kimball** "due to specialisation the product can be produced more cheaply and better than under the

older general methods". Similarly mechanisation makes mass production easy and convenient and thus helps in reducing cost. Scientific management increases the efficiency of workers and thereby productivity can be increased.

9. **Protection from trade cycle fluctuation.**
10. **Promotes industrial research:** Under rationalisation research is feasibly done.

### 8.5.2 Benefits to Workers are:

Rationalisation aims at securing maximum efficiency of labour with minimum effort. This leads to higher production, greater productivity and profits to the producer reduction in cost waste and in efficiency, provides an opportunity to the producer to raise the remuneration of workers.

Rationalisation also raises stability in the economy and ensures better working condition for its labourers. Rationalisation provokes mutual cooperation between workers and employers.

It is thus seen that rationalisation facilitates overall development of workers.

### 8.5.3 Benefits to Consumers are:

1. **Availability of Better Products:** The measures of rationalisation like standarisation, specialisation, mechanisation etc ensures the availability of better quality products to the consumer.
2. **Availability of cheaper products:** Rationalisation removes wastages and inefficiency, increases production and productivity and ultimately reduces cost of production and distribution. As a result the prices of products are reduced which in turn benefits the consumer in the form of cheaper products.
3. **Ease in product selection by** consumers since the products are uniform in nature.
4. **Higher Standard of having:** Rationalisation stresses on price reduction raising thereby the purchasing power capacity and rise in real income, this further ensures rise in standard of living.
5. **Prompt delivery:** Kimball and Kimball viewed that due to standarisation goods are delivered to the consumers promptly.

### 8.5.4 Benefits to the Nation are:

Benefits to the nation can be summarised as below:

1. **Effective and Economic use of Resources:** Rationalisation promotes effective and economical use of resources. It eliminates wastages of resources.
2. **Raises National Income:** One of the basic objective of rationalisation is to secure higher production. Higher level of production entails a hike in national income.

3. **Economic Prosperity and Stability:** Rationalisation promotes productivity, rise in production, rise in national income, reduces cost, inefficiency wastages, thereby promoting rise in stability.
4. **Rapid Industrial Development:** Rationalisation speeds up industrial development and also promotes export potentiality.

Rationalisation may therefore be regarded as a "process which brings together the advantages of planned production pooling of research and scientific and technical know-how, centralised regulation of finance modernisation of production, process, sales and optimum untilisation of man power".

## 8.6 CONCLUSION: RATIONALISATION ATTEMPTS AS SUCH

1. To bring stability to our industry by means of amalgamations and agreements; eliminating wasteful competition.
2. Process of manufacturing are simplified, standarised, reduntant type of production are eliminated. As such cost of production is reduced.
3. Improvement in technique assures rise in productivity .
4. Economies accure in centralised buying of raw material, fuels, stores etc. Unnecessary middlemen are eliminated.
5. Cost of distribution in marketing is reduced.
6. The benefits of common scientific and industrial research are passed on to the constituent units cheaply.
7. Planned production avoids wastages.
8. The credit worthiness of the units is enhanced as a result of the centralisation of finance.
9. Labourers enjoy the benefits of rationalisation since rationalisation provides better working condition and wage incentives thereby creating a congenial atmosphere to work. This enables the workers to work by earning more wages with less fatigue thus leading to higher standard of living.
10. Consumers gain by rationalisation by getting standarised products at cheap rates.
11. Rationalisation benefits the whole society by raising national income and standard of living.

## 8.7 THE ATTITUDE OF INDUSTRIALISTS

Despite the benefits arising from rationalisation the industrialist are still apprehensive towards rationalisation. They viewed that

1. Rationalisation would involve huge capital expenditure without an assurance of adequate return on investment. Further inadequacy of fund may also prove to be a barrier in the implementation of rationalisation.

2. There is a chance of conflict to arise amongst the employer and the employee regarding profit sharing.
3. The entrepreneurs are afraid of the threat of nationalisation from the government. They fear that if the industry becomes nationalised in near future then despite having spent huge amount they would not become ultimate beneficiaries.
4. Opposition is raised by vested interest if uneconomic and inefficient units in an industry are closed down.
5. Fear of obsolence may occur Rationalist favours continued research and development in industry the machines installed at high cost may become obsolete with the invention of new one within a short span of time. This requires further changes. This process of invention and obsolence would be involving huge cost. Therefore, the producer opposes rationalisation.

The advocates of rationalisation favours rationalisation since they feel that merits of rationalisation are greater since it ensures rise in income.

## 8.8 OPPOSITION FROM LABOURERS

Rationalisation involves a process of closing down uneconomic and inefficient units. Concentrating production with up-to-date machinery and labour saving devices in those units which are best suited for the said purpose. The immediate effect of these measures would be loss of employment for a large number of workers. The labourers therefore criticised rationalisation on the following grounds:

### 1. Danger of Large Scale Unemployment

**Shri V.V. Giri** rightly observed that “All schemes of rationalisation involving either an increase in the workload or the installation of modern machinery which will invariably require a small number of workers for the same output must inevitably lead to varying degrees of retrenchment”.

The danger or large scale unemployment is thus the major ground of workers opposition to the scheme. Rationalisation creates unemployment through retrenchment and reduction in employment opportunities. The introduction of sophisticated methods and machines reduces the quantum of work done by the human labour. This displaced labour who were trained on old methods and machines, would not generally be absorbed anywhere. Thus, they added to the already existing unemployment in the country.

However, this notion was attacked on the ground that unemployment created through rationalisation was temporary in nature. Further rationalisation boosts up employment in the long run by promoting industries Modern small scale units also offers more jobs.

### 2. Danger of Increased Workload

The labourers fear that workers retained in the industry even after rationalisation would be required to work hard because of the intensification of the processes.

All this puts excess strain on the workers which results in both physical and mental stagnation. Further rationalisation puts a barrier in the working condition of manufactures who tend to spend less on the ancillary aspects like working condition suitable training etc since there commitment would be heavy in rationalisation.

### 3. Share in Profits

Rationalisation raises production and profitability in the industry benefitting thereby the employees. The workers are denied due shares in increased profits. This is a major reason why workers oppose this scheme.

Rationalisation according to Hobson[9] leads to unemployment. Hobson said that "There can be no ground for holding that rationalisation as a whole tends to distribution of income favourable to the workers either through raising wages or lowering prices. All economic evidences showed that rationalisation carried with it a net diminution of employment and substitution of a large proportion of low skilled for high skilled workers and distribution of the product which increases the proportionate share of capital and reduces that of labour".

Another important thing to be noted was that due to rationalisation person in the age-group of 35 and over where retrenched. At this age when a person is over-burdened with family responsibilities it is not possible to undergo training and raise his skill, so that he is able to run automated machines. Infact a young employee is in advantageous position to adapt and bring a change in his skillful access. This statement was made in the report of the National Commission on Labour, Government of India[10].

Rationalisation is therefore regarded as unmixed blessing; a key to progress and prosperity.

## 8.9 RATIONALISATION AND SCIENTIFIC MANAGEMENT

Peter. F Drucker viewed that rationalisation performed the same function in Germany as scientific management did in U.S.A. Rationalisation is infact a development of scientific management. Both aim to use modern scientific methods of production and organisation in place of out moded methods with the objective of raising production, efficiency, productivity, along with proper utilisation, of material and human resources to the fullest extent. Both aimed to reduces wastages. Rationalisation initially meant the application of principle of scientific management. Rationalisation includes not only scientific management but many more things Rationalisation is concerned with the problem of the industry as a whole while scientific management is concerned

---

9. J.A. Hobson, *Rationalisation and Unemployment.* George Allenit Onium Ltd. London, 1930, 88.

10. *Government of India, The Report of the National Commission on Labour,* p.260.

with individual concerns alone Rationalisation dealt with standarisation mechanisation, simplifications, while scientific management was concerned primarily with increased efficiency of existing production. Rationalisation has got a wider scope than scientific management since it also covers financing and distribution along with integration of various units in an industry which has not been taken over under scientific management. *C.S. Meyers* said that "Rationalisation includes scientific management but it goes further, it aims not only at avoiding over production, it aims not only at avoiding waste within the single concern but also avoiding waste within a whole combine of concerns". Infact scientific management is a part of rataionalisation.

The difference between the two can be categorically studied in a tabular form:

| S.No. | Rationalisation | S.No. | Scientific Management |
|---|---|---|---|
| 1. | Rationalisation was discovered in Germany in order to revive the disastarous economy into a prosperous economy. | 1. | Scientific Management was discovered in U.S.A in order to maximise the efficiency of a plant. |
| 2. | The scope of rationalisation is wide. It includes scientific management. | 2. | The scope of scientific management is narrow. It is a constituent of rationalisation. |
| 3. | Rationalisation is industry oriented | 3. | Scientific management is applicable at individual plant level. |
| 4. | Rationalisation covers all activities of an industry such as production, finance, organisation, marketing personnel, social and human etc. | 4. | Scientifc management mainly covers production and organising activities. |
| 5. | Rationalisation encompasses several measures to raise productivity and production such as combination, mechanisation automation, reorganisation, industrial research, standardisation specialisation, intensification etc. | 5. | Scientific management encompasses measures like time study, motion study, fatigue study etc. |
| 6. | Rationalisation eliminates competition within an industry. | 6. | Scientific management strengthens competitive strength of a firm. |
| 7. | Rationalisation brings equilibrium between demand and supply. | 7. | Scientific management brings disequilibrium between demand and supply. |
| 8. | Seeks to eliminate waste and inefficiency of the whole industry. | 8. | Scientific management also seeks to eliminate waste and inefficiency within an individual plant. |
| 9. | The mechanisation of rationalisation is dynamic in nature. Hence it is not fixed and predetermined. | 9. | Scientific management has virtually well set and predetermined mechanism. |

It is thus obvious that there exists both similarities and dissimilarities between rationalisation and scientific management. The dissimilarities are viewed from point of view of objectives, scope, mode of application, mechanism etc.

## 8.10 RATIONALISATION AND AUTOMATION

Automation, is the continuation of the process of mechanisation of production initated by the industrial revolution. It is something which replaces direct manpower for mental or manual work or for both by self-regulating machines for example, application of computers. Automation infact is a part of rationalisation. Without any significant resort to automation it is possible to implement rationalisation but automation is necessarily the higher reach of rationalisation. Automation involves the application of automatic control mechanism with self-regulation. Automation promotes standardisation of products and acts as a labour saving element. It ensures simplicity and convenience of administration and precision in results. Goods and services will be produced at low cost which would thereby promote higher standard of living and rise in consumption.

## 8.11 RATIONALISATION IN INDIA

Rationalisation was adopted widely in various countries of the world. The government of India too realised that rationalisation should be adopted on organisational, managerial as well as labour side. A sub-committee of the Industries Development Committee of the Planning Commission consisting of employers and employees representative under the chairmanship of **Gulzari Lal Nanda** discussed the issue of rationalisation and arrived at the following conclusion in 1951:

1. Rationalisation should be introduced in Indian industries with a special care to avoid retrenchment of workers and to do this:
   (*a*) It was felt that vacancies caused by death and retirement should not be filled by advertising new vacancies but through;
   (*b*) Absorbing surplus workers in other departments without breaking the continuity of services.
   (*c*) Granting gratuity for voluntary retirements and
   (*d*) Extension of machinery wherever possible to absorb displaced personas.
2. Workload should be standardised and if there is any dispute it should be investigated.
3. The government should prepare a scheme for the rehabilitation of retrenched workers.
4. An equitable share in the gains of rationalisation should be given to the labourers.

*The second five year plan* observed that "Rationalisation should be attempted when it does not lead to unemployment and is introduced in consultation with the workers and is effected after improving the working conditions and guaranting a substantial share of gains to workers". *The Seventh All-India Conference of the Indian Institute of Personnel Management (*1957*)* said that rationalisation as far as possible be planned in such a way as to eliminate retrenchment and where retrenchment becomes inevitable, efforts should be made to secure alternative employment of those workers.

Rationalisation should be adopted by all major industries like cotton textile, jute, sugar, coal etc, so that it is well-equipped to meet the national and international demands, and competition. Rationalisation leads to betterment of workers and community as whole. Rationalisation should be widely implemented to boost the economic growth rate.

❑❑❑

CHAPTER 9

# Industrial Productivity

## 9.1 INTRODUCTION

In the process of economic growth, production and productivity are the two significant elements. Increase in productivity in an industry is an essential factor for stepping up the rate of economic growth especially in case of an under-developed country which suffers from inadequacy of capital, raw material and skilled manpower.

**Rise in productivity implies rise in production which reflects rise in National income and economic growth rate. Infact rise in productivity is just not sufficient** index of rise in growth, rise in productivity must be accompanied by reduction in cost of production of every additional unit. Expansion of output with **minimum input implies rise in productivity**.

**The concept of productivity:** The term productivity has been defined differently by different authors. **B.B. Lal** said that "Productivity refers to measurable relationship beteween well-defined output and input *i.e.*, between the production results and the relative production agents in both the financial and physical terms in relation to given time and condition" [1]. Productivity **refers to ratio between production that is (total output) and factors used in production that is (input).** Productivity implies that how by allocating rationally the resources maximum output is achieved thereby enhancing economic growth.

**Ewan Claugue** says that 'Productivity is a word which we use broadly to express the overall efficiency with which our industries perform[2]. This definition is not accurate since overall efficiency embraces all factors of production and measuring all the dissimilar factors of production in one group is impracticable.

---

1. B.B. Lal, *Industrial Productivity and Economic Growth* p. 1
2. Ewan Claugue, *Productivity, Employment and Living Standards*, Conference on Productivity, 4th June 1969, University of Wiscons in, U.S.A.
3. Russel W. Fenske, *Productivity, Measurement at the Work Centre,* N.P.C., Productivity Journal.

**Russel. W. Fenske**[3] defines the term **'Productivity' in five ways: They are:**

(*i*) Productivity is a form of efficiency.

(*ii*) Productivity is the utilisation of resources or effectivenes of utilisation of resources.

(*iii*) Productivity is a ratio.

(*iv*) Productivity is a ratio (rather than a phenomenon).

(*v*) Productivity is a rate of return (**primarily in monetary terms**).

**J.M.S. Risk** defines **'Productivity as a physical ratio**; it relates to the quality of goods produced or services given in comparison with the quantity of resources consumed"[4].

**The International Labour Office** defines productivity as the ratio between output and one of the factors of input is generally known as the productivity of the factors considered"[5]. This productivity means the ratio between output and any of the factors of production land, labour, capital and organisation.

**Measurement of Productivity:** Productivity refers to a relation between output and input.

**Symbollicaly it canbe connoted as such:**

1. $\text{Productivity} = \dfrac{\text{Net output}}{\text{Effort input}}$

2. $\text{Labour productivity} = \dfrac{\text{Net output}}{\text{Number of workers or Number of man hours utilised}}$

   Productivity of labour is thus a ratio between output and labour used or number of man hours utilised.

3. $\text{Productivity of capital} = \dfrac{\text{Net output}}{\text{Net Capital employed}}$

   It is a ratio between output and capital employed.

4. $\text{Productivity of machine} = \dfrac{\text{Net output}}{\text{Total machine hours worked}}$

5. $\text{Productivity} = \dfrac{\text{Net output}}{\text{Number of hectares of land}}$

Although productivity is measured in terms of all factors of production, that is output rises in proposition to rise in input, but labour is selected as most important element to measure the ratio of productivity. When output per worker is increasing, the economy would reflect rise in national income and rise in growth rate.

---

4. J. M. S. Risk, *Measurement in a Competitive Planned Economy, Management Accounting,* July 1970, p. 259.

5. *International Labour Organisation, Methods of Labour Productivity,* Statistics, 1951.

## 9.2 DEFECTS IN MEASUREMENT OF PRODUCTIVITY

Defects in measurement of productivity can be summarised as:

1. It is not possible to measure productivity of service industries like Banking, Insurances etc. as the output cannnot be directly measurable in terms of physical unit.
2. If the finished products are homogeneous in nature, measurement of productivity is easier but it is difficult to measure productivity of certain industries producing heterogeneous products like chemical engineering, electric, glass industries etc.
3. It is not possible to take account of **invisible and intangible output** or **associated services which** may have no bearing on current production while measurig productivity as in the case of maintenance of scientific and industrial research laboratories, market research bureau etc.
4. Measuring productivity through labour index lacks precision and clarity. The quality of labour force is not uniform in nature and therefore measurement based on labour force lacks accuracy.
5. The difficulty involved in the measurement of output is of technical character.
6. It is difficult to bring long term comparison. Through passing of time techniques, method of production changes which influences productivity.

### 9.2.1 Tools of Productivity

The following are the tools of industrial prodcutivity:

1. Use of scientific management technique and practises.
2. Work, time and motion studies for scientifically determining better and quickers ways of doing a job.
3. Developing better human relations including the modern concept of industrial sickness between the employer and the employee.
4. Provision of wages and bonus incentives, adoption of collective bargaining, management workers consultations, workers participation in management training of workers and labour welfare schemes.
5. Adoption of standardisation, specialisation and simplification programmes in the methods of production.
6. Adaption of control techniques (including production and planning control), cost control, quality control at each level.
7. Improvement in working conditions, material handling and plant lay-out etc.
8. Selection and training of personnel at the various levels of management.

### 9.2.2 Factors Influcencing Industrial Productivity

1. **Technical Factor:** Technologically innovation plays an important role in affecting productivity. The application of mechanical power, introduction of highly specialised and semi-automatic and automatic machines, improvement in the production process, more efficient co-ordination and integration of productive processes and specialisation are the factors which have contributed to the spectacular advances in raising of productivity. Infact, long term gains in productivity stem mainly from the advances in science and technology. The application of motive power and mechanical improvement to the process of production has accelerated the pace of industrialisation to an unprecedented degree and has given us the vision of the vast and unexplored frontiers that still lie ahead of us in the realm of science and technology"[6].
2. **Financial Factor:** Finance plays a dominating role in affecting productivity. Industrial productivity is dependent on innovation and technological improvements and innovation can be possible only where capital is available in abundance. Adequacy of finance would promote mechanisation and this would help to accelerate the pace of industrial productivity especially where labour is scarce.
3. **Natural Factors:** In case of agricultured industries, extractive industries like coal, mining, physical output is determined by geological, physical and topographical factors. Natural and climatic factors exercises a vital influence on the industrial productivity, climatic condition also influences the working capacity of a labourer *e.g.*, cotton textile industry is also dependent on good climatic condition."[7]. The geological and physical factors thus plays a very dominant role in determining the productivity of extractive industry like coal mining in which the physical output per head is greatly influenced by the depth of coal mines, the thickness of the coal seams, the topography of the region and the quality of coal available. In industries like tailoring hosiery, etc the geographical, geological, physical factors exercise little influence on productivity"[7].
4. **Managerial Factors:** Managerial factors today play a dominant role in influencing industrial productivity since under the present system of industrial production management plays a vital role. It performs a wide variety of function *i.e.*, decision making, laying down policy, organising, planning, directing, controlling staffing, coordinating, getting goods produced and selling. It has been said that 'never before in the history of industrial development was there a great need of energetic, enterprising, foresighted managerial talents imbued with the spirit of adventure of qualities of judgement, imagination and vigilance, as is today, for the individual units are destined to sink or swim with those who guide and govern their destinies"[8].

---

6. M.M Mehta, *Measurement of Industrial Productivity*. The World Press Ltd., Calcutta 1955, p. 12
7. M.M Mehta p. 58
8. *Ibid* p. 49.

5. **Social Factors:** The socio-economic institution plays an important role though not directly but indirectly to promote industrial productivity. The psychological attitude, behaviour of the investors, employers, workers, consumer, their social values, their attitude of pessimism, their attitude to adopt themselves to the new innovative dynamic changes influences productivity to a great extent. If the people are educated, progressive in thought and not backed by traditionalism, the level of productivity would surely increase. Thus the socio-economic factors such as the role of decision making capacity of the individuals or group of individuals, property rights, consumer's sovereignty, living condition, standard of living of the people, family system, religion, willingness to save etc may stimulate or dampen the urge for higher industrial productivity. Further the psychological attitude and behaviour of the investor, employers, workers, and consumers, their resilience to accept new innovation and products and the values that guide and govern their philosophies of and daily conduct and influence and the attitude towards community, may adjust or retard productivity.
6. **Adminstrative Factors:** The administrative and financial policies of the government also plays a vital role in influencing the industrial productivity. The goverment's industrial policy, taxation, tariff policies influences the productivity of industrial units. At times the policy of protectionism may prove to be a barrier to productivity and at times it may be benefical. Infact, this depends upon the nature of industry. The government may also play an important role in creating favourable atmosphere for saving, investment flowing capital from one industry or sector of production to another which will influence directly or indirectly the trends in industrial productivity.
7. **Quality of Labour Force:** The skill, experience, qualification, intensity of work etc of the worker have dominating pull in influencing the level of industrial productivity. There is a positive relation between the standard of living of a nation and the skill that the country's labour force can acquire. No spectacular gain in the industrial progress has been made in most of the under-developed countries due to lack of proper facilities necessary for the upkeep of body and mind of labour force. Thus wage, working condition, ability of worker influence productivity.
8. **Size of Industrial Unit:** Some economists say that increase in productivity is also due to economies of large scale. When other factors like technology, labour etc remain at the same level large scale unit as a rule should be more efficient than a small-scale unit. Large scale unit is at an advantageous position in obtaining the supplies of raw material at lower price. Further the large sized plant can derive the advantage of specialisation of managerial ability, marketing of products, utilising of by products etc. Generally large units spend substantial sum of money on scientific, tehnical and marketing research which leads to greater productivity.

### 9.2.3 Significance of Productivity Measurement

Industrial productivity is a **statistical measurement** on the basis of which we are able to measure compare, the industrial capacity of various industrial units and draw conclusion. Productivity indices reflect the industrial capacity of industrialist. It indicates the magnitude of change in the economic activity. Its scope entail all the facets of economic welfare.

Productivity indices at the national level have been used as an objective and scientific measure for forecasting the trends in the major sectors of the country's economy and in apparising the economic condition and prospects. Industrial productivity is considered as a **barometer or bench-mark of countries economic and industrial advancement**. On the national level, productivity indices are used to evaluate whether policy of protectionism or restriction should be adopted, against a particular industry. It also initates the framers to decide the taxation, industrial, fiscal policy, along with social labour welfare schemes in the limelight of industrial productivity indices. Productivity indices also assits in analysing, forecasting the economic trends, in evaluating the influence of technological changes on the volume of production, employment and in allocation of natural, financial human resources which would maximise national welfare.

The **international study** also suggests the competitive efficiency in the economic growth of the respective countries and their potentialities in capturing foreign markets. The productivity indices at the **inter regional level** thus reveals the differences in effectiveness of production between two regions in terms of output when similar products are produced. This stimulates the policy makers to analyse and formulate policy, disperse industries. Further even at **department and plant level productivity index helps in stimulation of policy of rationalisation and scientific management and in formulation of policies for future planning of production.**

Thus, we can briefly put the significance of productivity measurement as such:

1. Helps to make Comparative analysis.
2. Helps to make proper allocative distribution of resources.
3. Helps the government to formulate policies.
4. Helps to make an analytical apparisal of performances of an industry.
5. Helps in initation of cordial industrial relations.

## 9.3 MIS-INTERPRETATION OF PRODUCTIVITY

There is a mis-interpretation that productivity drive results in making the workers work harder or in displacement of workers. There is also another misconception that only management stands to gain from productivity. But the truth lies in the fact that the workers should recognise that productivity drive ultimately leads to their prosperity. No doubt, some sort of short run displacement of workers may be there. Infact measures should be taken by the management to see that the displacement would not result in loss of earning to the workers. Management also should evolve a proper scheme of sharing the benefits of productivity drive. **Dr. P.S. Lokanathan** the Founder Chairman of National productivity Council suggested that "It appears inevitable that the economy will either develop along these lines or will be made to do so. In an economy such as ours operating at such low levels of productivity, it should be immediately possible over a fairly wide front to link up increased productivity and higher remuneration for workers ... a rise of wages to the minimum level would be rapidly paid for by increased productivity, would have made an investment in the good will and contentment of its workers. This is good business". The formula suggested by Lokanathan, was as follow to share the gains of productivity technique:

| | **Percentage Share** | |
|---|---|---|
| | **Management** | **Labour** |
| where the wage is below the minimum wage | 0% | 100% |
| where the wage between the minimum wage and the fair wage | 20% | 80% |
| where the wage is at or above the fair wage level | 50% | 50% |

Having seen thus it would not be wrong to say productivity drive plays an important role in pacing the level of industrial development in the country. Thus, the main objective of productivity drive would be to raise production and improve:

1. quality, use modern techniques which aimed at fuller utilization of the available factors of production raising the standard of living of the people, and improving the working condition of labour.
2. Increase productivity which would help to raise employment opportunities and not displace workers.
3. The benefits of productivity be rationally distributed among capitalist, labourers, and consumers.
4. Productivity drive should cover all the large, medium and small industries whether they are in public or private sector.
5. Joint consultation, workers participation in management and promotion of mutual understanding between management and labour in each industry and each individual enterprise would help in increasing productivity.

**Productivity Movement in India:** In conclusion, we may say that the productivity drive in relation to India, through National Productivity Council (NPC) though attained significant momentum in the right direction yet the results were too poor to be adequate to the needs of the countries industrial development. India therefore requires more researchers, more practical men, for replacing the present preachers.

❑❑❑

CHAPTER 10

# Introduction to Cost Benefit Analysis

## 10.1 INTRODUCTION

Project evaluation is a microplanning technique which is used to assess the social desirability of a project in valuing public expenditure. It implies an assessment of a project as to its operational efficiency, technically, economically, financially and managerially. It is the evaluation of cost and benefits of each investment proposal meant for inclusion in a plan. Indian Planning Commission observes, that 'Evaluation is an aid to policy'. It may be considered as a branch of action programme. It is an integral part of development programme. According to **Hyman** "Project evaluation refers to the procedures of fact finding about the results of planned social action which in turn, moves the spiral of planning over upward. It is the proper methodological accompaniment of rational action."[1]. According to the second five year "Evaluation is an essential aid to policy. It may be considered to be a branch of research which is oriented primarily to the needs of an action programme".

"Project evaluation utilises principles similar to those....for the evaluation of industrial sectors, but it requires more extensive study of individual elements whereas sector analysis is applied only to the typical cost and demand conditions in the industry, project analysis takes into account a variety of supply and demand factors that are peculiar to the commodities and production technique under consideration"[2]. Thus, we may say that the technique of project evaluation is useful both for developed and under-developed countries. Since it helps to assess its success and failures and suggest further line of action. Project evaluation is a technique of optimisation.

1. Hyman, Wright and Hopkins, *Application of Methods of Evaluation,* 1962.
2. UN, ECAFE, *Formulating Industrial Development Programme,* 1961.

## 10.2 STAGES OF PROJECT EVALUATION

Project evaluation has four stages:

(*i*) To review the situation before starting the project.

(*ii*) To make appraisal of the project when it is started.

(*iii*) To suggest certain measures to improve the project in the light of its failure.

(*iv*) To evaluate the project ultimately in respect of its objectives.

## 10.3 METHODS OF EVALUATION/STAGES

The methods to evaluate are:

(*i*) Description of the technical and economic characteristics of each project.

(*ii*) Estimation of the impact of the project on the economy both during the construction phase and operational phase.

(*iii*) Evaluation of the consequences of project which may be direct or indirect.

(*iv*) Formulation of criterion for the selection of the project.

## 10.4 COST-BENEFIT ANALYSIS

The most significant and well-known method of project evaluation in our country is Cost Benefit Analysis. Regarding Cost Benefit Analysis Prof S.A. Marglin[1] advocated that the 'perspective and five year plan determine the broad strategy of growth by allocating of resources among sectors. But the strategy of growth embodied in the plans leaves many technical questions unresolved and it is these tactical decisions that are the province of cost-benefit analysis." Cost-Benefit Analysis provides superior criteria for project evaluation in planned economy. It helps the planning authority in making correct investment decision to achieve optimum resource allocation by maximising the difference between present value of benefit and cost of a project. Thus, cost-benefit analysis "purports to describe and quantify the social advantage and disadvantages of a policy in terms of a common monetary unit." Its objective function can be expressed as net social **Benefit NSB = Benefits – Costs**, where benefits and costs are measured in terms of "**Shadow**"* or '**accounting**' prices of input and outputs instead of in actual market price.

The entire cost-benefit analysis revolves around three steps:

(*i*) Enumeration of cost and benefits.

(*ii*) Evaluating cost and benefits.

(*iii*) Comparing them.

---

* Cost-benefit analysis was developed in U.S.A. for appraisal of investments in irrigation and transportation.

* Shadow prices reflect the intrinsic value of factors of productions.

### 10.4.1 Criteria for Cost-Benefit Analysis

The project evalution must be made on cost-benefit analysis to formulate optimal development plans. The social benefits of a project includes the conclusion that the project would make to the attainment of national goals.

**Cost:** Cost refers to the value of resources used in constructing the project and incurred in producing current output. The cost of capital, labour, salary of managers, natural resources, intermediate goods and advertisement constitute the total cost.

**Benefits:** Benefits refers to the addition to the flow of national output accuring from a project. A project may be regarded beneficial when it tends to increase the income of the people and that can be measured by the actual increase in production and consumption. Benefits may be real or nominal, tangible and intangible direct and indirect.

### 10.4.2 Evaluation on the Basis of Benefit

1. **Real Benefit** stands to be important since bounding of a river valley project increases irrigational facility to the cultivator which is just nominal benefit, but along with this it also promotes productivity and enhances a rise in real income of the agriculturist. This is real benefit. Therefore, if a project promotes both real and nominal benefit then it is beneficial.
2. **Direct Benefits** are those benefits which are directly obtainable from a project. For instance, a river valley project directly provides benefits like irrigational facility, power generation, flood control etc. But it also provides indirect benefits in the form of employment opportunities, construction of new railway line, road, tourist resort, establishment of factories etc. Therefore, in selecting a project only these projects should be chosen which promotes both direct and indirect benefits.
3. **Tangible Benefits** are those which can be measured in monetary terms while intangible benefits are those which cannot be measured in monetary terms. All benefits accuring from any river valley project are tangible and they can be easily valued in monetary terms.
4. **Intangible Benefit** refers to the individual valuation and they may be positive or negative. A good looking view of the Dam and recreational value of the Dam refer to the positive intangible benefits while the **negative intangible benefits** refer to all the losses of the people of that region accrued as a result of the Dam.

### 10.4.3 Evaluation on the Basis of Cost

1. **Real and Nominal Cost:** Cost may be real or nominal since they involve real sacrifice on the part of people or not. If money is borrowed from the people it is a case of **Nominal cost** but if people are required to construct project themselves they will be incurring real sacrifices and then it will be a case of **Real cost**.

2. **Primary and Secondary Cost: Primary Costs** are those which are directly incurred on the construction of a project. **Secondary Cost** includes the cost providing benefits to the people working on the project such as cost of constructing houses, schools, etc. at the sight of a project.
3. **Associated Cost:** They are the value of goods and services needed beyond those included in the cost of a project to make immediate products or services of the project available for use or sale. For example, the farmer's cost of producing irrigated crop other than any charge for water would be his associated cost of producing crops.
4. **Project Cost:** These are the value of resources used in constructing, maintaining and operating the project. This incudes cost of labour, capital equipment, intermediate good, natural resources, foreign exchange etc.

Thus, in evaluating a project we are to compute and compare its total benefits and total direct cost. If the **benefits are expected to be more than cost,** then only the **project is profitable** otherwise not.

The U.S. Sub-committee on benefit and cost has suggested four benefit-**cost criteria**. They are:

(*i*) $B - C$ (*ii*) $B - C/I$

(*iii*) $\Delta B/\Delta C$ (*iv*) $B/C$

where $B$ = Benefit, $C$ = Cost, $I$ = Direct Investment, $\Delta$ = Increament.

The formula $B–C/I$ is "for determining the total annual returns on a particular investment to the economy as a whole irrespective of to whom these accrue". If private investment is large then even high value of $B - C/I$ may be less beneficial to the economy. The second criteria of $\Delta B/\Delta C = 1$ is meant to determine the size of project. The criterion $B - C$ favours large project and makes small and medium projects less beneficial. Thus, this criterion helps in determining the scale of the project on the basis of the maximisation of the difference between $B$ and $C$. The most effective criterion for project evaluation of project is done on the basis of Benefit Cost Ratio. If $B/C = 1$ then the project is marginal because the benefits accruing from the project just covers the cost. If $B/C < 1$ the benefits are less than cost so the project is not acceptable. **Finally** $B/C > 1$ then offcourse the project becomes profitable and hence acceptable. **Greater the benefit the more profit oriented is the project.**

The criterion discussed does not account for the **time factor**. Future benefits and cost cannot be treated at par with present benefit and costs. Therefore, project evaluation requires **Discounting of Future Benefits and Costs because society prefers present to the future**. For this purpose economist have devised a number of 'decision rules' or criterion. But we shall discuss present value criterion and internal rate of return criterion.

## 10.5 NET PRESENT VALUE CRITERION

Net Present Value = Present Value of Benefit -Present Value of Operating and maintaing Cost- Initial Outlay. Thus, NPV of Benefit = Gross Present value of Benefit – Gross Present Value of Cost when NPV B > 0 then the project is socially profitable. But this criterion is not accurate method since it neglects time horizon. Capital investment gives benefit after a lapse of some time. Therefore, future benefits and cost cannot be equated with present benefit and costs. So it becomes essential to discount future benefits and cost since society prefers present to future. The discount factor is expressed as:

$$D = \frac{1}{(1+i)^t}$$

Here $i$ = social discount rate, $t$ = time period.

Thus,

$$NPV = \left[\frac{B_1}{(1+i)} + \frac{B_2}{(1+i)^2} + \ldots \frac{B_n}{(1+i)^n}\right] - \left[\frac{C_1}{(1+i)} + \ldots \frac{C_2}{(1+i)^2} + \ldots \frac{C_n}{(1+i)^n}\right]$$

$B_1, B_2 \ldots B_n$ = Series of Gross present benefits in period 1, 2...$n$.

$c_1, c_2 \ldots c_n$ = Series of Gross present cost in period, 1, 2,...$n$.

$i$ = Social rate of discount for annual compounding.

In making a choice projects either of the two rules be followed:

1. All projects where the ratio of present value of benefit to the present values of cost is > 1.

   **Expressed symbolically as such**

$$\frac{\frac{B_1}{(1+i)} + \frac{B_2}{(1+i)^2} + \ldots \frac{B_n}{(1+i)^n}}{\frac{C_1}{(1+i)} + \frac{C_2}{(1+i)^2} + \ldots \frac{C_n}{(1+i)^n}} > 1$$

2. Only those projects should be selected in which the present value of benefits exceed the present value of cost where symbolically

$$\frac{B_1}{(1+i)} + \frac{B_2}{(1+i)^2} + \ldots \frac{B_n}{(1+i)^n} > \frac{C_1}{(1+i)} + \frac{C_2}{(1+i)^2} + \ldots \frac{C_n}{(1+i)^n}$$

The NPV criterion is the most appropriate rule for the project evaluation.

### 10.5.1 The Internal Rate of Return Criterion

This criterion refers to the percentage rate of return implicit in the flows of benefits and cost of projects. **Marglin**[2] defines the IRR as the discount rate at which present value of return minus cost is zero. The mathematical formula for the computation of IRR is:

2. S.A. Marglin, *Public Inuestment Criteria,* 1967.

$$\frac{B_1 - C_1}{(1+r)} + \frac{B_2 - C_2}{(1+r)^2} + .... \frac{B_n - C_n}{(1+r)^n} = 0$$

where, $r$ = Internal rate of return. In case of mutually exclusive projects the project to be selected must have highest rate of return. The choice on the basis of changes in discount rate is called **"Switching" and "Reswitching"**.

This criterion has certain limitations:

1. It is not possible to change the rate of return assumed for the calculation of profitability of project .
2. It is difficult to calculate rate of return on long gestation project which does not yield benefit for many years.
3. It is not applicable to highly capital intensive projects.
4. It is difficult to calculate IRR in which the entire investment outlay cannot be made in the first period.
5. The use of IRR for public investment does not yield correct decision.
6. It is difficult to make choice between two alternative investment on the basis of their alternative IRR.
7. Since IRR depends on social rate of discount. The choice of projects depends upon discount rate if NPV of projects are given. This can be **explained diagrammatically**:

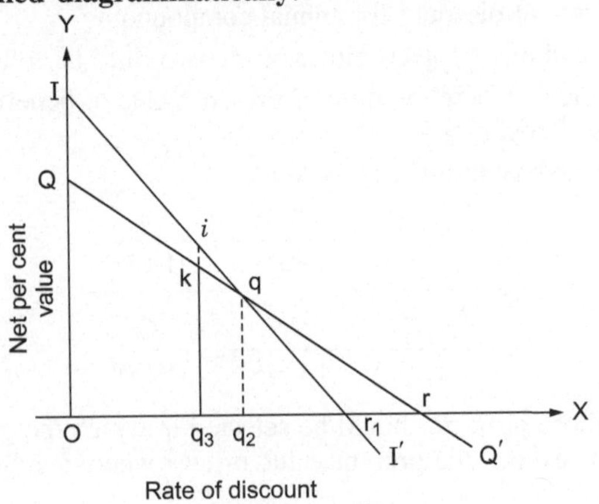


**Fig. 10.1**

The rate of discount is measured along OX axis and NPV, OY axis. The curve I I′ depicts investment of project I and QQ′ of project Q. The IRR of project Q is > than of project I because discount rate, or is > than or′. At $O_{q_2}$ the IRR of both projects are equal. But if discount rate falls below $O_{q_2}$ project I will be chosen because its NPV is higher by ik. Of the two criterion NPV is technically superior to IRR. Since IRR can give incorrect result in special circumstances[3].

3. M. D. Little, *Project analysis in relation to planning in a Mixed Economy in Development Problems,* 1967.

### 10.5.2 The Social Rate of Discount

The rate at which future benefits must be discounted to make them comparable with present benefit is called Social rate of discount. In other words, it is the rate of the premium which the society puts for prefering the present consumption to future consumption.

The **Social rate of discount is a constant rate over time** the choice of a discount rate affects the projects to be undertaken. "A discount rate of 5% might well lead to twice as much investment as one of 10% together with equivalent reduction in consumption"[4]. If the discount rate is high **short period projects with** higher **net benefits** are preferred. On the contrary when the **discount rate** is low, long period projects with lower, net benefits are selected.

Since benefits and cost are to occur in future they are discounted in order to find their present net worth, so there is a problem of choosing suitable rate at which future benefits are discounted. Generally, the market rate is used for this purpose but it fails to solve the purpose where there is multiplicity of rate of interest in market or the private and social rate of discount may not concede so there is no scientific way of choosing a suitable rate.

## 10.6 LIMITATIONS OF COST BENEFIT ANALYSIS

1. The correct estimation of benefits from a project becomes difficult due to uncertainties regarding future demand and supply of the products from a new project and their prices. Another problem is the assessment of external economics.

   The presence of external economics may lead to selling of the product at price equal to marginal cost and not equal to average cost which will create a deficit and efforts are made by a special levy on consumers or through Budgetary resources to cover the deficit.

   This method does not solve the problem in the best possible manner. In this method the different projects are measured by the scale. If one uses a shadow rate of exchange it would apply to all projects. This method does not consider external effects to be incurred on cost and benefits. **Prof Lewis** writes in this context "To calculate the true net social benefit of an investment calls for skepticism as well as skill. The figures submitted to government almost always involves exaggerated optimism and double counting. If one uses, low shadow image in valuing labour, when calculating costs, one must also, when calculating benefits give extra credit to the projects because it will relieve unemployment. Shadow prices may be applied to cost or to benefits, the same item should not appear in both. Again annual values and capital values should not be added together.[5] The gross benefit can neither be obtained by valuing increased output at a initial price nor can it be estimated by using new price.

4. Richard Layard, *Cost -Benefit Analysis,* 1972
5. Lewis *Development Planning,* p. 258.

2. The social rate of discount assumed for any project is arbitrary. There is no perfect method to find social discount rate. A small change in discount rate may change the full result of project evaluation. The arbitrarily large discount rate does not help in calculating the net present value of benefits of long term project.
3. This method ignores opportunity cost problems. Griffin and Enos states that if all prices reflect opportunity costs all projects for which $B/C < 1$ would be chosen.
4. The side effects of a project are difficult to be calculated. There may be technological and precuniary externalities of a river valley project such as the effects of flood control measures or a storage dam on the productivity of land at other places in the vicinity.
5. Another, problem arises with regards to choice of criteria. A wrong choice of criteria may lead to false conclusions.
6. It neglects joint benefits and cost arising from a project. There are a number of direct and indirect benefits flowing from river valley project but it is difficult to calculate and evaluate such benefits separately.
7. Cost estimates are made on the basis of choice of technique location and prices of factor services used. Market prices of factors of production are used for this purpose provided they reflect oppurtunity cost because there is fundamental disequilibria which is reflected in the existence of massive under-employment at the prevailing level of wages the deficiency of funds at prevailing interest rates and the shortage of exchange at current rates of exchange. The equilibrium level of wage rates will be considerably lower than market wage while equilibrum interest rates will be probably much higher than the market rates. To remove this problem, the use of shadow prices has been suggested. In the cost-benefit analysis we thus cannot take the oppurtunity cost of labour as zero.
8. It is difficult to obtain required data in Under-Developed Countries. It is not possible to assess the benefits that are likely to accrue to people from a particular project and hence the element of arbitrariness in cost benefit analysis may be quite high. In certain cases both tangible and intangible benefits are difficult to assess.
9. Further assessing the cost of a project is not easy task. Preliminary estimates of costs are made but they are either over-estimated or under-estimated. Rise in prices, shortage of rawmaterial and foreign exchange difficulties often stand in the ways of accurate cost assessment. According to **Prof. Lewis** "Assessing the cost and the benefits of new industrial enterprise is highly specialised work which is best left to experienced consultants. Without such specialised knowledge project analysis is bound to be wrong.

## 10.7 COST-BENEFIT ANALYSIS IN INDIA

The Cost-Benefit Analysis was started in the first two five-year plans in the multipurpose river valley projects. The pioneer studies in the field were namely, *Bhakra-Nangal Project* dealt by **Prof. K.N. Raj**; the benefits and cost of *Hira*kund Dam by **N.V. Sonani** and N. Rath; Survey of the Godavari Canal *System* in Maharashtra by **D.R. Gadgil**, and the *Sarda Canal project* in U.P. by *Balgit Singh.*

**Prof. K.N. Raj** centralised his attention on the discussion of the employment of the Bhakra-Nangal Project and on its growing effects in the form of indirect demand for consumption. He concluded that more labour for the Bhakra-Nangal could be employed but it would have rather increased the cost of the project, as the labour had to be supplied from the distant places. Secondly, the marginal propensity to consume of the local labour was less than that of the migrant labour. Raj's study though timely could not go further to use a social rate of discount to convert benefits and cost accuring at different point of time to commensurable units so the different margins of choice which existed in designing and implementing the project were not indicated.

The Government of India has been appointing committees from time to time but there is no uniformity in the application of cost-benefit technique in these studies. These studies have been made either on the basis of 'before' and 'after' techniques or the 'with' and 'without' techniques. The before and after techniques takes into account the benefits and cost before the introduction of the project and compares the same with the benefits and cost that have resulted after the introduction of the project. The with or without techniques makes a comparatiue study of the same project being benefits by the facilities.

## 10.8 SUGGESTIONS

To reduce the limitation of cost benefit analysis, certain suggestions have been made for the better appraisal of projects. The benefits ought to be measured both in their positive and negative aspects. Scarce factors used should be counted as negative benefits while positive benefits induced by investment in projects should make an addition to national product. Therefore, both direct and indirect benefits should be induced. Shadow prices should be used in evaluation of the project if the market prices do not reflect equilibrum prices. The influence of an investment project on the national product should not be measured in one year only but also in time, along with its influence on employment, balance of payments, regional income distribution etc. Weights should be given to each of these elements in order to mention the inclusion of the following factors into the evoluation procedure:

1. **Scale and Locational Effects:** In order to select the optimum scale of production for a particular project an estimate of the increase in demand over time is to be made. Further there are likely to be certain

diseconomies arising from over concentration of a project in a few centres, increase in transport cost and difficulties of operating large scale plants. Only some of these effects can be evaluated quantitatively.

2. **Variation in Range of Commodities Produced:** The different techniques of production produce different qualities of product. Small scale production techiques are generally more flexible than production techniques under large scale.
3. **Variation in Output Over line:** This factor is of special importance in the case of those projects which have long fruition lag such as river-valley projects take a long time to fruitfy. A discounting of future cost and prices is necessary for purpose of evaluation.
4. **Non Market Effects of Production differs:** The use of an advanced technology may be held in training labour and management for industrailisation in the long run. Although this fact is not reflected in the calculation of accounting prices. The social benefits which reduces undesirable waste must be considered.

## 10.9 CONCLUSION

Project Evaluation is a very useful technique, especially for under-developed countries since it assists the planners to get maximum possible benefits from limited resources. The use of the tool of planning imparts an element of rationality to the process of plan formulation.

The use of cost-benefit analysis permits decentralised decision making. Even if public sector is small, no single authority can hope to handle vast mass of technical information needed to decide on a number of specific projects. A separate authority is needed to calculate cost and benefits of each project.

Thus cost-benefit analysis is a practical way of assessing in the desirability of projects, where it is important to take a long view and wide view in the sense of allowing for side effects of many kinds on many persons, industries etc."[6]

❑❑❑

6. A.R. Prest and R. Turvey, *Cost-Benefit Analysis: A Survey.*

CHAPTER 11

# Industrial Policy and Indian Planning

## 11.1 INTRODUCTION

Industrial policy reflects the socio-economic and political ideology of development. To a large extent industrial policy has dominantly determined the pattern and direction of development of the economy. The Industrial Policy Resolution of 1956 was regarded as the base around which other industrial policies were framed. It was therefore, regarded by some as the **Economic Constitution of India.**

"Industrial Policy" is comprehensive and it covers all these procedures, principles, policies, rules and regulations which control the industrial undertakings of a country and thereby shapes the pattern of industrialisation. It incorporates fiscal, monetary policies, tariff, labour policy and Governments attitude towards external assistance, public, private joint, cooperative, small, medium, and large scale industries.

## 11.2 INDUSTRIAL POLICY RESOLUTION, 1948

**Main Features:** The Industrial policy resolution contemplated a (1) Mixed economy *i.e.*, both public and private. A number of sectors were given importance. (2) It divided the industries into a number of categories. (3) Role of cottage and small scale industry was given importance.

The industries were categorised as such:

### 1. Government Controlled Industries

The manufacture of arms and ammunition, the production and control of atomic energy and the ownership and management of railway transport were to be the exclusive monopoly of the Central Government.

### 2. State Monopoly

The second category covered coal, iron and steel, aircraft manufactures, ship building, manufacture of telephone, telegraph and wireless apparatus etc. New undertakings in these industries could henceforth be undertaken only by the state.

### 3. Private Industries Subject to State Regulation and Control

The third category was made up of industries of such basic importance that the central government would feel it necessary to plan and regulate them.

### 4. Private Enterprise

A fourth category comprising the remainder of the industrial field was left open to the private enterprise, individual as well as cooperative.

The main thrust of the Industrial Policy was thus

1. To establish a social order where justice and equality of opportunities could be assured to all people.
2. Promote rapid rise in the standard of living of the people through exploitation of latent and available resources of the country.
3. Accelerate production to meet the needs of growing population.
4. To provide opportunities for employment.

The features of Industrial Policy Resolution of 1948 is contemplated.

(*i*) As a mixed economy in which both public and private sectors were given importance

(*ii*) The government controlled industries

(*iii*) It divided the industries into a number of categories

## 11.3 REVIEW OF INDUSTRIAL POLICY, 1948

The industrial policy remained the same in force for eight years. It had a mixed reaction of the public. According to **Prof. Kuchall** "It was most useful policy." **Minoo Masani** further observed that "this policy laid foundation of democratic socialism". While the leftist felt that "The Industrial policy of 1948 was reflection of capitalist traditions". They said that there was doubt about the coordination between the public and private sector. Apart from certain criticism it was admitted that the pattern of mixed economy laid down by this policy was beneficial for the country's need at that time.

## 11.4 THE INDUSTRIAL POLICY RESOLUTION OF 1956

The Industrial Policy Resolution was presented to the Lok Sabha by the Prime Minister on the 30th April, 1956. The noteworthy factors that necessitated the Government to plan the new industrial Policy resolution were: the enactment of the Constitution of India guaranteeing certain fundamental rights to all citizens, the Directive Principles of State Policy, acceptance of 'socialistic pattern of society' as the objective of socio-economic policy the successful completion of the first five year plan and the need for placing the second five year plan before the country with rapid economic development as its objective. The main objective as such was:

(*i*) To accelerate the rate of economic growth, and speed up industrialisation of the country.

(*ii*) Develop heavy industries and machine making industries.

(*iii*) Expansion of public and cooperative sector.

(*iv*) Reduce disparities in income and wealth.

(*v*) Present private monopolies and the concentration of economic power in different fields in the hands of small number of individuals.

(*vi*) Encouragement to village and small scale industries.

## 11.5 MAIN FEATURES OF 1956 POLICY

### I. Classification of Industries

(*a*) **Schedule A: Government Enterprises:** Under Schedule A were listed seventeen industries which were the exclusive responsibility of the state. They were: arms and ammunition, atomic energy, iron and steel, heavy castings and forgings of iron and steel, heavy machinery required for iron and steel production, for mining, for machine tool manufacture, etc; heavy electrical industries, coal, mineral oils, mining, iron ore, and other important minerals like copper, lead, zinc, aircraft air transport, railway transport, ship building, telephone, telegraph, and wireless equipment, generation and distribution of electricity.

(*b*) **Schedule B: Mixed Enterprises** under Schedule B were those industries which were to be progressively state owned and in which the state would generally set up new enterprises, but in which **private enterprises would be expected only to supplement the effort of the state.** This schedule included twelve industries. They were: machine tools, ferro-alloys and tool steels, the chemical industry, antibiotics and other essential drugs, fertilisers, synthetic rubber carbonization of coal, chemical pulp, road transport, and sea transport.

(*c*) **Schedule C: Private Enterprises** under this all the remaining industries and their future development would in general be left to the initiative and enterprise of the private sector.

### II. Role of Cottage and Small Scale Industries

The Industrial policy had laid special emphasis on giving every encouragement to cottage and small scale industries. These industries give employment, facilitate effective mobilisation of resources, and equitable distribution of national income.

### III. Reduction in Regional Disparity

This policy aimed at regional development through transport development, power supply.

### IV. Labour Participation in Management

The resolution accepted that in a socialistic economy labour participation is essential in management. Some laws governing industrial relations have been enacted. The entrepreneur in public sector have been asked to set an example in this regard.

## 11.5.1 Basic Critical Appraisal of Features of the Industrial Policy, 1956

The allocation of industries into distinct categories does not imply that they are placed in water-light compartment and room; for exception could be made in appropriate cases, the private unit might produce an item in category one for meeting the requirements of the industry. On the other hand heavy industries in the public sector may obtain some of their requirements of lighter components from the private sector while the latter may rely upon the former for many of its needs. The same principle may apply in greater degree between large and small scale industries. Thus, both the state and private enterprises are expected to operate closely together inspite of the fact that the state is a major partner.

The industrial policy gave encouragement to the private sector and small scale industries. It tried to foster small scale industries through differential taxation and direct subsides. Financial assistance was provided for improving and modernising the techniques of production and thereby to raise the competitive strength.

Further, the resolution of industrial policy was to remove the disparities and thereby secure a balanced, coordinated development of the industrial and agricultural sector in each region and thereby secure a rise in the standard of living. The Resolution recognised that various **technical training facilities** through institutions be provided to raise the level of technical and management personnel. It also felt the need for foreign capital in the industrialisation of the economy. The government insisted upon the progressive Indianisation of foreign concerns.

The Industrial policy of 1956 is considered thus as a landmark in the economic history of India. Some say that it has laid down the economic constitution for the country. Infact **Nehru ji** said that " The government of India think that the new policy would obtain support from all quarters and will prove helpful in an earlier industrialisation of India." **H. Venkata Subbaiah** aptly criticised the policy saying that "The Resolution of 1956 superimposed a political philosophy on the economic philosophy of the resolution of 1948". Critics also went at length to say that:

1. This policy will not prove helpful in the establishment of socialistic pattern of society. 2. This policy had laid more emphasis on basic and heavy industries which is against Gandhian ideology. 3. This policy had laid emphasis on public sector which would give birth to red-tapism, and nepotism.

Infact despite the criticism it would not be wrong to say that this policy stands as a potent policy and has been regarded as a base in the formulation of other industrial policy and this resolution conceived that public and private sectors are complement to each other.

As compared to industrial policy resolution of 1948, this policy has considerably enlarged the area of operation of Public Sector. Jagdish Bhagwati and **Padma Desai**[1] have rightly observed that the "Second Industrial Policy Resolution despite its close similarity to the first appears to have been issued partly to reemphasise the importance of the public sector and the necessity to regulate the growth of the private sector in the light of the shift to a more explicitly socialistic instance by the government.

## 11.6 INDUSTRIAL LICENSING

To control and regulate the process of industrial development in the country, an Act was passed by the Parliament in October 1951, though it came into force on May 8, 1952. The Act was called as 'Industries Development and Regulation Act ' 1951 The main task of the Act was to:

(*i*) Regulate industrial investment and production according to plan priorities and targets.

(*ii*) Protect small enterpreneur against competition from large industries.

(*iii*) Prevent monopoly and concentration of ownership of production.

(*iv*) Balance regional development with a view to reducing disparities in the levels of development of different regions of the economy. It was hoped that through the instrument of industrial licensing the state would be able to direct investment into the most important branches.

(*v*) Correlate supply and demand in the domestic market.

(*vi*) Eliminate competition.

(*vii*) Ensure the optimum utilisation of social capital.

Industrial units employing less than 100 workers and having a fixed asset of less than Rs. 10 lakhs were not required to obtain any license what so ever.

## 11.7 HAZARI COMMITTEE REPORT ON INDUSTRIAL LICENSING POLICY

**Dr. R.K. Hazari** reviewed the working of the Industrial Licensing under the Industries Development and Regulation Act, 1951. The study had two objectives:

1. Jagdish Bhagwati and Padma Desai, "Planning for Industrialisation"

(*i*) To review the operation of licensing under the Industries Act. Broadly over the last two plans period and more closely over the last six or seven years including the orderly phasing of licensing with reference to targets of capacity.

(*ii*) To consider and suggest in the light of the present stage of economic development where and in what direction modification may be made in the licensing policy.

**Hazari** made some disclosure:

1. Some leading houses especially the Birlas followed the practice of multiple applications for the same product and for a wide variety of products which were meant to foreclose licensable capacity.
2. For the purpose of sanctioning licence the principle of chronological selection *i.e.*, on the basis of standing in the queue. This procedure helped the big industrial houses to foreclose capacity.
3. Industrial licensing did not bring about balanced regional development. The gains in term of balanced regional development and wider distribution of entrepreneurs are, at least, moderate. The licensing has served to channelise investment appears doubtful.
4. The absence of follow up action once the license were issued was a sordid feature. The Birlas did not utilise even 50% of the licenses issued to them.

To sum up, the licensing policy encouraged the foreclosure of the licensed capacity by influential and powerful industrial houses who could not afford to sit tight on unutilised license. In the absence of a policy of revocation of license issued, the large industrial houses prevented the entry of new entrepreneurs while they did not fulfill the targets laid down in the plans. Consequently industrial licensing which was supposed to act as an instrument of industrial development became an impedient.

## 11.8 INDUSTRIAL LICENSING POLICY ENQUIRY COMMITTEE (DUTT COMMITTEE)

The Government of India appointed Industrial Licensing Policy Enquiry Committee in July, 1967. Under the Chairmanship of **Mr. Subinal Dutt** to inquire into the working of the licensing system in India. The committee submitted its report in July, 1969. It said that:

(*i*) The Licensing authorities were bought over by large industrial houses For instance, 73 large industrial houses accounted for 56% of the total proposed investment on machinary by the entire private corporate sector. Similarly 60% of the value of import of capital goods by the entire private corporate sector was accounted for by these 73 large industrial houses.

(*ii*) The licensing authorities ignored the objectives of the Industrial policy (1956) and the reasons for the adoption of licensing system.

(*iii*) The areas reserved for the public sector under the Industrial policy Resolution of 1956 were opened to private sector under one pretext or the other. For example, in the case of synthetic rubber and chemical pulp all the licenses were allowed to the private sector. Similar was the case with aluminium and machine tool industry. In fertiliser alone while public sector was granted 12 licenses private sector was granted 42 licenses.

(*iv*) The licensing system could not favour the industrial backward states since 62% of the total licenses was gained by industrially advanced states of Maharashtra, West Bengal, Gujarat and Tamil Nadu.

(*v*) Out of 720 products in which foreign collaborations were permitted not less than 70 were consumer goods.

(*vi*) Out of the total assistance provided by the public sector term lending institution during the period 1955 to 1966, 73 large industrial houses accounted for 44% and 20 large houses for 17%. As against this public sector companies received only 9% of total financial assistance.

Public Sector Investment institutions like the LIC and UTI favoured large industrial houses. 20 large industrial houses received nearly 43% of the total funds loaned out by these institutions. Banking institutions also showed a heavy preference for large industrial houses.

The Dutt Committee reviewed that the Industrial licensing system was a failure since it could not regulate concentration of powers in the hands of big industrial houses. It failed miserably to achieve the objectives of planned economic development. Infact this policy worked as a negative instrument. The committee demanded for adoption of proper fiscal and monetary policy to achieve the goal of development and at the same time noted for the continuance of the licensing system so as to make it a policy instrument of industrial growth.

## 11.9 NEW LICENSING POLICY AND PROCEDURES, 1970

As against the recommendations of the Administrative Reform Committee (ARC), the Industrial Licensing policy Enquiry Committee (Dutt Committee) and the Planning Committee (Dutt Committee) and the Planning commission, a new Industrial licensing policy was announced in February, 1970 by the Government of India. This policy aimed at giving much greater freedom to private enterprises; as well as fresh entrants in the industrial field and small entrepreneurs. Elimination of excessive concentration of economic power was sought to be achieved through modyifing licensing policy with regards to large industrial houses and through the enactment of **Monopolies Restrictive Trade Practises** Act which came into operation from June, 1970.

The Industrial Licensing Policy Enquiry Committee also recommended that there should be a list of core industries in the economy. The industries in the core list as are included in schedule A of the Industrial policy resolution, 1956 and (as amended from time to time) are reserved for the public sector.

Except for industries reserved for the public sector under industrial policy resolution of 1956 large industrial houses foreign companies subsidiaries or branches of foreign companies were allowed to participate in the core and heavy investment sector leaving the opportunities in the remaining sector primarily to other class of entrepreneurs. Later on liberalisation was made by the Government in the licensing procedures in favour of large industrial houses.

## 11.10 THE INDUSTRIAL POLICY STATEMENT OF 1977

On the 23rd December 1977, Sir George Fernades, the Union Industries Minister presented a New Industrial Policy statement stating that though 1956 policy is valid one yet the result of actual policies in the industrial field have not been up to the expectations of the declared objectives. The growth of P.C.I. during the last ten years has been about 1.5% per annum, which is inadequate to meet the needs of the developing economy. Unemployment has increased. Rural-Urban disparities have widened and the rate of real investment has stagnated. The growth of industrial output in the last decade has been not more than 3 to 4% per annum on an average. Industrial sickness has widened, along with rise in cost, and prices has been distorted: The New Industrial Policy aimed at removing these lacunas. To initate this priority was accorded for generation and transmission of power. Along with this cement and steel was required to build our irrigation projects, the implements for ploughing and preparing the land, the equipment for processing high quality seeds, fertilisers, pesticides oil and power, a wide range of industrial products are essential for increasing production. It is by a process of reinforcement of the agricultural and the industrial sectors that employment can be found for the large numbers of the rural population who cannot be absorbed in the agriculture sector.

## 11.11 MAIN FEATURES

### 1. Small Scale Sector

Promotion of cottage and small scale industries was the main thrust of the Industrial policy. The policy also paid stress on the development of 'Tiny Sector' within the small-scale sector. All those units with an investment in machinery and equipment upto Rs. 1 lakh and situated in a town with a population of less than 50,000 as per 1971 census and villages will be considered to be in the tiny sector. The policy statement indicated that the government will consider the introduction of special legislation for the protection of cottage and small-scale industries.

To promote small and rural entrepreneur and to provide them guidance the policy involved a 'District Industries Centre' for each district Measures such as purchase preference and reservations for exclusive purchase by the government departments and public sector undertaking will also be used to support the products of small-scale units.

Further the list was expanded to cover 800 items. The list of reserved items for the small scale sector was expanded from 180 items to 504 items. The government also launched special programmes to improve the productivity and earnings of khadi spinners and weavers. Separate wing of Industrial Development Bank of India was formulated to deal with credit needs of the small, village, cottage industry.

## 2. Large Scale Units

Large scale industries were given importance. Amongst these large scale industries are basic industries which are essential for providing infrastructure as well as for the development of small and village industries such as steel, non-ferrous metal cement, oil refineries, capital goods industries for meeting the machinery requirement of basic industries as well as small scale industries, high technological industries which requires large scale production and which are related to agricultural and small scale industrial development such as fertiliser, pesticides and other industries which are outside the list of reserved items for the development of the economy such as machine tools, organic and inorganic chemicals.

It will be the policy of the government to ensure that no unit or business group acquires dominant or a monopolist position in the market .The present industrial activities of the large houses will be scrutinised so that any unfair practice arising out of manufacturing inter linkages are avoided.

## 3. Public Sector

The public sector socialises the production in strategic areas along with providing the countervailing power to the growth of large enterprises in the private sector. The public sector will be charged with the responsibility of encouraging the development of a wide range of ancillary industries and contributing to the growth of decentralised production by making available its expertise in technology and management to small scale industries The government further attaches importance to the building of a professional cadre of managers in the public sector who would be given the necessary autonomy and entrusted with task of providing dynamic and efficient management to such enterprises.

## 4. Appropriate Technology

The Industrial policy ensured an effective and coordinated approach for the development and wide spread application of suitable small and simple machines for improving the productivity and earning capacity of workers in small and village industries. The government therefore recognised the necessity for continued inflow of technology so that it is used for development of research and development facilities.

### 5. Foreign Investment

The new policy promoted foreign investment and emphasised that the government will allow the Indian entrepreneurs to set up joint ventures abroad mainly in the form of machinery and equipment structure and also technical knowhow and management expertise. Further many Indian firms are even today in a position to compete successfully in international field and Indian economy enjoys a favourable position in foreign exchange reserves.

## 11.12 CRITICAL ASSESSMENT OF 1977 POLICY

The Industrial policy statement of 1977 did not carry any radical changes regarding foreign companies and multinationals. Despite the limitation this policy was favourable one since it stressed on cottage, small scale sector along with public sector.

## 11.13 THE INDUSTRIAL POLICY STATEMENT OF 1980

In July, 1980 the Congress Government announced a new Industrial Policy basing on the fact that "Industrialisation is the *sine qua non* of economic progress". The features of new policy were:

### 1. Revised the Definition of Small Scale Units

1. The investment limit for small scale units was raised from Rs.10 lakhs to Rs. 20 lakhs.
2. For tiny units from Rs. 1 lakh to Rs. 2 lakhs.
3. For ancillary units from Rs. 15 lakhs to Rs. 25 lakhs.

### 2. Village Industries

Handloom, Handicraft, khadi and other village industries were to receive priority to achieve faster rate of growth in villages.

### 3. Regularisation of Excess Capacity

To maximise production particularly in the industries assuming national interest or those engaged in the production of mass consumption goods, it is proposed to regularise such excess capacity on a selective basis.

### 4. Public Sector

This policy aimed to create more competitive environment for the operation of public sector units through appropriate procedures and developement of a proven cadre of professional management.

### 5. Industrial Sickness

The new policy proposed to root out the causes of mismanagement which led to industrial sickness and to offer additional financial incentives to sick units merging with healthier units. The government would only take over sick units if it fails in its attempt to revive itself.

### 6. Relaxation of Industrial Licensing

Non MRTP and non-FERA companies could not be required to obtain industrial license under Industrial Resolution Act, for projects involving investment in fixed asset upto Rs. 50 crore if they were located in centrally declared backward areas and upto Rs. 15 crore if they were located in the non-backward areas. The number of industries requiring compulsory licensing was reduced from 56 to 26.

### 7. Industrialisation of Backward Areas

To promote industrialisation in backward areas new industrial undertakings established in declared backward areas were entitled to the income tax relief under Section 80 HH of the income tax act.

### 8. Promote export

The new policy proposed to promote export oriented units such as liberal import of technology, creation of capacity large enough to make the unit competitive in the world market.

Thus, the main objectives of 1980 policy were:

1. Optimum utilisation of the installed capacity.
2. Maximising production, productivity, employment.
3. Correction of regional imbalance through development of industrially backward areas.
4. Development of agro based industries.
5. Development of export industries.

## 11.14 CRITICAL ASSESSMENT OF 1980 POLICY

Thus the main thrust under the 1980 Policy is towards growth rather than toward enlarging, employment or curbing monopoly. The redefinition of small scale industries, regularisation of installed capacity beyond the limit of licensed capacity and scheme of automatic expansion has thus opened new vistas for large and big houses. In other words, it will result in the promotion of capital-intensive pattern of development.

## 11.15 A GLIMPSE ON INDUSTRIAL POLICY UPTO 1991

**Characteristics**

### 1. Reservation of Industries

(*i*) Most of the import industries was exclusively reserved for the public sector.

(*ii*) Manufacture of a large number of (around 850) items was reserved for the small scale sector.

### 2. Pre-Dominance to Public Enterprises

The Industrial Policy 1948,1956 aimed at promotion of public sector in order to promote socialistic pattern of society.

### 3. Entry and Growth Restrictions

On the private sector there were restrictions imposed. A license was mandatory for establishing new units with investment above a specific limit Large firm and dominant undertakings had to obtain clearance under the MRTP Act in addition to the industrial license for establishing new undertakings, substantial expansion and manufacture of new items. There were also restrictions on import of capital goods.

### 4. Controls on Foreign Assistance

Foreign capital and technology was restricted. A ceiling of 40% was subjected to the total equity. Operation of Foreign companies in India and issue of securities abroad by Indian companies were regulated under the Foreign Exchange Regulation Act (FERA) 1973.

## 11.16 INDUSTRIAL POLICY, 1991

The Industrial Policy, 1991 marked a big departure from the old policy. The changes were announced in two parts–the first part was announced on 24$^{th}$ July 1991, it was basically concerned with large industries including the medium sized industries. The second part was announced on 6$^{th}$ August, 1991 which dealt with small industries.

The industrial policy reforms were 'drastic', 'dramatic' and revolutionary'.

## 11.17 OBJECTIVES AND MEASURES

The new policy set before itself certain major objectives:

1. **Progressive Economy:** The aim of the policy is to achieve a sort of development which makes industries dynamic in their growth and which rendered justice to the people. It involves a struggle for social and economic justice to end poverty and unemployment and to build a modern, democratic, socialistic and forward looking India." The policy aimed at utilizing fully the indigeneous capabilities of

entrepreneurs fostering research and development efforts for the development of indigeneous technologies, raising investment, improvements in efficiency and productivity, controlling monopolistic behaviour, assigning the right areas for the public sector undertakings and ensuring welfare as also skills and facilities to the workers to enable them to deal with the inevitability of technological change." It placed greater emphasis on building up our ability to pay for our imports through our own foreign exchange earnings.

2. **Market Orientations:** The policy envisaged the use of market in a big way by dismantling the restrictive and regulatory system and thereby to unshackle the industrial economy from the cobwebs of unnecessary bureaucratic control. This would allow private entrepreneurs to make their commercial decisions on their own with no government judgment to bind them. The upshot of the whole set of means is that the market and the private entrepreneur and not the bureaucrat will govern the industrial development with Public Sector Undertakings (PSU) providing the support indirectly.
3. **Strengthening Private Sector:** This policy threw open a number of activities which had so far been exclusively in the realm of the public sector. The Public sector had been left with just 6 industries with the remaining having been opened for private sector. Most of the provisions of the MRTP Act pertaining to concentration of economic power were scrapped.
4. **Dispersal of Industries:** The new policy aimed at decentralisation of the industrial activities geographically. The thrust of the policy was to shift industries away from big congested cities to the rural and backward areas. It was also intended to promote investment in infrastructural development so that the areas which are lagging in industries are helped Besides this the new policy also favoured the expansion of agro-based industries near the farming areas.
5. **Redefinition of the Role of Public Sector:** The role of the public sector was redefined and the scope of the public sector had been drastically abridged. The number of industries reserved for the public sector was reduced to eight** and it was later pruned in stages to two (atomic energy and railway transport).

   Apart from this the industrial policy also laid stress on upgrading of PSU units. Public enterprises which were chronically sick and which were unlikely to be turned around will for the formulation of revival

** 1. Arms and Ammunition and allied items of defence equipment, 2. Coal and lignite, 3. Atomic Energy, 4. Mineral oil, 5. Mining of iron ore, manganese ore, sulphur, gold, diamond, 6. Minerals specified in the schedule to the Atomic Energy, 7. Railway transport.

be referred to the Board for Industrial and Financial Reconstruction (BIFR) or other high level institutions created for the purpose. A social security mechanism will be created to protect the interest of workers likely to be affected by such rehabilation packages.

In order to raise resources and encourage wider participation a part of the government shareholding in the public sector would be offered to mutual funds, financial institution general public and workers.

There will also be greater thrust on performance improvements through the Memorandum of Understanding (MOU) system through which managements were granted autonomy.

6. **Liberalisation of Foreign investment:** The policy towards foreign capital and technology had been modified significantly. The new policy expected significant contribution from foreign entrepreneurs and for that liberal provisions were made for easy entry into the country. It was said that approval would be given for direct foreign investment upto 51% foreign equity. The industries in which automatic approval was granted included a wide range of industrial activities in the capital goods and metallurgical industries, entertainment electronics, food processing and the service sectors having significant export potential. The limit was subsequently raised from 51 to 74% and then to 100% for many of these industries along with inclusion of certain new industries. Foreign investment, was initially under the new policy allowed in all sectors excepting arms ammunition, atomic energy, railway transport, coal, lignite, mining of iron, manganese, copper, zinc gold, diamond. As such this would make us planned under the new policy to bring about transparency and attract companies to invest easily in India.

   Apart from foreign direct investment the new policy also seeked help from foreign trading companies. In the field of exports from India, it was stressed in the policy that the government would encourage foreign trading companies to assist us in our export activities. A special Empowerment Board would be constituted to negotiate with a number of large international firms and approve direct foreign investment in selected areas.

7. **Foreign Technology Agreements:** (*a*) Automatic permission will be given for foreign technology agreements in high priority industries upto a payment of Rs. 1 crore, 5% royalty for domestic sales and 8% for exports, subject to total payments of 8% of sales over a 10 year period from date of agreement or 7 years from commencement of production. The prescribed royalty rate are net of taxes and will be calculated according to standard procedures.

(*b*) In respect of industries other than those listed for automatic approval of foreign technology agreements and 51% of foreign equity, automatic permission will be given subject to the same guidelines as above if no free foreign exchange is required for any payments.

(*c*) All other proposal will need specific approval under general procedure in force.

(*d*) No permission will be necessary for hiring of foreign technicians, and for testing of indigenously developed technologies.

8. **Monopoly Restrictive Trade Practice Act (MRTP Act):**

(*a*) Removal of MRTP restriction was an important feature of the new industrial policy. Under the MRTP Act, all firms with asset above a certain size (Rs. 100 crores since 1985) were classified as MRTP firms. Such firms were permitted to enter selected industries only and this also on a case by case approval basis. In addition to control through industrial licensing, separate approvals were required by such large firms for any investment proposals. The government felt that this was having a poor effect on many large firms in their plans for growth and diversification. The new policy therefore scrapped the threshold limit of assets in respect of MRTP and dominant undertaking. These firms will now be at par with others and not require prior approval from the government for the delicensed industries. The MRTP Act was accordingly amended. The Amended Act gave more emphasis to the prevention and control of monopolistic, restrictive and unfair trade practises so that consumers are adequately protected from such practises.

(*b*) **Delicensing:** About 18 industries were freed from licensing. Later is was reduced to six[*2]. The industries subject to industrial licensing account for only a very small share of the value added in the manufacturing sector. The number of items reserved for public sector has been kept to a minimum of only 4 items**.

9. **Promoting Small Scale Industries:** The most important feature of the policy is to provide financial support to the small scale sector. Besides providing credit needs of industrial units this provision also

---

* **Industries free from licencing** (*i*) Distillation and brewing of alcholic drinks, (*ii*) Cigars and cigarettes of tobacco and manufactured tobacco substitute, (*iii*) Economic aerospace and defence equipment, (*iv*) Industrial explosives (*v*) Hazardous chemicals, (*vi*) Drugs and pharmaceutial

---

** **List of industries reserved for public sector.** (*i*) Arms and ammunation, (*ii*) Atomic energy, (*iii*) Railway transport, (*iv*) The substances specified in the schedule March 15,1995 of the Government of India.

---

(2) **Source:** Report on Currency and Finance (1998, 99, RBI)

includes identification of select industries in large clusters which would be provided financial support by Small Industries Development Bank of India. The National equity fund scheme have been enlarged to provide larger funds to projects involving larger capital outlays.

In orderly, the new policy allowed equity participation by other or non-SSI industrial undertakings. In the SSI sector upto 24% of the total shareholding was allowed. This was done to provide small units acess to the capital market and to encourage modernisation, technical upgradation.

Thirdly a limited partnership was to be allowed which would limit the financial liability of the new and non-active partners to the extent of capital invested. This would enhance the supply of risk capital to the SSI sector.

*Fourthly*, provisions have been made to ensure speedy payments arising from the scale of products of the SSI sector. One such provision called factoring service involves payment to the SSI by SIDBI and by agencies to be operated by the commercial bank before these are collected from the buyers by these agencies. This will to a great extent solve the problem of delayed payment to the small-scale sector by the large units. Legislation was done to ensure prompt payment of small industries unit.

## 11.18 SUPPLY OF RAW MATERIAL AND MARKETING

The SSI units would be accorded priority by the government while allocating these materials. It is also to be ensured that the small sector gets adequate and fair share of raw material available. Both indigeneous and imported promotion of market by cooperative pubic sector and other agencies was envisaged. It was also provided that the National Small Industries Corporation would concentrate on marketing of mass consumption items under a common brand name in association with the State Small Industries Development Corporation (SSI DC). Further SIDO (Small Industries Development Corporation) would augment export activities including the improvements in productivity of the SSI sector.

## 11.19 TINY SECTOR

The investment limit in plant and machinery in a unit had been raised from Rs. 5 lakhs to Rs. 25 lakhs obviously to provide for the increase in the prices of capital good.

**Handloom Industry** was also given importance under the policy framework. Various schemes were launched to promote marketing of handloom products in the domestic and industrial market. The role of National Handloom Development Corporation and Craft Development Centre was enhanced.

## 11.20 EVALUATION OF THE INDUSTRIAL POLICY, 1991

The 1991 industrial policy brought about certain radical changes. Until 1991 industrial policy of India was characterised by a monopoly, and dominant role was ushered to public sector in strategic basic and heavy industries, preference for small scale units, cooperative, and joint sector. A restrictive attitude towards private sector, foreign capital and technology was done.

However, the New Industrial policy in July, 1991 along with bringing forth economic policy changes and measure brought dynamic economic reforms in India. Restrictions implemented to growth and entry of private sector was narrowed down. The policy towards Foreign capital and Technology had been substantially liberalised along with import.

The policy made a bold attempt to free the Indian Industry from the shackles of abortive and crippling controls. The policy environment in India was made conducive for both domestic and foreign investment. Development since 1991 have demonstrated the growth and competitive impulses that the liberalisation can generate.

Table 11.1 gives a bird eye view of the important policy changes:

**Table 11.1** Industrial policy changes

| Pre 1991 policy | Industrial policy (1991) |
|---|---|
| • Industrial licensing was the rule. | Licensing is an exception. |
| • Public sector, monopoly dominance in strategic, basic and heavy industries. | All but two industries are open to the private sector. |
| • MRTP act restrictions on entry and growth of large companies. | No such restriction |
| • Foreign Investment allowed only in selected Industries that too subject to normally a ceiling of 40% of total equity and prior permission. | Foreign investments allowed in a large number of industries including upto 100% of equity in many of them. Automatic route available subect to specified conditions. |
| • Restrictive policy towards foreign technology. | Liberal policy towards foreign technology. |
| • Reservation of large number of products for small scale sector. | Reservation list is being pruned. |

## 11.21 INDUSTRIAL POLICY REFORMS, 1992-93 ONWARDS

After the introduction of new industrial policy in 1991, industrial policy reforms were carried further in 1992-93. The capital market was freed from government control and the office of the controller of capital issue was abolished. Foreign exchange regulation act was amended and investment restriction or FERA companies were substantially removed. Foreign investment was further liberalised by removing the conditionality of dividened balancing for the non-consumer goods. Private investment in exploration and refining was allowed in the hydrocarbon sector. The textile control board was also repealed.

The new industrial policy 1991 eliminated a large number of government induced entry restriction, licensing requirements and controls on corporate behaviour. The trust of the policy reforms undertaken in 1992-93 has been to deepen these reforms and extend them to other sectors of the industry. The changes introduced since April, 1992 had made imported inputs cheaper and more accessible for industry and at the same time exposed larger segment of Indian industry to international competition.

The process of industrial de-regulation and structural reform has been carried further during 1992-93. The directions for further policy action has been established.

## 11.22 EXIT POLICY, NATIONAL RENEWAL FUND AND VOLUNTARY RETIREMENT SCHEME

In order to safeguard the interest of workers who may be affected by technological upgradation of industry or closure of chronically sick units, the government established a National Renewal Fund (NRF) in February 1992. It marks the launching of a process of industrial restructuring in the wake of new economic policies and aimed at making the country globally competitive. The government has decided that the structural adjustment would be done with a **human face**" though it does not mean keeping loss making units intact. Thus the government has mentioned in its budget that NRF would provide a safety net for workers, while an 'exit policy' formulated to give recognition of the right to 'exit' when a unit cannot be run economically or is terminally sick. Thus the NRF is designed to be safety mechanism which would provide retraining and rehabilation of workers adversely affected by structural adjustment and technological change. The size of NRF has to be therefore large.

### 11.22.1 Objectives of NRF

1. To provide assistance to firms to cover the cost of retraining and re-deployment of employees arising as a result of modernisation and technological upgradation of existing capacities and from industrial restructuring.

2. To provide funds for compensation to employees affected by restructuring or closure of industrial units both in public and private sectors.
3. To provide funds for employment generation schemes in the organised and unorganised sectors in order to provide a social safety net for labour. The department of Industrial development which administers NRF, has now taken up the first set of cases relating to the national textile corporation units.

To implement the NRF schemes an empowered authority has been made and a provision of Rs. 700 crores has been made in the budget for the year 1993-94. Additional amount of Rs. 320 crores was approved for NRF in the supplementary budget in December, 1993. An amount of Rs. 786.24 crores was released from NRF (upto October1993) and an estimated number of 60, 000 workers had opted for voluntary retirement under the scheme. A major portion of the amount has been utilised in the textile sector.

## 11.23 VOLUNTARY RETIREMENT SCHEME (VRS)

The Voluntary Retirement Scheme (VRS) was introduced simultaneously and at the initial stage it was known popularly as **Golden handshake scheme**. The unviable public sector units have been empowered to introduce the scheme in their units to have the way for voluntary retirement of workers and staff accepting the on-time compensation instead of continuing as a sick entity.

The government encourages PSU'S to promote VRS by raising money from banks against government guarantees and interest subsidy, PSE's would also be encouraged to issue bonds to workers opting for VRS with the government guaranteeing the repayment of such bonds and fully reimbursing interest payment. Upto 31$^{st}$ March, 1997, 2.17 lakh employees of PSU's have opted for VRS and an amount of Rs. 2, 373.37 crores has been paid to them as compensation money.[3] The PSU's, where more than 5000 employees have opted for VRS include the Bharat Coking Coal Ltd with 12,188 employees central Coal Fields Ltd with 5736 employees. SAIL with 17,128 employees, Heavy Engineering Corporation Ltd with 5472 employes. National Textile Corporation with 61,066 employees, Eastern Coal Fields Ltd with 7330 employees and Hindustan Steel Works Construction Ltd with 7400 employees.

The central government has spent Rs. 2310 crores on the implementation of VRS in 85 public sector units till 1998-99. The scheme offered full gross salary for the remaining period of service after voluntary retirement. Giving such excessive benefit is perhaps one of the important reasons for large scale exodus. It seems that the scheme does not appear to have properly planned redevelopment of surplus workers. Thus, it is imperative on the part of the government to re-examine the scheme.

---

3. Economic Survey – 1998-99 PP. 100–101

## 11.24 NEW VRS POLICY FOR PSU'S

The government approved a VRS for all public sector units on March 16,2000. As per the new VRS policy, financially viable public sector units which are capable of meeting their enhanced costs will now be allowed to implement their own variant of VRS. A marginally loss or profit making PSU whose viability can be restored and whose performance can be improved with a little effort can now adopt-'Gujarat pattern' of VRS which offers three different schemes. While enterprises which have been declared terminally sick can now adapt the VRS scheme enunicated by the department of heavy industries in 1988. Within a specific time period stipulated for exercising the VRS employees who completed 10 years of service or attained the age of 40 and are working in terminally sick units can avail VRS scheme. Those opting for this scheme will be entitled not only to terminal benefits but exgratiapayment equivalent to one and a half month's pay plus dearness allowance (DA) for each year of completed service otherwise they can avail monthly pay plus Dearness. Allowance at the time of retirement multiplied by the months of service left whichever is less.

For the marginally sick or profit-making companies the so called Gujarat pattern of VRS offers three different schemes, In addition to the terminal benefit, person who wish to avail of the VRS can either take 35 days of salary for every year of completed service or they can settle for 25 days of salary. Finally person can settle for Rs. 2, 500 for every year of service left. In the Gujarat pattern the salary includes basic pay plus DA, personal allowances, house rent allowance.

Finally to make VRS attractive for person working in the profit making organisation the government has added new incentives for person willing to avail of VRS and those who have completed 30 years of service a maximum of 60 months salary as compensation will be granted.

## 11.25 IMPLEMENTATION OF INDUSTRIAL POLCY REFORMS RESULTED IN

1. **Industrial Growth Rate:** Rise in industrial growth rate at 2.3% during 1992-93 to 6.0% in 1993-94 and further to 9.6% in 1994-95. In 1995-96 it rose to 12.8%. In 1996-97, 1997-98, 1999-2000 and 2006-07 the industrial growth came down to 6.1%, 6.7%, 6.7% and 11.6% respectively.
2. **Investement:** The overall investment scenario in the country continues to be buoyant and promising. The number of Industrial Enterpreneurs Memorandum (IEM) and letters of intent (LOIS) filed from 1991 to December 2005 totalled 62,508 with overall investment intention of Rs. 17,76, 870 crores and estimated employment of 11.1 Mullion[4].

4. *Economic Survey*, 2005-06, p.138

3. **Foreign Direct Investment:** The actual inflow of FDI from 1991 to September, 2004 stood at Rs 1,31, 385 crores of which nearly.15% has come during 1997 itself [5]. In terms of aggregate annual inflow FDI, maintained its declining trend for the second successive year. After 1997-98 FDI inflow was in 2003-04 (US 2, 776 million). Which was lower than the previous year ($, 3, 134 million). Inflows in the current year 2004-05 however are showing signs of improvement. During April to December aggregate FDI inflows have been higher (US $ 2, 549 million) than the comparable period of 1999-2000 (US $ 1489 million).
4. **Industrial Employment:** The industrial employment also rose in recent years. In the manufacturing sector it rose from 32.70 in 1990-91 to 33.380 in 1994-95. In SSI it rose from 12.53 in 1990-91 to 14.66 in 1994-95.

**Table 11.2** Overall employment in Industries

| Year | Manufacturing | Small-scale | ASI factory |
|---|---|---|---|
| 1990-91 | 32.70 | 12.53 | 8.16 |
| 1991-92 | 33.10 | 12.98 | 8.19 |
| 1992-93 | 33.40 | 13.41 | 8.71 |
| 1993-94 | 33.80 | 13.94 | N.A. |
| 1994-95 | N.A. | 14.66 | N.A. |

**Source.** Economic Survey, 1996-97, p. 119.

5. **Government Initative:** The ministries initatives during the year have been to integrate its programme and policies with those of the state government with a view to expanding and facilitating implementation of industrial approvals as also on measures which would reduce difficulties faced by entrepreneures and investors.

## 11.26 INDUSTRIAL POLICY 2000-2001 (INITATIVES)

Industrial policy initatives during 2000-2001 had the following **characteristics:**

1. Rationalisation of excise duty by introduction of Central Value Added Tax (CENVAT) and reducing the number of rates of excise duty.
2. Extension of the maximum retail price based excise duty to an increasing number of items which will lead to simplification of the excise procedure.
3. The Security and Exchange Board of India has been made the single regulator for venture capital funds.
4. Permission of raise FI equity funds to 40% through a special resolution by shareholder.

5. Economic Survey, 2004-05, p.161.

5. Limit for providing collateral to obtain finance raised from Rs.1 lakh to Rs. 5 lakhs. for SSI units in the tiny sector.
6. Reduction of import duty on cinematic camera and other related equipment for use in the entertainment industry and 100% exemption on export profits extended to non-corporate assesses.
7. Reduction in custom duty on several items of the IT and telecommunication sector.
8. Enhancing the corpus of Rural Infrastructure Development Fund (RIDF) VI and reducing the interest charged on this by half a per cent.
9. MODVAT credit of CVD paid on project imports allowed upto 100%.

## 11.27 CONCLUSION

The new policy though attracts foreign investment and gave boost to domestic investment, it was doubtful whether it would boost employment and production.

❑❑❑

CHAPTER 12

# Multinational's in India

## 12.1 MULTINATIONAL'S IN INDIA

Multinational corporation may be defined as a company or an enterprise which undertakes the foreign direct investment. Multinational corporations are also known by such names as 'international corporation, transational corporation, global corporation (or firm, company or enterprise) etc'. The essence of such a company is that it takes its principal decision in a global context.

According to World Investment Report 1997 there were about 45,000 MNC with some 280,000 affiliates, while in 2004 there were over 61,500 of them with about 926,950 affiliates. Only less than 12% of these affiliates were in the developed countries. The MNC growing with rapidity accounted for a significant share in worlds investment, production, employment and trade. They extended their industrial and marketing operations through a network of their branches or their Majority Owned Foreign Affiliates (MOFAS).

## 12.2 ORIGIN

The concept of MNC is not a new one. Its history can be traced back to the period of mercantilist period. Hudson's Bay Co, Royal African Co, and East India company are some important examples of this kind which went out of their land in search of markets for their products. These corportion possessed huge capital resources, latest technology, alongwith world wide goodwill. The fact is that people of less developed countries are more crazy for their products. In the pre-second world war period a large number of colonies were dominated by the giant corporations. They thought of exporting to developing countries. USA emerged as a most dominant single country exporting capital in the form of direct investment. But in the post-independence period these MNC especially USA entered into foreign collaborations in different countries**. Critics of

** Now there are a large number of Japanese and European MNC. In the list of 10 or 20 largest MNC'S Japan has the largest number. MNC has been emerging from the developing countries. South Korea has *e.g.*, a well known MNC like Samsung, Hyundai, LG and Daewoo.

MNC said that this was a clever attempt of the developed countries to penetrate into the economy of our country in different ways so as to gain control over some essential areas of organised production. As the MNC are guided by profit maximisations motive thus it result in drawing away of resources through repatriation of profits, royalty payment, commissions, and technical constancy fees. Thus, it is for these reasons that the development of MNC has now been considered as neo-colonialism. Which has been extended to various developing countries of the world.

## 12.3 DEFINITION

As the concept of multinational has several dimensions there is no single universally agreed definition of term MNC. According to an **ILO report** "the essential nature of the multinational enterprises lies in the fact that its managerial headquarters are located in one country (referred to for conveniences as the (home country) while the enterprise carries out operations in a number of other countries as well (host countries)"[1]. Obviously, what is meant is " a corporation that controls production facilities in more than one country, such facilities having been acquired through the process of Foreign Direct Investment. Firms, that participate in international business however large they may be solely by exporting or by licensing technology are not multinational enterprises[2] Sanjoya Lal and Streetan[3] defined from economic point MNC as such "A typical MNC is one with net sales of 100 million dollars to several thousand million dollars having direct foreign investment in manufacturing usually accounting for at least 15 to 20% of companys total investment. Direct foreign investment means at least 25% participation in the share capital of the foreign enterprise.

In its organisational definition "MNC is that which (1) acts as an organisation maximising one overall objective, (2) treats the whole world as its operational area, (3) is able to coordinate all its functions in any way necessary to achieve (1) and (2)".

The motivational definition highlights corporate philosophy and motivation in laying down criteria for multinationality. Thus multinationality is indicated by a lack of nationalism or a concern with the firm as a whole rather than with any of its constituent units or any country of its operations. On this basis firms are distinguished between home oriented, host oriented and world oriented on the basis of attitude revealed by their executives.

**Lal** and **Streetan** defined MNC "as a very large firms with widespread operations which are clearly international in character and have more than five foreign subsidiaries or more than 15% of total sales produced abroad, and acting in a collusive manner to achieve maximisation profits or growth."

1. ILO, Multinational Enterprises and Social Policy, ILO, Geneva, 1973, p. 3.
2. Leonard Gomes International Economic Problem, 1978, p. 119
3. Sanjay Lal and Streetan, Foreign Investment, 1877

Among the various other benchmark sometimes used to define 'multinationality' are that the company in question must[4]—

- Produce is (rather than just distribute) abroad as well as in the headquarters country.
- Operate in a certain minimum number of nations (*e.g.*, six).
- Derive some minimum percentage of its income from foreign corporations (*e.g.*, 25%)
- Have a certain minimum ratio of foreign to total number of employees or of foreign total value of assets.
- Posses a management team with geocentric orientations.
- Directly control foreign investment (as opposed to holding shares in foreign companies).

### 12.3.1 Characteristics of MNC's

1. **Giant Size:** The sales and assets of MNC's run into billions of dollars and due to this reason they earn super normal profit. For example, *I.T.* has 708 subsidiaries in 67 countries.
2. **Oligopolistic Structure:** A MNC acquires powers through the process of merger and take-over etc. The very process of a MNC makes it oligopolistic in character.
3. **Collective Transfer of Resources:** MNC facilitates a multilateral transfer to reasources which takes place in the form of package. It includes the technical know how, raw materials, finished products, managerial services etc. It also comprises complex modern technology ranging from production, marketing, finance and management.
4. **International Operations:** The control of such institution resides in the hands of a single institution but its interest and operations sprawl across national boundaries. It operates through a parent corporation in the home country.
5. **Spontaneous Evolution:** Generally, MNC grow in a spontaneous manner. They often grow through creeping incrementalism. Many firms have become international by chance.

### 12.3.2 Types of MNCs

MNCs are of three types:

(*i*) Domination of MNC, (*ii*) Industrywise distribution of Foreign Capital, (*iii*) Foreign collaborations.

**Domination of MNC:** MNC have a strong hold over the Indian economy. Infact these corporations controlled 53.7% of the assets of the giant sector

4. Rogner Bennett, *International Business,* 2000, p. 162

during sixties and seventies. In India, Industrial Licensing policy Enquiry Committee of 1966 has recorded that there were 112 companies in India with asset worth of Rs. 10 crores or more, of these 48 companies were branches of foreign companies or were subsidary companies. Besides this there were 14 companies where either a substantial amount of foreign capital was invested or which had obtained substantial foreign loans for conducting their operation. These MNC's have obtained a substantial portion of investment resources from within the country. The share of MNC in world GDP rose from 24.2% to 26.8% from 1982 to 1992. The aggregated profits of MNC stood at the huge level of $ 73.4 billion in 1992 Out of this the share of ten largest MNC was to the extent of $ 34.8 billion which comes around 47% of the profits of the 200 mega corporations. These MNCs are exercising a huge control on the business of world economy. Due to its possession of huge capital resources, latest technology and worldwide reputation, these MNCs are diversifying the market of their products in various countries and can sell easily whatever products they manufacture. The people of under-developed countries have their craze for the products of MNC instead of their indigeneous products, this tendency has helped the MNC to expand the market of their products in such developing countries.

### Industrywise Distribution and Foreign Collaboration

Investment in foreign branches and subsidiaries has been increasingly concentrated in manufacturing industries and capital goods. It was 49.2% in 1990 against to share of 26.7% in 1948.

### 12.3.3 Factors Responsible for their Growth

MNCs have manifold reason for their growth. Some of them are listed below:

1. **Product Innovations:** MNC's possessed adequate research and development facilities. They are busy in developing new products and superior designs of existing products. Therefore, they have greater production opportunities than the national companies.
2. **Market Superiorities:** MNC avails more market superiorities such as (*i*) efficient warehousing facilities, (*ii*) market reputation, (*iii*) reliable market information (*iv*) effective advertising, and (*v*) promotion techniques etc over the national firms.
3. **Technological Superiorities:** Due to technical superiority MNCs have been encouraged by under-developed countries to participate in their industrial development. These countries consider transfer of technology useful due to (*i*) The UDC's have to face severe competition to sell their products in international markets (*ii*) Industrialization represents the most way out of under development (*iii*) The resources of these countries are insufficient to sustain the industrial progress on their own. (*iv*) Local manpower materials, local

capital equipment etc have to be optimally exploited and UDCs are unable to accomplish this task. Unless the products produced by the UDCs earn quality specification and standard they cannot be sold in the international competitive markets. In this regard MNC help to promote marketing for such commodities.

4. **Expansion of Market:** Being a large sized firm MNC expands its operation in a wider market and consequently they earn international reputation which further seeks more extension of its activities beyond the physical boundaries of the country in which it is incorporated. This urge for the expansion of business activity are responsible for the growth of MNC in different countries.
5. **Financial Superiorities:** MNC enjoys the following financial superiorities over the national firm (*i*) easier assess to external capital, market, (*ii*) international reputation, (*iii*) utilisation of high level of funds, (*iv*) huge financial resources etc.

### 12.3.4 Importance of MNCs

MNC has a important role on the international economy. Its main benefits are :

1. **Transfer of Superior Technology:** The MNC serves as an agent to transfer the superior technology to the UDCs.
2. **Transfer of Capital:** MNC helps to transfer capital from countries where it is abundant to countries where it is scarce.
3. **Linkage Effect:** The UDCs back sufficient degree of linkage with other industries. Thus, the MNCs produce linkage effect in the host countries.
4. **Effect on Balance of Payment:** The operation of MNCs have a favourable effect on the balance of payments of a country. They possess a global marketing organisation by which they can promote export from developing countries.
5. **Employment Oppurtunities:** MNC creates large scale employment opportunity. Basically employment generation is a function of two variables *viz,* (*i*) growth of investment, (*ii*) **nature of technology** MNC has encouraged investment in productive channels to raise employment.
6. **Development of Human Resource Capital:** They provide sophisticated technology and improved skills and knowledge to under-developed countries.
7. MNCs **provides an efficient mean of integrating national economies**.

### 12.3.5 Demerits of MNCs

Demerits of MNCs are:

1. **Profit Oriented:** As **Leonard Gomes** points out that the MNC technology is designed for world-wide profit maximisation, not for the development needs of poor countries, in particular employment needs and relative factor scarcity in these countries. In general it is asserted that the imported technologies are not adopted to (*a*) the consumption needs, (*b*) the size of domestic markets, (*iii*) resource availabilities, and (*c*) stage of development of many LDC's; MNC's are reluctant to tolerate any obstacles that prevents them from maximising their profits.
2. **Transfer of Technology a Costly Affair:** The transfer of technology proves costly affair. They charge extra-ordinary in the form of fees, royalty and other charges.
3. **Corrupt Practises:** MNC at times resorts to corrupt business practises.
4. **Production of Non-essential Goods:** MNCs prefer to participate in the production of mass consumption and non-essential items.
5. **Promote Regional Disparities:** The MNC encourage regional disparities. They set their plants in big cities/town in LDCs, where infrastructural facilities are available. Thus, they accentuate sectoral inequalities and strengthen dualism in such countries.
6. **Capital Intensive Technology:** MNC brings in capital intensive technology.
7. **Exploitation of Labour:** MNCs exploit cheap labour available in UDCs. They are interested in maintaining a gap between the wages prevailing in their home country and the host country.
8. **The Staff of MNC are Paid High:** This leads to social inequality. It breeds unrest among the workers employed in indigeneous industry.

## 12.4 Control over MNC

Government agencies have been entrusted with the responsibility of controlling the activities of MNC. These agencies include the (*i*) RBI, (*ii*) Company affairs Ministry, (*iii*) the Ministry of Industrial Development, (*iv*) Ministry of Finance. But due to lack of coordination of these agencies there is not systematic control over the operation of MNCs. The government tried to tighten the MNC in the following ways:

(*i*) Restricting the import of foreign technology totally in respect of the production of inessential article and also in those areas where domestic technology is considered adequate enough .

(*ii*) The maximum rate of royalty on permissible foreign technology was laid down.

(*iii*) In respect of some designated industries foreign investment were allowed in principle only after getting sanction from the administrative body on a case by case basis.

(*iv*) The normal permissible period of agreements was reduced from ten to five years.

(*v*) Restriction on export.

(*vi*) Inorder to consider the application for approval of technology imports the CSIR was allowed to look into it and such technology import may be with held or delayed if it so desires.

In 1973, FERA (Foreign Exchange Regulation Act) was passed which put effective curb on the operation of foreign companies particularly on the MNC's and in 1999. FEMA (Foreign Exchange Management Act) replaced FERA in its working FERA was reviewed in 1993. FEMA aimed at regulation and management of foreign exchange. The act stated that no person resident in India shall acquire hold, own posses/or transfer any foreign exchange or any immovable property situated outside India. Thus, the main purpose of FEMA was to facilitate external trade and payments. It helps to "promote the orderly development and maintenance of foreign exchange market in India."

## 12.5 EMERGING GLOBAL COMPETITION AND INDIAN INDUSTRY

### Globalisation

According to **Deepak Nayyar** "Globalisation can be defined simply as an expansion of economic activities across political boundaries of nation state. It refers to a process of deepening economic integration, increasing economic openness and growing economic interdependence between countries in the world economy. It is associated not only with a phenomenal spread and volume of cross-border economic transaction, but also with an organisation of economic activities which straddles national boundaries."[1] Globalisation as I.M.F. defines is "The growing economic interdependence of countries worldwide through increasing volume and variety of cross-border transaction in goods and services and of international capital flows and also through the more rapid and widespread diffusion of technology" As **Mitchel** succinctly puts it "globalisation for better or worse has changed the way the world does business. Though still in its early stages it is all but unstoppable. The challenge that individuals and business face is learning how to live with it, manage it and take advantage of the benefit it offers".

Globalisation may be considered at two levels *viz*, at the macro level (*i.e.*, globalisation of the world economy) and at the micro level (*i.e.*, globalisation

---

**1. Deepak Nayyar.** "*Globalisation: What does it Mean for Development in Bibek Debroy (ed) Challenge of Globalisation* p. 15

of the business and the firm) globalisation of the world economy is achieved quite obviously by globalising the national economy globalisation of economics and globalisation of business are very much interdependent.

Globalisation infact grew between 1870-1913. However, since 1980's the new phase of globalisation became pronounced. The thrust to globalisation process in India was provided by the new economic policy introduced by the government of India in July, 1991 at the behest of the IMF and the world Bank and the subsequent extension of these reforms carried out in the later years.

At the corporate level, globalisation in its true sense is a way of corporate life necessitated, facilitated, and nourished by the transnationalisation of the world Economy and developed by corporate strategies, globalisation is an attitude of mind- it is a mind which reviews the entire world as a single market so that the corporate strategy is based on the dynamics of global business environment. International marketing or international investment does not amount to globalisation. Unless it is the result of such a global orientation. Normally, a firm passes through different stages of development before it becomes a truly global corporation. Typically, a domestic firm starts its international business by exporting later it may establish joint ventures or subsidiaries abroad. From an international firm it may then develop into a multinational firm and finally into a global one. A truely global corporation views the entire world as a single market it does not differentiate between domestic and foreign markets. In other words, there is nothing like a home market and foreign market- there is one market the global market.

There are however some essential conditions on the part of the domestic economy as well as the firm for successful globalisation of the business. They include, business freedom, required facilities, governmental support, resources competitiveness and proper strategic orientations. Economic liberalisation is regarded as a first step towards facilitating globalisation. There should be proper infrastructural facilities, financial resources, technology along with competitive advantage. A firm may derive competitive advantage from any one or more of the factor such as low cost and price, product quality, product differentiation, technological superiority, after sales service, marketing strength etc. Sometimes small firms may have an edge over others in certain aspect or times of business.

## 12.6 PROS AND CONS OF GLOBALISATION

Globalisation affects different countries, sectors, industries and sections of people. While developing countries which in the past were against globalisation have widely opened their doors for globalisation, many people in developed countries like U.S.A are angry against globalisation because of de-industrialisation, job cuts etc. Globalisation, has infact become a buzz-word with Indian firms now and many are expanding their overseas business by different strategies.

Globalisation promotes productivity; raises living standards, controls, price, promotes innovations with new ideas from abroad and export. Jobs often pay more than other jobs. While, on the other hand it also cuts jobs due to competitive pressure, workers face pay cut demand from employers which often threatens to export jobs.

As such although globalisation can benefit the developing countries in several ways, irregulated globalisation will cause serious problems for developing countries. The almost universal acceptance of the market economy and the globalisation driven by private enterprises tends to aggravate in the absence of proper regulation most of the harmful effects traditionally attributed to neo-colonolism.

## 12.7 GLOBALISATION OF INDIAN BUSINESS

India's economic integration with the rest of the world was very limited because of the restrictive economic policies followed until 1991. Indian firms confined themselves by and large to the Indian market. Foreign investment by Indian firms was very insignificant.

With the new economic policy 1991 there had been a change. Indian firms expanded their overseas business by different strategies.

The Indian business suffered from a number of obstacles, for instance governmental policy and procedures are not encouraging, inputs are costly with poor inadequate infrastructural facilities, obsolete technology. There are also several socio-political factors which resist change and this comes in the form of poor quality products. Further, Indian companies due to low production capacities is unable to accept large orders and keep up delivery schedules.

However, there are many factors which encourages globalisation of Indian business such as advantage of human resource, a wide resource and industrial base, growing entrepreneurship growing domestic market, and competition, expanding foreign markets, economic liberalisation in other countries, scope for marketing, resources of N.R.Is economic liberalisation. The growing competition both from within the country and abroad provoked many Indian companies to look to foreign markets seriously to improve their competitive position and to increase the business. Sometimes, companies enter foreign markets seriously to improve their competitive position and to increase the business. Sometimes companies enter foreign market as a counter-competitive strategy *i.e.*, to fight the foreign company in its own home market, to weaken its competitive strength.

## 12.8 GLOBALISATION STRATEGY

Indian industry can move towards globalisation by different strategies such as developing exports, foreign investment including joint ventures and acquisition, strategic alliances, licensing and franchising.

## I. Exporting

Exporting is an important way of globalisation. All international transactions do not constitute globalisation. If the governmental policy does not permit an Indian exporter to source materials globally the export cannot be regarded as global. In a truely globalised environment the exports will also be global, the source of financing, inputs will be global, based on purely business consideration. A number of products exported from several countries are more global. For instance, a product exported from Japan may consist of part and other materials produced in other countries which are sourced globally by the exporters.

In order to be competitive in the global market a company should be able to adopt a globalisation strategy, in all aspects of business including production. In India export progress has been low due to inadequacy of production capacities, deficiencies of product development, encompassing design, quality, finish and packaging, technological factors etc.

However, with the right policy and reforms and institutional support with technological upgradation and modernisation and enlargement of production facilities with thrust on quality and value added products, with improvement in infrastructure and with right marketing strategy great strides could be made in the export of many of the products.

One of the most important consideration in export should be to achieve maximum unit value realisation. Value added exports is necessary to enhance the foreign exchange earnings. For instance, while 20 million kg of tobacco exports can earn India Rs. 100 crores foreign exchange if converted to cigarette the same quantity of tobacco would earn Rs. 400 crores foreign exchange. India's export are mostly in bulk form and progress achieved in value added exports is not anything significant. Supply constraint is another major hurdle which comes in increasing exports. An important oppurtunity is market riching.

## II. Foreign Investment

Foreign Investment by Indian companies has so far been very limited. The attractiveness of the domestic market, lack of global orientation, government regulation etc have been responsible for this. With economic liberalisation and growing global orientation many Indian companies are setting up manufacturing/trading/assembling bases abroad either wholly or in partnership with foreign firms. Indian companies have also been making huge investment abroad on acquisitions. For instance, Aditya Birla group has been establishing manufacturing basis abroad.

These overseas investment aims not only at expansion of production base and business abroad. But also at consolidation of the domestic business. The Ballarpore Industry of the Thapars are setting up a giant paper mill in Indonesia at an estimated cost of Rs. 1800 crores. A plantation put up on 2,50,000 hectares of land will feed the mill. Any surplus pulp may be exported to India to feed

Thapar paper mills here. The significance of it should be viewed against the possible wood and pulp shortage in future in India.

Indian companies are also establishing production facility abroad to get entry into regional trade blocs. For instance, Cheminor Drugs one of Dr. Reddy's lab's groups of Companies Act Jersey has set up a subsidary unit in New Jersey.

### III. Mergers and Acquisition

It may be used to acquire new technology and reduce competition. Merger and acquisition provides instant access to market and distribution network. For example, Vijay Mallya's U.B. group acquired a small British Company Wiltshire Brewery. The attraction of Wiltshire for UB was that the former offered a ready made chair of 300 pubs throughout Britain which could be used for marketing of UB's brand of beer like King Fisher. The UB group has gone for such acquisition in U.S.A. and South Africa.

With the growing of global orientation of the Indian companies there has been a flurry of buy-outs abroad both big and small.

### IV. Joint Venture

Joint venture has been adopted as an important foreign market strategy employed by Indian firms like Ranabaxy, Core, Lupin, Reddy etc. Essar Gujarat's joint venture in countries like Indonesia and Bangladesh to manufacture cold rolled (CR) steel which have resulted from a strategy to create an assured market for its hot rolled (MR) coil mother plant at Hazaria [(HR) coils are inputs for manufacturing (CR) steel products]. The ESSEL PACKAGING has taken the joint venture route to expand the business abroad.

Today, the number of companies on joint venture has been increasing.

### V. Strategic Alliance

Strategic alliance provides enormous scope for the Indian business to enter/ expand the international business. This is important for the technology acquisition and overseas marketing. Alliance is indeed an important international marketing strategy employed by several Indian firms.

### VI. Licensing and Franchising

Under licensing a firm in one country (the licensor) permits a firm in another country (the license ) to use its intellectual property (such as, patent, trademarks, copy rights technology, marketing skill or some other specific skill for a fee or royalty). Franchising is a form of licensing in which a parent company grants another independent entity (the franchise) the right to do business in a prescribed form. This right can take the form of selling the franchise products using its name, production and marketing techniques or general business approach. Franchising involves the franchiser supplying an important ingredient (part, material etc) for the finished product.

## 12.9 SUMMARY

The intent of globalisation is efficiency improvement and market oppurtunities taking advantage of the opportunities of the global environment. Therefore, in many cases Indian companies have to globalise to survive and grow in the emerging competitive enviornment.

The limitations of the national markets, the diversity and uneveness of resource endowments of different nations, complexity of technological development, demand patterns, differences in production efficiency, cost, technological revolution in communication and other field etc mandates globalisation. If the Indian firms have the facility to obtain the latest technology in the world to raise finance input from the cheapest source then they are on equal footing with the foreign firms in many respect. Incase, if the Indian firm muster over foreign firms in labour cost/productivity/product cost/quality that could be a competitive advantage. The growth plans of many Indian companies indicate a great leap forward. The increase in size could keep the companies on a strong footing to make dent into both the domestic and foreign market Reliance turnover was seen to have doubled.

Several Indian companies are infact leading players. The Ispat group of Mittals which has units in U.S., Canada, Indonesia, Trinidad, is the largest sponge iron producers in the world. The Aditya Birla group is the world's largest players in viscose fibre and Carbon Black and also the largest refiner of oil (palm). The ESSEL-PACKAGING, Arvind mills (largest denim cloth) producer are making trust. When the projects are implemented. Reliance industries would be the second largest texturiser in the world to be fully integrated from naptha to fabrics. India is also a major producer of some of the agro-goods, two wheelers, and bicycle.

The liberalisation in India and in other countries poses a real challenge to the Indian business to prove its mettle.

❑❑❑

CHAPTER 13

# Problem's of Large Scale Industries in India

In this chapter, we shall probe into the problems relating to the growth of some major large scale industries in India.

## 13.1 IRON AND STEEL INDUSTRY

Iron and steel industry forms the base of all industrial activity. The development of all manufacturing and consumer goods industries depends upon the extent of development of iron and steel industries. The most important among the industries directly dependent on iron and steel industries are engineering, wagon building, tractor, agricultural tools, tubewells etc. Steel was a symbol of the strength of the economy and a potent of the glory of India and the future. Steel production has thus a multiplier effect on the development of all other industries. Further, it brings employment for thousand of people (approximately 3 lakh workers).

Today India is the fifth largest crude steel producing country in the world. The crude steel production in the country during 2004-05 was 43.44 million tonnes as compared to the production of 38.73 million tonnes in 2003-04 and 34.71 million tonnes in 2002-03. It ranged to 46.46 million tonnes in 2005-06 and rose to 50.82 million tonnes in 2006-07. According to 2007-08 (2007-08) provision crude steel production was 53.92 million tonnes (*see* Table 13.1).

**Table 13.1**

| year | Crude Steel Production in India (million tonnes) |
|---|---|
| 2002-03 ⟶ | 34.71 |
| 2003-04 ⟶ | 38.73 |
| 2004-05 ⟶ | 43.44 |
| 2005-06 ⟶ | 46.46 |
| 2006-07 ⟶ | 50.82 |
| 2007-08 ⟶ | 53.90 |

**Source:** JPC (Joint Plant Committee)

The production of finished (carbon steel) during 2002-08 is stated below in Table 13.2.

**Table 13.2:** Production for sale of total finished steel (in million tonnes)

| Item | 2002-03 | 2003-04 | 2004-05 | 2005-06 | 2006-07 | 2007-08 |
|---|---|---|---|---|---|---|
| Main producer | 14.509 | 15,363 (5.9) | 15,814 (2.9) | 16,406 (3.7) | 17,599 (7.3) | 18017 (2.4) |
| Major and other producers | 22,657 | 25,346 (11.9) | 27,699 (9.3) | 30,160 (8.9) | 34,930 (15.8) | 37,250 (6.6) |
| Total | 37,166 | 40,709 | 43, 513 | 46,566 | 52,529 | 55,267 |

**Source:** Joint Plant Committee.

The sponge iron industry had been specially promoted so as to provide an alternative to steel melting scrap which was increasingly becoming scarce. Today, India is the largest producer of sponge iron in the world. The production of sponge iron was 7.86 million tonnes during 2002-03 and 9.88 million tonnes during 2003-04. In 2005-06 it rose to 14.82 million tonnes and 18.35 million tonnes in 2006-07. During 2007-08 it was 19.2 million tonnes (provisional)

In India though the countries production of iron and steel is sufficient to meet the domestic demand some quantity of steel is always needed to be imported especially those grades and qualities which are required in small quantities and therefore do not justify setting up of production capacities. Over the last few years India had been annually importing about 1 to 2 million tonnes of finished carbon steel. Indian steel companies have marked their diversified presence in the global market effected mainly through the establishment of the state of the-art plants, continuous modernisation and improved energy efficiency of plants. Additional capacities of nearly 6 million tonnes have been commissioned for finished (carbon) steel in the current year. The observed growth in import is mainly in hot rolled coils, cold rolled coils, semis and steel scrap. Imports of finished (carbon) steel during the year 2002-03 was 1.510 million tonnes which rose 4.4 million tonnes in 2006-07 and to 5.05 million tonnes during 2007-08 on account of supply-demand gap in the domestic market. The Eleventh Five Year Plan Document points out that the problems faced by the industry include depleting of iron ore resources, inadequate availability of coal, inadequate sintering and pelletization capacities and poor transport infrastructure for movement of raw material (Table 13.3).

**Table 13.3:** Production, consumption, export and import of steel and pig iron (m tonnes)

| Item | 2004-05 | 2005-06 | 206-07 | April-December | |
|---|---|---|---|---|---|
| | | | | 2006-07 | 2007-08 |
| Production<br>Finished carbon steel<br>pig iron Exports | 44.54(9)<br>3.23 (-14) | 48.9(10)<br>4.69 (45) | 55.15 (13)<br>4.99 (6) | 39.29<br>3.67 | 41.7 (6.1)<br>3.96 (7.9) |
| Finished carbon steel | 4.38 (-10) | 4.48 (2) | 4.89 (9.3) | 3.53 | 3.67 (4) |
| pig iron Imports | 0.39 (-25) | 0.44 (13) | 0.71 (61) | 0.49 | 0.53 (8.2) |
| Finished carbon steel | 2.11 (37) | 3.85 (82) | 4.44(15) | 2.94 | 4.7 (60) |
| Pig iron | 0.08 (300) | 0.03 (-63) | 0.03 (0) | 0 | 0.01 |
| Consumption<br>Finished carbon steel | 34.39 (10) | 39.18 (14) | 44.33 (13) | 31.48 | 35.51 (12.8) |
| Pig iron | 2.79 (-14) | 4.14 (48) | 4.34 (4.8) | 3.16 | 3.42 (8.2) |

**Note:** Figure in parenthesis indicates variation over previous year.
**Source:** Economic survey-2007-08 p.193). *Provisional estimate.

The total volume of finished carbon steel exported during the year 2002-03 was 4.506 m tonnes, 4.835 m tonnnes during 2003-04. It rose to 4.381 m. tonnes during 2004-05, and 4.350 m. tonnes during 2005-06. The volume of total finished steel exported during 2007-08 was 5.05 m. tonnes (povisional) as against 5.24 m tonnes in 2006-07.

In recent years there has been a significant improvement in areas of iron and steel making processes, upgradation of raw material, product development, increase in productivity, reduction in energy consumption by the in-house. Research and development -activities however, expenditure on *R* and *D* still remains low at 0.2% (approximately) of the total turn over of steel plants. The government therefore decided to spend upto Rs. 150 crores from the interest incurred on Steel Development Fund (SDF) loans, given to SAIL (Steel Authority of India limited) and TISCO (now Tata steel limited).

Reforms in the iron and steel sector consisted of liberalisation of import and export of steel materials abolition of price and distribution controls, and successive reduction of import duties on iron and steel products. The iron and steel industry in now faced with a competitive environment. The competitive pressures are likely to increase with further liberalisation in trade policy. It is the government's belief that the Indian steel industry which has access to the source) of best quality iron ore from domestic mines and also substantial portion of cooking coal could improve her efficiency and face foreign competition successfully. With a view to augment the supply of steel the Government reduced the custom duty on seconds and defective steel from 20% to 10% and provided exemption from custom duty to all coking coal. The custom duty on alloys and stainless steel was reduced to 5% in January, 2007.

## 13.2 SOME MAJOR PROBLEMS FACED IN IRON AND STEEL INDUSTRY-A SUMMARY

1. **Rise in Input Cost:** Over the years rise in prices of pig iron, coal and power has risen considerably, a small hike in input cost has had considerable impact on the cost of production.
2. **Shortage of Coal and Power:** The steel plant faced the problem of obtaining adequate quantity of the coking coal. In addition Indian coking coal has a high ash content. This brings down the production of blast furnaces. Dependence on imported coal rose, leading to rise in cost of production. Further, power shortage also affected the functioning of steel plant adversely.
3. **Government Control and Pricing Policy:** Indian Iron and steel industry was state regulated since 1941. Both prices and distribution of steel was under governmental regulation. Due to demand for various items of steel, price control and distribution of steel led to black marketing and acute shortage of steel.

   The government decided to remove statutory control over the prices and distribution of all, but on a few categories with effect from 1st March, 1964. On the basis of the recommendation of the Raja committee a Joint Plant Committee (JPC) consisting of representatives of the main producers of steel and the railways was set up by the government in March 1964. The JPC periodically fixed a set of prices for various items of steel, keeping in mind the need to avoid a price spiral through cost-push factors. It also aimed to ensure a reasonable return to the main producers and reduce the burden of the consumers. The administered price regime has been dismantled and the industry in now free to fix prices.
4. **Technological Obsolescence:** It is due to technological obsolescence that energy consumption in Indian steel mills still continues to be considerably higher than in steel mills of the developed countries. For instance, Japan has neither iron ore deposit nor coal but imports all its basic raw material and still is able to produce high quality steel at low cost. Japan has been successful mainly because of its high level of technology *i.e.*, the improved integrated process of control of blast furnace. Absence of technical know how and shortage of technical personal bottlenecks, stood in the way of iron and steel-industries development and hampered the production schedules.

However, the Indian steel industry needs to reduce the cost of production by improving factor productivity and catching up with the technology of the rest of the world.

## 13.3 JUTE INDUSTRY

Jute industry occupies an important place in the national economy especially in W. Bengal. Jute meets all the standards for 'safe' packaging since it is a natural, renewable, bio-degradable and eco-friendly product.

India, stands as the second largest exporter of jute goods and this sector provides employment to 40 lakh farm families as well as direct and indirect employment to 4 lakh workers. There are 78 jute mills in the country of which 61 are in West-Bengal, 3 each in Bihar and Uttar Pradesh, 7 in Andhra Pradesh, 1 each in Assam, Tripura and Madhya Pradesh. Annually the export of jute product ranges between Rs. 1075-1100 crores.

The production of raw jute varies between 90-100 lakh bales and the domestic consumption of jute good is in the range of 13.5-14.5 lakh million tonnes. The ratio of domestic consumption to exports is 80: 20. In 2005-06, the production of raw jute was 85 lakh bales, in 2007-08, it was expected to be 100 lakh bales.

The government announced the first National Jute Policy on 15 April 2005, with the objective of achieving compounded annual growth rate of 15% per annum, improving the quality of jute fibre, ensuring value addition through diversified jute product, ensuring remunerative prices to jute farmers and enhancing the yield per hectare.

As envisaged in the National Jute Policy, 2005, Steps were taken to implement a Jute Technology mission on June 2, 2006 at an estimated cost of Rs. 355.55 crores and it established a National Jute Board at Kolkata by merging the Jute manufactures Development Council (JMDC) and National Centre for Jute Diversification (NCJD). Steps have also been initiated to set up a national institute of Natural Fibre and a National Jute and Jute Geo-Textile Museum.

The minimum support price (MSP) for raw jute has been increased to Rs. 1000 per quintal in 2006-07 from Rs. 910 per quintal in 2005-06, with a view to protect the jute farmers from seasonal uncertainties and help to prevent distress sales by farmers.

The volume of jute import declined from 790,000 tonnes to 250,000 tonnes between 1951-1998. This is due to rise in domestic consumption. The government boosted up jute export to Soviet-Union, Japan, U.S.A. to some extent.

## 13.4 PROBLEMS OF JUTE INDUSTRY

1. **Problem of Raw Material:** The problem of raw material is the basic problem of jute industry. The fluctuations in the production of raw jute have continued since decades. This necessitates imports to supplement domestic production of raw jute.

2. **Obsolete Machinery:** The industry did not accumulate internal resources for modernisation of plant and machinery. The government recently announced a package of assistance of Rs. 150 crores under the Jute Modernisation Fund scheme to improve the situation.
3. **The Emergence of Substitutes:** The Indian jute industry is constrained by competition from synthetic materials, paper, cloth, etc. A whole range of rival packaging material offer stiff competition to jute goods. As a result, India's jute exports are facing competition from countries like Bangladesh and China.
4. **Irregular Power Supply:** Severe power crises in West Bengal in a number of years resulted in power cuts in jute industry. This hampered the production of jute.
5. **Cost of Production:** The jute industry experienced rise in the cost of production since there was rise in the prices of dyes, chemicals, power charge etc.

Thus, in the last few years jute industry did not farewell. The output of jute textile had declined. The government therefore enacted Jute Packaging Material Act, 1997 to protect the interest of the jute sector. The government allowed 'nil' state of excise duty on all jute products. As a consequence, the export of jute manufacture rose to Rs. 694 crores in 1997-98. This showed slight changes.

## 13.5 SUGAR INDUSTRY

Sugar industry is very important to the Indian national economy. It is the fourth major sugar producing country in the world (next to Russia, Brazil, Cuba.) with 15% share of the world's sugar production and second largest agro-based industry in the country. It ranks as the third largest industry in terms of its contribution to the net value added by manufacture and employs nearly 3.25 lakh workers besides creating employment indirectly for 45 million farmers. Around 7.5% of the rural population is involved in the cultivation, harvesting and ancillary activities of sugar cane. Besides 0.5 million skilled and semi-skilled workers mostly from rural areas are engaged in the sugar industry. The sugar industry in India has been a focal point for socio-economic development in the rural areas by mobilising rural resources, generating employment, raising income, and promoting transport and communication facilities. Sugar industry is also an important source of excise duty. There are now 506 sugar factories in India (as against 138 during 1950-51) with a total installed capacity of 17 million tonnes. Against this 436 factories were in operation.

Sugar industry is predominantly localised in Uttar Pradesh, particularly in the district of Meerut, Saharanpur, Bijnour, Baraiely, Muzaffarnagar, Moradabad, and Rampur. Apart from U.P. it is also located in Andhra Pradesh, Bihar, Maharashtra.

Production of sugar rose from 11.34 lakh tonnes in 1950-51 to 51.48 lakh tonnes in 1980-81, 132.77 lakh tonnes in 1991-92, 189.08 lakh tonnes in 2002-

03 but fell to 162.90 lakh tonnes in 2003-04. It rose to 193.21 lakh tonnes in 2005-06 and to 281.99 lakh tonnes in 2006-07 (provisional). However, in 2008-09, sugar production was assessed to be 150 lakh tonnes, as against the demand of 225 lakh tonnes.

## 13.6 PROBLEMS OF SUGAR INDUSTRY

1. **High Prices of Sugar:** The fluctuation in the production of sugar has been attributed to the fact that it is an agro-based industry and its output fluctuated with the vagaries of monsoon. The inefficiency and uneconomic nature of production in sugar mills, low yield and short crushing season, the high prices of sugarcane, heavy excise duty levied by the Government are responsible for high cost of sugar in India. The prices of Indian sugar is considerably higher than the world price of sugar. Hoarding, speculation and black marketing of sugar in India by wholesale dealers are rampant in India.
2. **Problem of Production of Sugar:** The low yield sugarcane, short crushing season unsatisfactory location of the industry in U.P. and Bihar and inadequate supply of cane-all these create problems of production of sugar in India. Besides Indian sugar factories have low milling efficiency, and recovery of sugar from sugarcane is low. One reason for that is the uneconomic character of many of the sugar mills. Further Indian sugar mills do not have sugar plantation of their own and hence do not have control over the quantity and quality of sugarcane supplied by the cane growers.
3. **Problems of Mounting Losses:** Sugarcane prices have been increasing over the years as the cost of production have been rising on the one hand and on the other hand the government feels that a remunerative price policy is a must for growers so that the incentive to grow more remains. Since cane prices account for 60% of the cost of producing sugar, this in truth leads to rise in cost of production of sugar. However, the realisation from the sale of sugar are not rising adequately to meet these increasing cost resulting in heavy losses to sugar units.
4. **Fixation of Higher Sugarcane Prices by the State Government:** The pricing of sugarcane is affected by Statutory Minimum Prices (SMP) and State Advised Prices (SAP). SMP is the price of sugarcane as fixed by the central government and SAP is the price fixed by the state government taking into account the specific recoveries and condition in that particular state. Sugarcane pricing infact, has become a highly **political** issue and it has been observed that the basis of fixing SAP is arbitrary.
5. **Competition from Jaggery Production:** In India 10 tonnes of sugar are obtained from 100 tonnes of cane but in case of khandsari only 7 tonnes of sugar are derived. Thus, a net loss to the country by the

use of cane for khandsari and jaggery. The recovery content of gur is only 5%. The jagger factories deprive the community by 25-40% of sucrose when they divert the cane required by sugar mills. While the price of sugarcane supplied to the factories is fixed by the Government there is no price fixation for sugarcane used for jagger. The obvious result is that the production of jagger increases at the cost of sugar. It is seen that price fixation policy, distribution of sugarcane among the producers of sugar, jagger and khandsari is not done on a fair basis. Therefore 'price' competition between the three be avoided.

6. **Problem relating to Obsolete Machine:** Sugar factories in U.P. and Bihar still are in the grip of use of outmoded machines. Replacement of modern technique is necessary.
7. **Higher Excise and Other Duties:** Basic cost shot up due to the various statutory provisions like the implementation of the second Wage Board Award, higher rates of depreciation under the income tax rules, increased cane freight charges etc. The local levies in certain states has therefore gone up.
8. **Policy Measures:** The government of India set up B.B. Mahajan Committee to study the development and growth of sugar industry in India *vis-a vis* other sugar producing countries and suggested modifications, amendments or repel of existing laws and controls in order to raise production and efficiency and in its report in 1998 made certain recommendations.
   1. Complete decontrol of sugar in order to provide level playing field to the domestic industry *vis-a vis* imported sugar.
   2. Discontinuation of sugar through PDS so as to prevent PDS sugar entering the open market.
   3. Setting up of a board for determining statutory minimum prices (SMP) for sugarcane in the month of September every year.
   4. Prescribed a minimum distance of 15 kms instead of the existing 25 kms between an existing sugar mill and a new sugar mill.
   5. Continuance of import of sugar under OGL in order to protect the consumer against any unusual rise in prices.
   6. Abolition of existing incentives for a new factory.

The government has however announced the decision to remove the sugar industry from compulsory licensing under the provision of Industries Development and Regulation Act, 1956 and to maintain a distance of 15 km between an existing Sugar mill and a new mill in order to avoid unhealthy competition among sugar factories to procure sugarcane.

In 1982, Sugar Development Fund was setup under the Sugar Cess Act and was funded by transfer of proceeds of sugar cess imposed at the rate of Rs. 14 per quintal or sugar produced by all sugar factories. The fund was utilised for advancing loans at concessional rate of interest for the rehabilation and modernisation of sugar industry and for the development of sugarcane in the sugar factory area. The Sugar Development Fund makes grants for undertaking research projects for development of sugar industry. The fund was used to defray expenditures for the purpose of building up and maintenance of buffer stock of sugar with a view to stabilising its prices.

## 13.7 CEMENT INDUSTRY

Cement is one of the advanced industries in the country. After the complete decontrol of prices and distribution in March, 1989 and introduction of other policy reforms cement industry has made rapid strides both in capacity/ production and process technology. The Indian cement industry not only ranks second in the production of cement in the world but also produces quality cement which meets global standards. In 2008 April, there were 159 large cement plants with an installed capacity of 11.10 million tonnes per.annum. The production during 2006. April was 99.99 million tonnes which rose to 107.71 million tonnes during April, 2007 and rose to 168.03 million tonnes during 2008 registering a growth rate of 7.83% over the previous year. Export of cement and clinker was 6.02 million tonnes in 2007-08.

Expansion of cement capacity and production has been assuming great importance in view of the growing demand from the infrastructure sector. Cement capacity and production are targeted to grow by 11.5% annually during the eleventh plan. Thus, capacity and production are likely to increase to 269 million tonnes from 166 million tonnes at the end of the Tenth Plan. However, the Eleventh Five year plan document observes that the achievement of targets is crucially dependent on factors like adequate availability of limestone, coal, power and facilities for transport of limestone. The small number of bulk cement terminals poses another challenge.

India is producing different varieties of cement like Ordinary Portland Cement (OPC), Portland Pozzdona Cement (PPC), Portland Blast Furnance Slag Cement (PBFS), oil well cement, white cement etc. These different varieties of cement are produced strictly under BIS specification and the quality is comparable with the best in the world.

The cement industry has kept pace with technological advancement and modernisation. The introduction of advanced technology has helped the industry immensely to conserve energy and fuel and to save material substantially. Export of cement was 9.19 m tonnes in 2005-06. Improvement in quality of cement has found its ready market in Indonesia, Bangladesh, Malaysia, Nepal, Middle-East countries, Burma, Africa and South-East Asian countries.

## 13.8 PROBLEM OF CEMENT INDUSTRY

1. **Power Shortage:** Power cuts, unsteady and inadequate power supply from state electricity boards have created serious problems for cement units.

2. **Raw Material :** To produce 1 tonne of cement, 1.6 tonnes of limestone and clay 0.35 tonnes of gypsum and 0.5 tonnes of coal are required. At present there is shortage of raw material but the problem is the availability of the material at an economical distance. With the introduction of industrial waste product for the manufacture of cement such as sludge from fertiliser factories and blast furnance slag from steel works, the aforesaid problem has been solved to a certain extent.
3. **Regional Imbalance:** Though the industry developed very well, there is significant regional imbalance in the sphere of production. In the case of eastern and northern regions there have been shortfalls, while in the case of western and southern regions there were surpluses. Cement being a resource tied industry the factories are concentrated at points in close proximity to the regions where extensive deposits of cement grade limestone which is the prime raw material used in cement production are located. Hence, a large number of cement factories have come up in the Southern and Western regions in the country. On the other hand, the demand for cement in Northern and Eastern region of the country is far in excess of the production of the units located in these regions. As such, smooth flow of cement from surplus to deficit regions will have to be ensured by some way or other so that the available capacity is fully utilised to meet the demand for cement in the country as a whole.
4. **Transport:** Transport bottleneck is another problem faced by the industry.
5. **Finance:** The problem of finance is closely associated with the problem of profitability in cement industry. Profitability, is closely related to the problems of distribution and marketing as well as with the cost of production. Even during the early years the rate of return was low because of depressed prices and during the later years the industry was not allowed to take advantage of the improved market conditions because of the governmental controls and regulations. As such the financial position of the cement industry was badly affected. Cement, being a capital intensive industry the fixed assets account for a major part of its total assets. It has not been able to build resources for financing expansion of existing units due to low profitability. The industry is presently depending on borrowed funds for its expansion.
6. **Partial Control and Dual Pricing Policy:** The government benefitted the most due to price control of cement.
7. **Unrealistic Distribution Policy:** The government introduced permit system of distribution which never worked properly.

## 13.9 CONCLUSION

In order to increase the production of cement a massive modernisation programme is being chalked which involves Rs. 2400 crores. Further, the government introduced partial decontrol policy.

## 13.10 PAPER INDUSTRY

The paper industry has a vital role to play in socio-economic development of the country. The per capita consumption of paper is generally considered as a benchmark of a countries modernisation. The Indian paper industry which is century old has made steady progress and witnessed a moderate production growth rate. There are more than 700 paper mills producing nearly 6.3 million tonnes of paper and paper board in 2007-08 and around 1.04 million tonnes of newsprint (2007-08) as against an estimated operational capacity or nearly 7.5 million tonnes of paper and paper board and about 1.44 m. tonnes of newsprint respectively. The projected demand for the paper, paper board and newsprint is expected to touch 8.3 m. tonnes by 2010. The per capita consumption of paper which is the benchmark of modernisation of any country stands at 7.2 kg for India.

The paper and newprint industry is fragmented with installed capacity ranging from 2 tonnes to 800 tonnes per day. The turnover of the industry is 16,000 crores and contributes about 2500 crores to the national exchequer. The Indian paper industry employs three lakh persons directly and 10 lakh persons indirectly.

One fact that however needs to be emphasised is that paper and paper products have been subjected to wide annual fluctuations in growth. After growing at 15.6% and 10.5% respectively during 2003-04 and 2004-05 their growth came down to 0.9% during 2005-06. The rate of growth picked upto 8.7% during 2006-07 but dropped to 1.6% during April-November, 2007.

The eleventh plan document has however observed that despite the fact that India is self-sufficient in most forms of paper, the industry is affected by difficulties like high production cost problems related to handling pollution, less than acceptable quality and shortage of raw materials forcing there increased imports.

In the wake of economic liberalisation the Indian paper industry thus found itself confronted with global competition which has an evolutionary effect on the traditional Indian management style resulting in redesigning of strategies. Looking, into the serious concern about the competitiveness of the Indian paper industry the department of industrial policy and promotion, ministry of commerce and industry, government of India commissioned a study on global competitiveness of Indian paper industry by an international consulting agency of repute to understand various issues relating to the growth and susceptibility. Based on the recommendation the major issues confronting the industry are:

## 13.11 PROBLEMS OF PAPER INDUSTRY

1. **Inadequate Availability of Raw Material:** The larger paper mills are based on conventional raw material *viz.*, bamboo, hardwood. Due to deforestation there has been problem of inadequacy of raw materials. It was with this view to conserve the forest resources and to maintain ecological balance that the government encouraged the setting up of small units using unconventional raw material *viz.*, agricultural waste such as straw, begasse, stalks etc. The availability of these material is easier.
2. **High Cost of Production:** The price of capital equipment required by paper industry has risen up. Other cost too have been rising quite fast-power and coal; likewise chemical, raw material has also risen up. Royalties on bamboo and hardwood has also risen up. The acute shortage of local timber, paper control order of 1978 and the heavy excise duties has all burdened the paper industry. For those units situated near the forest the transport cost are high.
3. **Finance:** After the decontrol of paper from May 1968, the industry has done better and generated its own resources but still the saving available for plough back are not adequate to finance the gigantic crash programme before it. As a results of mounting cost of production there has been a decline in the return on the capital employed. It was estimated that to set up an integrated 150-200 tonnes per day pulp and paper unit it was estimated that an investment of Rs. 25 crore is required. In the present capital market with the profitability obtaining in the industry it appears to be almost an impossible task for any entrepreneur.
4. **Machinery:** Lack of modern equipment is one of the acute problem faced by paper industry. Even the available supplies are not in a position to meet the entire machinery needs of the industry, further more whatever plant and machinery is manufactured in India it is available at high cost.
5. **Technology and Research:** The industry still depends an import for most of its modern equipment as indigeneous capacity has yet to be developed. Though the government has made all the possible arrangements to develop the indigenous know-how yet the industry finds it difficult to secure high yielding pulping equipment and faster machines for manufacturing paper. It is therefore necessary to make available foreign exchange for existing units for expanding the production and the new units to secure the modern foreign developed know-how.
6. **Chronic Shortage of Newsprint:** There is serious shortage of newsprint. 70% of our requirements are met by imports. On an average

India imports about 200,000 tonnes of newsprint every year. The main suppliers of newsprints are Canada, Finland, Norway, Sweden, Poland and Russia. Production of newsprint in India are done by NEPA, Mysore paper mills and in Kerala. Newsprint project were launched in 1981-82. Hindustan Paper Corporation also contributed to the production of newsprint.

Thus, the major issue before the Government was to resolve the problem. These identified issues were addressed by the government of India through National Manufacturing Competitiveness Council (NMCC). The Government has taken up various measures which included. Excise rebate to small units, abolition of custom duty on the import of paper grade pulp and wood chips, removal of statutory control over production, price and distribution of white printing paper, providing infrastructural support by way of increased allocation of coal and wagons. Along with it the concept of broad banding has been extended to paper and pulp products whereby the firms will have the freedom to manufacture any variety of papers within the overall limit of licensed capacity.

## 13.12 TEXTILE INDUSTRY

The Indian textile industry has a overwhelming presence in the economic life of the country. It plays a pivotal role. Apart from providing the basic necessities of life the textile industry also contributes to industrial output, employment generation and export earnings of the country. In 2007, it contributed approximately 14% to industrial production 4% to Gross Domestic Product, 17% to countries export earnings. It provided direct employment to about 35 million people which includes a substantial number of SC/ST women.

Textile industry is thus the second largest provider of employment after agriculture. Thus, the growth and all round development of this sector has a direct bearing on the improvement of the economy of the country. The cotton textile industry is the largest organised industry in the country. Besides, there are a large number of subsidiary industries dependent on this sector, such as manufacturing machinery, accessories stores, ancillaries, dyes and chemicals. As on 31 January, 2006 there were 1779 cotton/man made fibre textile mills in the country.

Over the years the production of cloth in the organised mill sector has been stagnating. It has declined from 1714 million square metres in 1999-2000 to about 1503 mn sq. mtrs in 2004-05 and is anticipated at 1515 mn sq. metrs in 2005-06. The total production of cloth by all sectors *i.e.* mill, powerloom, handloom, hosiery and khadi, wool and silk has however shown an upward trend in recent years. The IIP data shows that during April-November 2007 cotton textiles grew by 5.5% (cotton yarn by 5.7% and cotton cloth by 4.2%) wool, silk and man-made fibre textiles by 4.5%, compared to the corresponding period in 2006 (Table 13.4).

**Table 13.4:** Industrial production by broad industry groups-growth rates (per cent)[a]

| Industrial group | IIP Weight | 2005-06 | 2006-07 | Apr-Nov 2006-07 | Apr-Nov 2007-08 | Point contribution Apr-Nov 2006-07 | Point contribution Apr-Nov 2007-08 |
|---|---|---|---|---|---|---|---|
| **Sl. No. Manufacturing** | **79.4** | **9.1** | **12.5** | **11.8** | **9.8** | **91.21** | **89.87** |
| **Rate of growth higher than for total manufacturing during April-November, 2007** | | | | | | | |
| 1. Wood products | 2.7 | -5.7 | 29.1 | 2.4 | 72.6 | 0.20 | 6.62 |
| 2. Other manufacturing | 2.6 | 25.2 | 7.8 | 10.8 | 19.1 | 3.09 | 6.43 |
| 3. Basic metals | 7.5 | 15.8 | 22.9 | 20.5 | 15.6 | 14.41 | 14.05 |
| 4. Jute textiles | 0.6 | 0.5 | -15.8 | 2.3 | 13.3 | 0.06 | 0.38 |
| 5. Leather products | 1.1 | -4.8 | 0.6 | -3.4 | 12.2 | -0.25 | 0.94 |
| 6. Machinery, equipments | 9.6 | 12.0 | 14.2 | 15.0 | 12.2 | 18.27 | 18.16 |
| 7 Rubber & petroleum | 5.7 | 4.3 | 12.9 | 12.0 | 10.8 | 5.79 | 6.22 |
| **Rate of growth lower than for total manufacturing during April-November 2007** | | | | | | | |
| 1. Beverages & tobacco | 2.4 | 15.7 | 11.0 | 13.0 | 9.5 | 5.20 | 4.56 |
| 2. Chemicals | 14.0 | 8.3 | 9.6 | 9.2 | 9.4 | 14.56 | 17.28 |
| 3. Non-met min product[b] | 4.4 | 11.0 | 12.8 | 13.6 | 8.4 | 6.71 | 4.99 |
| 4. Food products | 9.1 | 2.0 | 8.6 | 2.5 | 6.8 | 1.32 | 3.98 |
| 5. Cotton textiles | 5.5 | 8.5 | 14.8 | 13.0 | 5.5 | 4.26 | 2.17 |
| 6. Textile products | 2.5 | 16.3 | 11.5 | 12.2 | 4.9 | 3.34 | 1.58 |
| 7. Wool, silk, MM textiles | 2.3 | 0.0 | 7.8 | 7.7 | 4.5 | 1.83 | 1.25 |
| **Very low/negative rates of growth during April-November 2007** | | | | | | | |
| 1. Transport equipments | 4 | 12.7 | 15.0 | 16.3 | 2.7 | 8.67 | 1.77 |
| 2. Paper products | 2.7 | -0.9 | 8.7 | 8.8 | 1.6 | 2.30 | 0.48 |
| 3. Metal products | 2.8 | -1.1 | 11.4 | 6.9 | -4.4 | 1.36 | -0.99 |

**Source:** Central Statistical Organsation.

[a] Based on the index of industrial production. Base: 1993-94 = 100.

[b] Non-metallic mineral products.

**Note:** Growth rates are estimate over the corresponding period of the previous year.

Figure based on the IIP data, suggests that the production of cotton textiles may have been affected cosiderably by the recent appreciation of rupee against

US dollar. Textile products may also have been affected to a lesser extent as shown in (Figure 13.1) and (Figure 13.2).

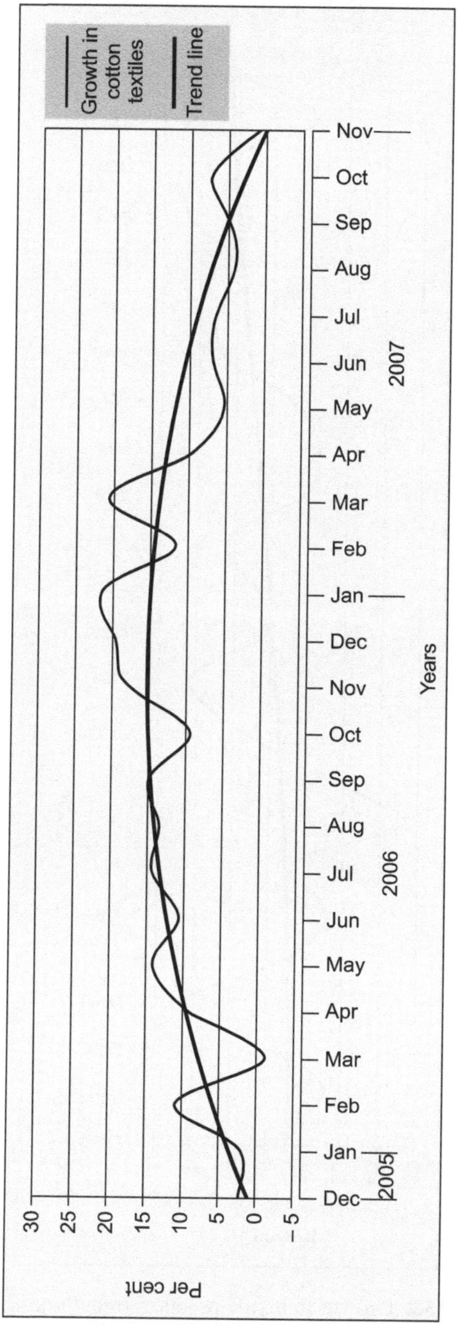


**Fig. 13.1** Growth in cotton textiles (month-on-month).

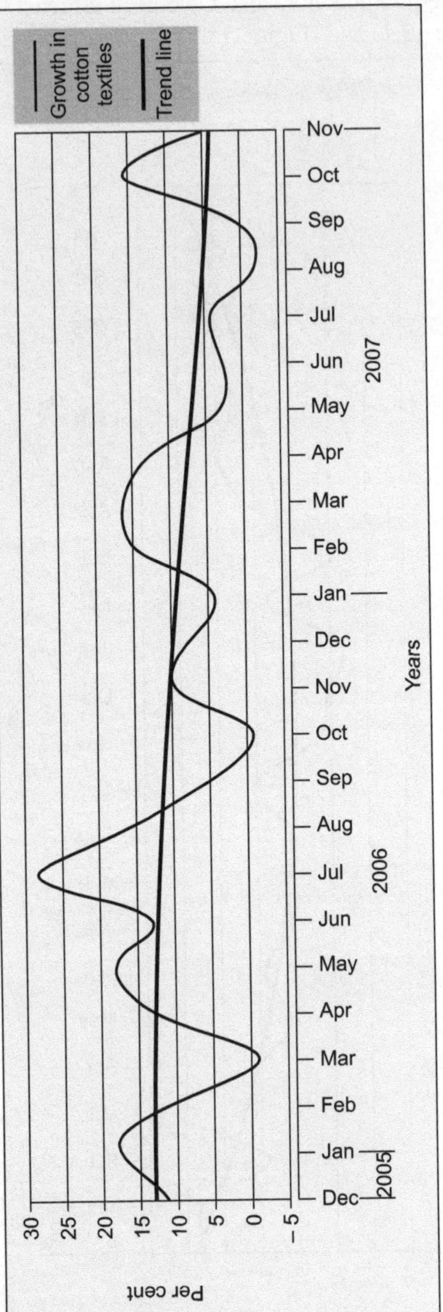


**Fig. 13.2** Growth in textile products (month-on-month).

The Overall production of textile fabrics increased by 7.7% during 2006-07 and then recorded a slower growth of 3.4% upto December, 2007 on year-on year basis by 2007-08 (provisional), the production of textile fabric was 4.9%, this burther declined to –1.9% during 2008-09. During 2006-07 the total production of cloth was 53 billion sq. metres compared to-50 billion sq. metres in 2005-06 and 45 billion sq. metres in 2004-05. During 2007-08, the production of cloth was 56 billion sq. meters which came down to 54 billion square meters in 20080-09. During 2004-05 the per capita availability of cloth was 32.63 sq. metres and in 2005-06 it was 36.10 sq. metres and in 2006-07 it was estimated to be 39.60 sq. metres.

Textile exports during 2006-07 recorded an increase of 6.9% over 2005-06. During April-Oct, 2007 textile export increased marginally by 1.49 on year basis. (Table 13.5).

**Table 13.5:** Export of textiles (US$ million)

| Item | 2004-05 | 2005-06 | 2006-07 (P) | April-October 2006 | 2007(P) | Growth April-Oct., 07(%) |
|---|---|---|---|---|---|---|
| Ready-made garments | 6,024.5 | 7,986.4 | 8,075.6 | 4643.6 | 4413.9 | –4.95 |
| Cotton textiles | 3,544.2 | 4600.8 | 5,485.0 | 2817.0 | 2816.3 | –0.03 |
| Wool and woollen textiles | 417.1 | 455.9 | 445.5 | 271.3 | 377.5 | 39.14 |
| Man-made textiles | 2,050.7 | 2,039.6 | 2,361.2 | 1328.5 | 1689.9 | 27.20 |
| Silk | 594.6 | 693.3 | 689.6 | 395.4 | 384.8 | –2.68 |
| Handicrafts | 1,013.9 | 1,314.5 | 1,259.2 | 803.8 | 719.2 | –10.52 |
| Coir and coir manufactures | 105.6 | 133.4 | 156.4 | 80.5 | 92.2 | 14.62 |
| Jute goods | 276.3 | 296.3 | 257.5 | 176.4 | 179.0 | 1.48 |
| **Grand Total** | **14,026.7** | **17,520.1** | **18,729.9** | **10,516.5** | **10,672.8** | **1.49** |

**Source: DGCI and S, Kolkata** **P = provisional**

Though the textile sector seemed to have gathered momentum consequent to the termination of the quota regime in December, 2004 yet the export performance of the Indian textile continues to lag substantially behind that of China in the post-quota era, in terms of rate of growth of exports and share in world textile exports (*See* Table 13.5). Despite steady growth in production, the textile industry has been plagued by factors like high transaction and power costs, technological obsolescence and labour issues.

The government launched two flagship schemes namely Technology Upgradation Fund Scheme (TUFS) launched in 1999 and Scheme for Integrated Textile Parks (SITP) launched in 2005, which have been approved for continuation in the eleventh five year plan. Under TUFS loans worth Rs. 27,449 crores were disbursed to 10,216 applicants upto March 2007. Under SITP 30 integrated textile parks of international standard covering weaving, knitting, processing and garmenting sectors with project proposal worth Rs 2893.42

crore have been sanctioned. These projects were to be completed by March 2008. Besides in November, 2007 the government announced package which reduced basic custom duty on certain items relating to the textile sector and extended refund of service tax paid by exporters on taxable services linked to exports. A support package for providing relief to export sectors like textiles which have low import intensity was also announced with additional subvention of 2% in pre-shipment and post-shipment credit to textiles including readymade garments and carpets but excluding man-made fibre.

## 13.13 PROBLEMS OF TEXTILE INDUSTRY

1. **Availability of Raw Material:** The industry has the largest area under cotton in the world but ranks fourth as the producer. This is because the yield of cotton per hectare is very low in India compared to U.S.A., U.S.S.R, Egypt etc. Around 80% of the crop is raised under monsoon conditions and 60% falls under Asiatic types of cotton. Adverse weather condition has therefore been the main reason for the sharp decline in production. Uncertainty in the rawmaterial market and in particular fluctuations in the price of raw cotton are two major causes of sickness and consequently closure in textile industry.
2. **Substitution Effect:** Rapid strides in the field of science and technology resulting in a variety of synthetic materials are giving a stiff competition for cotton textile. With the increase in standard of living the demand for better quality fabric will increase. As a result it is necessary to meet the special requirement of the textile industry.
3. **Competition from the Decentralised Sector:** The share of the mill sector declined from 79 to 30% between 1951-2004 while the share of decentralised sector has been rising and is around 97%.
4. **High Cost and Competition in Foreign Market:** The cotton textile industry has been facing increasing competition in the world market. This is largely due to low productivity and high cost and consequently high prices of Indian textiles. It is paradoxical that in a country where wages are low and cotton is internally available production cost should be high. But the advantage of low wages is offset by high cost of raw material and inefficiency in production caused by use of outmoded technology (machine).
5. **Outmoded Plant and Machinery:** The mill sector has been working with obsolete machinory Over 80% of the machinery in the cotton textile mills is obsolete and needs replacement with modernised machines. In 1986, however the government set up textile modernisation fund of Rs. 750 crore and asked the IDBI to operate it.
6. **Government Control and Heavy Excise Duty:** The government control in price, the distribution of yarns, pattern of production etc created problems in the growth of the textile sector. The yarn distribution scheme 1972 made it obligatory on all mills to supply

50% of the production of yarn to the decentralised sector at reduced rates. The duty on imported cotton was quite high and it not only made import of cotton quite expensive but exercised an upward pressure on the price of cotton. The excise duty on different varieties of cotton cloth were quite heavy and discriminatory.

## 13.14 PETROLEUM INDUSTRY

Petroleum oil industry is one of the major industry of our country. Petroleum liquid gold is the basis of chemical industries developed in our country. The oil resources in India are Naharkatiya- Moran area of upper Assam-offshore Mumbai high fields, and the basin structure of North-Gujarat fields and Gandhar fields in South, Gujarat. In India, the demand for crude mineral oil has been increasing. "Total production of crude mineral oil which was 0.26 million tonnes in 1950-51 rose to 6.8 million tonnes in 1970-71 and then increased to 10.5 million tonnes in 1980-81 and then sharply to 34.1 million tonnes in 1989-90, it again declined to 33.02 million tonnes in 1980-81 and then in 2006-07 it rose to 34.0 million tonnes and in (April-November 2007-08) it was 22.69 million tonnes as against 22.56 MT during the corresponding period in the previous year, showing a marginal increase of 0.60% (Table13.6). Correspondingly natural gas production at 21.35 billion cubic metre during April-November, 2007 showed an increase of 2%. The domestic refining capacity was 148.97 m. tonnes per annum as on April 1, 2007. The refinery production during April-November, 2007 stood at 103.06 MT which showed an increase of 8.3% as compared to April-November, 2006.[1]"

The expenditure in the petroleum sector has been rising and this indicates the need for an ongoing liberalisation measure for private sector participation. Oil and Natural Gas Commission was established in 1956 for the exploration of oil in India.

**Table 13.6:** Petroleum industry production

| Item | Unit | 2004-05 | 2005-06 | 2006-07[a] | 2007-08[b] |
|---|---|---|---|---|---|
| Reserves (Balance recoverable) | | | | | |
| (*i*) Crude oil | MT | 739 | 786 | 756 | N.A |
| (*ii*) Natural gas | BCM | 923 | 1101 | 1090 | N.A. |
| Production | | | | | |
| (*i*) Crude oil | MT | 33.98 | 32.19 | 33.99 | 22.69 |
| (*ii*) Petroleum products[d] | MT | 120.82 | 121.94 | 137.35 | 84.41[f] |
| Consumption | | | | | |
| (*i*) Crude oil[e] | MT | 127.42 | 130.11 | 146.55 | 103.06 |
| (*ii*) Petroleum products | MT | 111.63 | 113.21 | 119.55 | 66.52[f] |

1. Ecomonic Survey 2007-08 p. A-32 and India 2008 p. 473.

| Item | Unit | 2004-05 | 2005-06 | 2006-07[a] | 2007-08[b] |
|---|---|---|---|---|---|
| **Refinery: Installed capacity** | MT | 127.37 | 129.91 | 136.04 | 99.31[g] |
| Refinery production | | | | | |
| (*i*) Public sector | MT | 93.11 | 96.95 | 108.17 | 74.56 |
| (*ii*) Private sector | MT | 34.31 | 33.16 | 38.38 | 28.50 |
| **Total (*i* & *ii*)** | | **127.42** | **130.11** | **146.55** | **103.06** |
| Natural gas | | | | | |
| (*i*) Gross Production | BCM | 31.763 | 32.202 | 31.747 | 21.35 |
| (*ii*) Utilizaton | BCM | 30.775 | 31.325 | 30.791 | 20.79 |
| Exploratory drilling | | | | | |
| (*i*) Wells | No. | 117 | 114 | 96 | NA |
| (*ii*) Metreage | 000' | 329 | 342 | 263 | NA |
| Wells & metreage drilled | | | | | |
| (*i*) Wells | No. | 333 | 301 | 297 | NA |
| (*ii*) Metreage | 000' | 839 | 801 | 742 | NA |

Source : Ministry of Petroleum and Natural Gas.

*a* = provisional. *b* = Up to November, 2007.
*c* = As on April 1 of the initial year. *d* = Includes LPG production from Natural gas.
*e* = Refinery crude throughput. *f* = Upto Oct. 2007.
*g* = Prorated figure.
NA = Not available. RBF = Refinery Boiler Fuels.
MT = Million tonne. BCM = billion cubic metre.

of oil in India. Since its inception the commission conducted successful drilling operation in Assam, Gujarat, Bombay High Cambay area and Rava offshore area. Another agency for the exploration of oil in India is Oil. India limited. Its exploration activities are mostly concentrated in Eastern and North-Eastern regions of the country. The government offered medium and small sized oil and gas fields for development to private companies for accelerating the production of petroleum crude. Moreover the government also encouraged acquisition of exploration and development acreages abroad to national oil companies ONGC Videsh Ltd. (a wholly owned subsidary of ONGC) which has a venture in offshore Vietnam where gas discoveries have been made. The Government has also approved a proposal of ONGC Videsh Ltd. to take a participating interest in a venture in Egypt currently held by a consortium Ltd by Britain gas, U.K.[2].

In India there are 19 oil refineries of which 17 are in the public sector and 2 in the private sector due to rise in the refining capacity. Because of modernisation programmes introduced in Indian refineries the country has

2. Ecomonic Survey 2007-08 p. 190

turned as net importer of petroleum products such as gasoline, Naptha/ natural gasoline liquid high speed diesel and gas oil. Liquified Petroleum Gas (LPG) is also exported in limited, quantity in Nepal. The import of petroleum product was 8.0 million metre ton in 2003-04 and the export was 14.62 MMT in 2003-04. During 2006-07 the countries total import bill on the import of crude mineral oil and petroleum product was Rs. 2,58,572 crores as against Rs. 25,173 crores in 1995-96.

## 13.15 PROBLEMS OF PETROLEUM INDUSTRY

1. **Shortage of Petroleum Crude:** Petroleum industry has been suffering from the shortage of raw materials *i.e.* petroleum crude. Total refining capacity has risen up in recent years which led to rise in demand for imported petroleum crude. Due to the increasing volume of demand-supply gap the petroleum refineries in India have failed to utilise their production capacity fully.
2. **Dependence on Foreign Countries:** The dependence of petroleum industry on some foreign countries for meeting its requirement of various drilling and refining machines was a major problem.
3. **Price Hike:** The prices (international) of petroleum goods have been maintaining a constant hike since 1973-74 leading to a rise in import bill on petroleum goods. In 1997-98, total import bill on petroleum oil and lubricant was to the tune of Rs 30, 538 crores as against Rs. 5,587 crores in 1980-81. In 2006-07, it rose to Rs. 2,58,572 crores.
4. **Technical Problem:** The petroleum industry is suffering from numerous technical problems in respect of production of middle distillates activating its fire fighting system etc which needs to be created and updated at the earliest possible time. The RD facilities in the industry should be expanded with the maximum possible limit to face these technical problems.
5. **Pollution:** Pollution is another basic problem of this industry.
6. **Lack of Market Determining Pricing System:** The lack of well functioning market determined pricing system partly because of the lack of vibrant competition among the companies with diversified ownership continues to constrain the performances of the petroleum industry. Despite the surge of international prices of petroleum touching record level the petroleum companies are not allowed to revise their market price of petrol and HSD accordingly and allowed only a limited freedom to revise the prices as per revised methodology. This has resulted in serious drain of the financial resources of the petroleum companies.

## 13.16 RECENT GOVERNMENT MEASURES

1. **Dismantling the APN: Administered Price mechanism:** The government has dismantled the administrative. Price mechanism (APM) in the petroleum sector and the first phase of such dismantling. APM commenced in April, 1998. The cost plus formula for indigeneous crude oil producers and for shipping of crude oil have been withdrawn with a minimum floor price fixed as temporary measure. Retention pricing for refineries has been abolished. However, consumer price of MS, HSD, SKO for PDS, LPG for domestic use and ATF are still administered.
2. **Other Measures:** Other measures in the sector include a recommendation in the custom duty on crude oil from 27% to 22% from June, 1998. In order to boost refining capacity for meeting future needs tax holidays, were extended upto 2003 for new refineries set up after October 1, 1998. In another major step, petroleum and its distillation products have been removed from the list of industries reserved for public sector and have also been delicensed.

❑❑❑

CHAPTER 14

# Small Scale Enterprises

## 14.1 DEFINITION

Small scale industrial sector is a vital constituent of India's industrial sector. It contributes significantly to India's gross domestic product, export earnings and employment oppurtunities. The SSI sector covers (*a*) Small scale industrial undertakings, (*b*) ancillary industrial undertakings. (*c*) export oriented units (*d*) tiny enterprises, (*e*) Small scale service enterprises, (*f*) small scale service business enterprises (*g*) artisan, village and cottage industries, (*h*) women entrepreneurs enterprises *i.e.* a small scale unit where one or more women entreprenecurs have not less than 51% financial holding[1].

In 1950, the Fiscal commission laid down the basis for the distinction between the small scale and cottage industries. A **cottage** industry is one which is carried on wholly or primarily with the help of members of the family either as a whole or as a part time occupation. A small scale industry on the other hand is one which is operated mainly with hired labour usually 10 to 50 hands. Accordingly, the Industries (Development and Regulation Act, 1951) exempted small scale units employing less than 50 workers with power and with 100 workers or less than 100 workers without power from the system of registration. These industries which were exempted were termed as SSI units.

Industrial policy resolution 1948, 1956, 1977 have offered development of SSI in India. The fixed capital investment limit initially was restricted to Rs. 5 lakhs but in course of time the limit had been raised to Rs. 10 lakhs, then Rs. 15 lakh, and Rs. 35 lakhs during the year 1975, 1980, 1985. Similarly the limit for ancillary units were risen from Rs. 15 lakhs in 1975 to Rs. 20 lakhs in 1980 and Rs. 45 lakhs in 1985. In 1990, the limit for small scale units further rose to Rs. 60 lakhs and Rs. 75 lakhs for ancillary units and for the tiny unit the limit was raised from Rs. 2 lakhs to Rs. 5 lakhs. In 1996-97, under the Industrial policy reform the limit was raised from Rs. 60 lakhs to Rs. 75 lakhs and further to Rs. 3 crores for plants and machinery for small scale

1. Reserve Bank of India, *A Handbook of Statistics on the Indian Economy,* Explanatory Notes p 496.

industries and ancillary units and that for tiny sector it was raised from Rs. 5 lakh to Rs. 25 lakh. Again in 1999-2000 the investment limit for small scale and ancillary undertaking was reduced from Rs. 3 crores to Rs. 1 crore. The union Budget 2007-08 proposed to raise the exemption limit of small scale industry from Rs. 1 crore to Rs. 1.5 crore. Further the number of items reserved for small scale unit was 239 on 22nd January, 2007. The process of de-reservation of items for small-scale sector has continued and only 35 items would continue to be manufactured in SSI sector.

### 14.1.1 Distinction between Cottage and Small Scale Industry

Cottage industry are household industries mainly located in villages and run by the members of the family while **small** scale industries are run by hired labourers and located in urban and semi-urban areas. The level of investment in cottage industry is less and are working with simple tools while small industries invest uptill Rs. 3 crores and have machines which are run by power.

### 14.1.2 Present Position of Small Scale Industry in India

In India, small scale industry is an important sector of the economy with a noteworthy contribution to GDP, industrial production, employment generation and exports. The performances of small scale industry sector based on final results of the Third All India Census of SSI is given in (Table 14.1). It is observed from the table as per census of registered and unregistered units there were in all 25.71 lakhs SSI units in the country in 1994-95 out of which 19.44 lakhs were registered units and 6.27 lakhs were unregistered units. Again total number of such SSI units in 2004-05 increased to 118.59 lakhs showing a growth of 4.1% over the previous years out of which 17.53 lakhs were registered unit and 101.06 lakhs were unregistered units. It is estimated that the number of SSI units during 2006-07 has increased to 128.44 lakhs registering a growth of 4.1% over the previous years. The value of production of SSI units in India at current prices has increased from Rs. 2,98,886 crores in 1994-95 to Rs. 4,18,263 crores in 2004-05 and to Rs. 4,76,209 crores in 2005-06 registering a growth rate of 16.9% and 13.9% respectively over the previous year. Again total value of production of SSI sector at constant prices has increased from Rs. 2,66,054 crores in 1994-95 to Rs. 2,51,511 crores in 2004-05 and then to Rs. 2,77,668 crores in 2005-06 registering a growth rate of 10.0% and 10.4% respectively over the previous year Again total value of production of SSI sector calculated at 2001-02 prices increased to Rs. 4,71,663 crores registering a growth rate of 12.6% over the previous year. Total number of persons employed in SSI unit has also increased from 146.55 lakhs in 1994-95 to 287.55 lakhs in 2004-05 and then to 312.52 lakhs in 2006-07 showing a growth rate of 4.1% and 4.2% respectively over the previous year.

**Table 14.1:** Performance of micro small scale sector

| Year | No of Units (Lakhs) Registered | Unregistered | Total | Production (Rs crores) At current prices | At constant prices | Employment (In Lakhs) | Export (Rs. Crores) |
|---|---|---|---|---|---|---|---|
| 1994-95** | 19.44 | 6.27 | 25.71(7.66) | 2,98,886 (23.69) | 2,66054(10.10) | 146.55(5.15) | 29.068(14.86) |
| 1994-95 | 11.61 | 67.99 | 79.60(4.1) | 1,22,210(23.7) | 1,09,166(10.4) | 191.40(4.8) | 29068(14.9) |
| 1995-96 | 11.57 | 71.27 | 82.84(4.1) | 1,48,290(21.3) | 1,21,649(11.5) | 197.93(3.4) | 36,470(25.5) |
| 1996-97 | 11.99 | 74.22 | 86.21(4.1) | 1,68,413(13.6) | 1,35,380(11.3) | 205.86(4.0) | 39,248(7.6) |
| 1997-98 | 12.04 | 77.67 | 89.71(4.1) | 1,89,178(12.3) | 1,47,824(9.2) | 220.55(3.5) | 44,442(13.21) |
| 1998-99 | 12.00 | 81.36 | 93.36(4.1) | 2,12,901(12.5) | 1,59,407(7.8) | 213.36(3.5) | 48,979(10.2) |
| 1999-2000 | 12.32 | 84.83 | 97.15(4.1) | 2,34,255(10.0) | 1,70,709(7.1) | 229.10(3.9) | 54,200(10.7) |
| 2000-01 | 13.10 | 88.00 | 101.10(4.1) | 2,61,289(11.5) | 1,84,428(8.0) | 239.09(4.4) | 69,797(28.8) |
| 2001-02 | 13.75 | 91.46 | 105.21(4.1) | 2,82,270(8.0) | 1,95,613(6.1) | 249.09(4.2) | 71,244(2.1) |
| 2002-03 | 15.91 | 93.58 | 109.49(4.1 | 3,11,993(10.5) | 2,10,636(7.7) | 263.68(4.5) | 86,013(20.7) |
| 2003-04 | 16.97 | 96.98 | 113.95(4.1) | 3,57,733(14.7) | 2,28,730(8.6) | 275.30(4.4) | 97,644(13.5) |
| 2004-05 | 18.34 | 100.35 | 118.59(4.1) | 4,18,263(16.9) | 2,51,511(10.0) | 287.55(4.5) | 1,24,417(27.4) |
| 2005-06 | 19.30 | 104.12 | 123.42(4.1) | 4,76,201(13.9) | 2,77,668(10.4) | 299.85(4.3) | 1,50,242(20.8) |
| 2006-07 | 20.32 | 108.12 | 128.44(4.1) | N.A. | 4,71,663(12.6) | 312.52(4.2) | N.A. |

**Source:** Ministry of small scale Industries and Economic Survey 2007-2008 p. 198.

** These data relate to figure given by ministry of SSI earlier.

Exports from SSI sector accounted for about 35% of the total value of exports. Total value of exports of SSI units in India has risen from Rs. 29,068 crores in 1994-95 to Rs. 1,5,0,242 crores in 2005-06 registering a growth of 20.8% in the previous year. Again the total value of exports in U.S. dollar terms from the SSI sector has increased from $ 8.07 billion in 1993-94 to $ 10.90 billion in 1995-96 and then to $ 13.13 billion in 2000-01.

The total value of production of SSI units accounted for nearly 40% of the total value of industrial output of the country in general.

## 14.2 ROLE OF SMALL SCALE INDUSTRIES IN INDIAN ECONOMY

Small scale industry has been playing a vital role in our economy, since about 40% of the gross value of output has been coming from this sector in general and the generation of employment by small scale sector is more than five times to that of large scale sector.

The total number of registered small scale units has been increasing rapidly from 19.44 lakhs in 1994-95 to 20.32 lakhs in 2006-67. These small scale units in recent years has been producing consumer goods and manufactured sophisticated electronic goods. The reserved list of small scale unit at present is 35.

### 14.2.1 The Contribution of Small Scale Units can be Classified as such

1. **Employment Generation:** Small scale industries basically are labour intensive and thus have been generating employment opportunities Total employment generated by these small scale industries has risen form 39.7 lakhs in 1973-74 to 96.0 lakhs in 1985-86, 129.8 lakhs in 1991-92, 312.5 lakhs in 2006-07 showing an increase of 4.2% over the previous years[2].
2. **Output:** Total production of small scale unit has risen from Rs. 7,200 crores in 1973-74 to 57,100 crores in 1985-86, and to 4,71,663 crores in 2006-07 showing an increment of 12.6% over the output of Rs. 41,8,884 crores in 2005-06[3].
3. **Contribution to Export:** The contribution of SSI sector towards export has been increasing at a massive rate. The value of exports of the produced by the SSI sector has risen from Rs. 393 crore in 1973-74 to Rs. 9,100 crores in 1990-91 then to Rs. 150,242 crores in 2005-06. The value of export rose from $8.87 billion in 1993-94 to $13.13 billion in 2000-01. The share of export from small scale sector in the total export has risen from 9.6% in 1971-72 to 35% in 2000-01.

---

2. Economic Survey, 2007-08 p. 198.
3. Economic Survey, 2007-08 p. 198.

4. **Investment:** Investment in SSI has been increasing at a faster rate. The total amount of investment in SSI unit has increased from Rs. 2233 crores in 1972-73 to Rs. 4431 crores in 1978-79. This investment has been shifting upwards and in 1985-86 it was Rs. 9585 crores.
5. **Distribution of Equitable Income:** Small scale and cottage industrial has been resulting in equitable distribution of income and wealth. The relation between the employer and the employee are harmonious.
6. **Taping Latent Resource:** The small enterprises are able to tap latent resources like hoarded wealth, entrepreneurial ability etc **Dhar and Lydall** felt that mobilisation of hoarded wealth is only a once for all gain. The entrepreneurial class requires an environment which provided by small scale enterprises encourages a growing network of feeder and complementary relation among plant and firms. It is in this environment that latent talents of individual entrepreneur finds self expression in localised innovaion and cost saving measures. The growth of a large number of small firms in the post independence period only highlights the fact that given the basic condition such as supply of power and credit facilities, the latent resource of entrepreneurship can be tapped by the growth of small enterprises significantly.
7. **Regional Dispersal of Industries:** Another argument which favours small scale unit is the **Decentralisation** that is the necessity of regional dispersal of industries. Large enterprises are mostly concentrated in metropolitian cities. The smaller towns and the country side in order to benefit from modern industrialisation must encourage small scale enterprises. Decentralisation of industries helps in tapping local resources *e.g.*, rawmaterial, idle saving, local talents and thereby also raises the standard of living in backward regions. Moreover, decentralisation helps to solve the problem of congestion.
8. **Better Industrial Relation:** SSI are maintaining better industrial relations between employer and employee and this can lessen the frequency of industrial disputes. Thus, loss of mandays are less in SSI.
9. **Miscellaneous:** Where artistic skill is required small scale has always proved to be efficient than large scale.

To sum up we may say that the government should help to create conditions which facilitates their growth. **Aldous Huxley** said that "The ownership of the means of small scale production has none of the disastrous political, economic, psychological consequences of large scale production, loss of independence, enslavement to an employer, insecurity of terms of employment.

## 14.3 PROBLEM OF SMALL SCALE INDUSTRIES IN INDIA

The small scale industries faces a number of problems. Many small scale units turned sick and large number had to close down. In March, 2003 as many as 1.68 lakh of these units were sick and the amount of Rs. 5,706 crores of bank credit was blocked in them, only 3,626 of these units have been identified by the banks as potentially viable. A number of unviable SSI units are eventually closed down.

Small enterprises are handicapped by an inequitable allocation system for scarce raw material and improved components, lack of provision of credit finance, low technical skill. According to a Report of the Second All India Census of Small Scale Industrial unit "Finance problems was stated as the reason for the closure of 35% of the units. This was more or less the case in every industry. In case of 14.4% of units "marketing problems" was stated as the reason for the closure. "Raw material non-availability" was stated as the reason for the closure by 5.6% of units, 2.2% was reported to have closed down due to labour problem. While 1.9% were reported to have closed down for other reasons" (*see* Table 14.2).

**Table 14.2:** Reasons for the closure of small-scale sector units (Period 1980-1988 Combined)

| Reasons | Per cent |
|---|---|
| Financial problem | 34.7 |
| Marketing Problem | 14.4 |
| Raw material problem | 5.6 |
| Dispute among owners | 3.7 |
| Natural calamity | 3.4 |
| Labour problem | 2.2 |
| More than one reason (combined) | 16.5 |
| Other reasons | 19.4 |
| Total | 100.0 |

**Source:** Complied and computed from the date provided in the report of the Second All India Census of Small Scale Industries unit p.159.

The problems of SSI are analysed as such :

1. **Raw Material:** It is estimated that the raw material alone accounts for nearly 70% the ex-factory price of the products in the small scale sector and most of these industries have to depend heavily on the open market for the supply of scarce raw material where prices are more than double the controlled prices. Large scale industries take away most of the raw material. The inequity in the struggle for the existence of the small scale units against large scale units is too glaring owing to the government faulty distribution policy of raw materials.

The seventh plan expressed its deep dissatisfaction in this regard. "While various measures have been taken for the supply of raw material to the small scale units through state small industrial development corporation, import quota, etc in actual, practice the sector gets more or less a 'residuary treatment in raw material distribution/allocation".

2. **Credit and Finance:** The biggest problem for cottage and small scale is that of obtaining finance. The artisan requires finance for buying raw materials for stocking the same and for holding his finished article. It is difficult for him to obtain the money that he requires from the banks or even from corporative credit societies for his assets are negligible and so he cannot furnish sufficient security. This was recongnised by the industrial planning team 1955. "Considering the vital role of small industries within the Indian Industrial Economy, the total amount of loans granted to small industries forms a very small part of the total loans to Indian industry[4]. The flow of credit to SSI sector from public sector banks has gone up from Rs. 38,110 crores in March, 1998 to Rs. 49,743 crores in March 2002. However as a percentage of SSI advances to net bank credit a declining trend was observed from 15.6% in March, 1998 to 12.5% in March, 2002. Nevertheless, there is a need for a positive change in the outlook and approach of our financial institution towards small scale enterprises. Their credit worthiness should not be judged in terms of the value of the assets but in terms of the ability of an enterprise to do the job and earn profit. This required the evolution of a system of integrated credit whereby longterm loan, capital and short term credit are provided adequately at a reasonable rate of interest.
3. **Marketing Assistance:** Another important problem faced by small scale unit is that of marketing, due to lack of proper marketing channels. Further, the products of these industries are at times imperfect to a certain extent due to lack of market information. The products are not in accordance with the change in fashion of the customers in many cases. The government could come forward to provide a fair market for the products of small scale industry by showing discrimination in the purchasing policy.
4. **Technical Assistance:** The development of small scale enterprise is hampered by the presence of low level of technology, shortage of trained and experienced supervisory personnel. The Planning Commission has also admitted that the development of small industires has been hampered by the low level of technology. It has also been pointed out that more than the availability of credit, lack of technical consultancy services at all level has been pointed out as the biggest obstacle in the development of small scale industry by a survey

4. The Second Report of the International Team, p. 10.

conducted by Reserve Bank of India. Recognising the need the Government set up the small industries service institute but technical assistance provided by these 'small industries service institute' is neither adequate nor effective. Testing laboratories need to be implanted.

5. **Infrastructural Constraint:** Many productive activities are constrained by inadequate infrastructure and of this power, is the most severe constraint. Capitve generation at a reasonable cost is out of question for small firms. Therefore, they have to depend on state electricity board for meeting their requirements which do not supply regular and adequate power. Transportation, communication and water supply are also infrastructural constraint.[5]
6. **Poor Database:** Another problem is lack of accurate statistical information. The Small Industries Development Organisation (SIDO) and Central Statistical Organisation (CSO) are not in a position to provide complete information. Further these organisation conducts survey at an interval of 5 years. The SIDBI report stated that "There is an urgent need to evolve a regular system for the upgradation and collection of data on the SSI sector in view of the rapid growth and substantial contribution of the SSI sector. Upkeep of latest information is critical for policy decisions"[6].
7. **Heavy Taxation:** Cottage and small industries raw material are subjected to octroi duties and their finished products to sales tax. Thus, they bear heavy burden of taxes.
8. **Adverse Effect of Economic Reforms and Globalisation:** SSI are increasingly exposed to competition from foreign goods from MNCs (Multinational Corporations).

## 14.4 REMEDIAL MEASURES

Small scale industries occupy an important place in the countries industrial structure. Therefore, steps need to be taken to remove the problems.

The remedial measures are:

1. Conducting detailed survey of existing small industries and drawing productive programme for them.
2. Improvement in technique and adoption of modern technology in these SSI units.
3. Imparting proper education and training to workers engaged in small scale units.
4. Regular supply of inputs at a reasonable rate.
5. Adequate credit facility.

---

5. Keeshab. Das and Sebastian Morris, *Infrastructural constraint and small.* Firms", pp. 216-220.
6. SIDBI. Report on Small Scale Industrial Sector, 1999, pp, 28-29.

6. Provision of regular and cheap power.
7. Proper marketing channels.
8. Conducting research.
9. Maintaining standards and quality of output produced by the SSI units.

If these steps are taken up effectively small scale industries will be able to utilise huge development potential available in the country and prove itself a vibrant sector of the economy.

## 14.5 SMALL SCALE AND COTTAGE INDUSTRIES DURING THE PLAN-GOVERNMENT POLICY

**Policy Prior to 1991:** A large number of steps were initiated by the Government of India after independence for the development of small scale and cottage industries. These included the building up of organisational structure, increase in the outlay for the development of small scale and cottage industries, reservations for production, credit and marketing facility concessions, exemptions etc.

1. **Organisation Structure:** Cottage Industry Board was set up in 1947. This was split into the following three boards during the first five year plan- All India Handloom Board, All India Khadi and Village Industries Board, All India Handicraft Board. In addition of this small scale industries board, Coir Board and Central Silk Board were also set up. National Small Industrial Corporation Ltd (NSIC) were set up in 1955 to provide machinery to small scale units on hire purchase basis and to assist these units in procuring order from the government Department and offices. In 1954, Small Industries Development Organisation SIDO was also set up. It functioned as an apex body in the formulation of policies and coordination of institutional activities for sustained and organised growth of small scale industries. The programmes of industrial estate was imitated in 1955. It aimed at providing factory accommodation and a number of common facilities like power, water, transport etc at one place. The district industries (1979) also aimed at providing and arranging a package of assistance and facilities for credit guidance, raw material, training, marketing etc including the necessary help to unemployed educated young entrepreneurs.

The government also made an attempt to raise the level of expenditure during the plans from Rs. 42 crores to Rs. 7,266 crores in 1992. The government further set up SIDBI in 1989. The major activities of SIDBI was refinancing of loans, advances, discounting and rediscounting of bills, extension of loans, providing services like factoring, leasing etc and extending of financial support to state Small Industrial Development Corporation. Council for Advancement of Rural Technology (CART) was also set up in October, 1982 to provide necessary technical input to the rural industries.

### 14.5.1 New Small Enterprise Policy, 1991

On August 6, 1991 the government announced its new small sector industrial policy. The main objective of this new policy is to inject higher degree of vitally and growth impetus to this sector in order to attain a higher growth rate in respect of its output, employment, export. The **main features of this industrial policy are**:

1. Deregulation, debureaucratisation simplification of rules, regulation and procedures in connection with the establishment and maintenance of these small scale units.
2. Enhancement of the investment limit in fixed capital assets of 'tiny' enterprises from Rs. 2 lakhs to Rs. 5 lakhs irrespective of the location of the unity.
3. Recognising industry related services and business enterprises within small scale industries irrespective of their location with investment upto Rs. 5 lakhs.
4. Arranging adequate and regular flow of credit on a normative basis and to improve the quality of its delivery for the smooth and viable operation of the small scale sector.
5. Arranging a suitable legislation to ensure prompt payment of small industries bill.
6. Introducing a scheme of integrated infrastructural development for small scale units.
7. Setting up of a Technology Development Cell in Small Industries Development Organisation for providing technology input for improving productivity and competitiveness of the products produced by small sector.
8. Establishing a export development centre in Small Industries Development Organisation.

The Government thus restricted the registration of new SSI units for the manufacture of certain items. Further, an ordinance was promulgated on 23rd September, 1992 making payment of interest obligatory on delayed industrial payment to small scale and ancillary ancillary industrial undertakings. The central government appointed the Nayak committee to examine the problem of credit, sickness and other problems in the SSI sector. In order to ensure timely credit to SSI unit the government on July 3, 1993 announced a special package of measures and incentives for SSI. The salient Features of this package are:

(*a*) Banks should give preference to village industries, tiny industries and other small scale units in that order, while meeting the credit requirement of the SSI sector.

(*b*) Banks should raise the credit flow to meet the requirements of the SSI sector.

(*c*) A grievance cell within each bank which can be approached by the SSI in case of difficulties would be set up.

(*d*) Banks should adopt the 'single window clearance scheme' of SIDBI to meet the credit requirement of the SSI sector.

(*e*) A new scheme of Integrated Infrastructural Development was launched recently to strengthen infrastructural facilities in 50 centres in rural backward area.

(*f*) A quality certification scheme was launched in 1994 to improve the quality standards of the SSI products. Modification were effected in the single window scheme operated by SIDBI. The project qutlay under the scheme was raised from Rs. 30 lakhs to Rs. 50 lakhs as a whole. The government announced the setting up of an expert committee to probe into the problem of the SSI sector.

### 14.5.2 Policy Measures Taken up During 2004-05

1. The National Commission on Enterprise in the unorganised informal sector was set up in September, 2004. The committee will *inter-alia* recommend measures considered necessary for improvement in the productivity of these enterprises, generation of large scale employment oppurtunities on a sustainable basis, linkage of sector to institutional framework in areas like credit, raw material supply, infrastructure, technology upgradation marketing facilities and skill development.
2. 193 items reserved for exclusive manufacture in the SSI sector were de-reserved in March, 2005. The total number of items now stands at 506.
3. To facilitate technology upgradation and enhancing competitiveness the investment limit (in plants and machinery) has been raised in October, 2004 from Rs. 1 crore to Rs. 5 crores in respect of certain sports goods (7 items) reserved for manufacture in small scale.
4. The Small and Medium Enterprises Fund (SMF) of Rs. 10,000 crores was opertionalised by SIDBI since April, 2004. 80% of the lending from this fund will be for SSI units at an interest rate of 2% below the prevailing PLR of the SIDBI.
5. The RBI enhanced the composite loan limit for the SSI sector to Rs. 1 crore from Rs. 50 lakhs.
6. With a view to integrate small and medium enterprises facilitating their growth and enhancing their competitiveness a suitable legislation is being finalised along with a new "**Promotional package**" for small enterprises. This would include measures to provide adequate credit, incentives for technology, upgradation infrastructural and marketing facilities etc.

### 14.5.3 Policy Initiatives and Measures Undertaken During 2006-07

The Government of India enacted the micro, Small and Medium Enterprises Development Act, 2006 (MSMED) which provided the first ever legal framework for recognition of the concept 'enterprise' (comprising both manufacturing and services) and integrated the three tiers of these enterprise *viz.* micro, small and medium. The investment limit for manufacturing enterprises at micro enterprises is fixed at Rs. 25 lakhs, for small enterprises above Rs. 25 lakhs to Rs. 5 crores and for medium enterprises above Rs. 5 crores to Rs. 10 crores. In case of service enterprise the investment limit for micro enterprises is fixed up to Rs. 10 lakhs, for small enterprises upto Rs. 2 crores and for medium between Rs 2 crores to Rs. 5 crores.

The Act included (*a*) establishment of specific funds for the promotion and development, and enhancement of competitiveness of these enterprises, (*b*) notification of scheme programmes for the purpose, (*c*) progressive credit policies and practices, (*d*) preferences in government procurements to products and services of the micro and small enterprises, (*e*) introducing effective mechanism for mitigating the problems of delayed payment to micro and small enterprises, (*f*) simplification of the process of closure of business by all three categories of enterprises.

The government approved a package for the promotion of micro and small enterprises to address the problem of credit, infrastructure, technology, marketing and support of women entrepreneurs. Empowered group of Ministers under the Chairmanship of the external affairs minister was set up to lay down a comprehensive policy for cluster development and its implementation in February, 2007. Further, to make "Credit Guarantee Scheme" more attractive the following modifications were made (*a*) enhancing eligible loan limit from Rs. 25 lakhs to Rs. 50 lakhs (*b*) raising the extent of guarantee cover from 75% to 80% for (*i*) micro enterprises for loans upto Rs. 5 lakh (*ii*) MSE operated/owned by woman (*iii*) all loans in the North-East region and (*c*) reducing one-time guarantee fee from 1.5% to 0.75% for all loans in the North East Region.

The phased deletion of products from the list of items reserved for manufacture by micro and small enterprises was reduced from 125 items in 2007 to 114 items in 2008. Further, 79 items where de-reserved through a notification dated February 5, 2008.[7]

**SIDBI (Small Industries Development Bank of India)** was set up in response to along standing demand as an apex level national institution for promotion, financing and development of industries in the small scale sector. SIDBI ever since its inception has given due attention to identify and launch various promotional and development activities. Rural industrialisation is one of the thrust areas in the development initatives of the bank.

7. Economic Survey 2007-2008 p 1/98. 99

## 14.6 CONCLUSION

A change of policies would help to reduce the problems of small industries. The government must encourage the cottage and small scale industries by providing various concessions to them as regards the supply of raw matarial, finance, power, tax concessions etc. The other is to restrict the entry of large units into some sectors reserving such sectors exclusively for small scale sector. Various concessions like financial aids, provisions of sites on hire purchase basis in industrial estate, power at cheaper rates, preferences in governments purchases policy are being given to small scale units. Thus, this reservation is mainly aimed at as a measure of protection to the small scale sector from the large scale sector.

The development of small scale industry will rebuild rural India and accelerate the pace of economic growth and well-being of the people. The government would raise employment opportunity if cottage and small scale industries are developed. Since they are labour-intensive, quick yielding, well dispersed and capable of bringing more jobs and more consumer goods to backward areas of the country. According to the data provided by economic survey 2007-2008, Micro and Small enterprises (MSEs) provided employment to an estimated 31.2 million persons in the rural and urban areas of the country. During 2003-07, the MSE sector registered continuous growth in the number of enterprises, production, employment and exports (Table 14.3).

**Table 14.3:** Performances of micro and small enterprises

| Year | Number of Units (in lakhs) | | | Production (Rs. crores (At 2001-02 price) | Employment (in lakhs) | Export |
|---|---|---|---|---|---|---|
| | Registered | Unregistered | Total | | | |
| 2002-03 | 16.03 | 93.46 | 109.4 (4.1) | 3,06,771(8.7) | 263.68(4.5) | 8,6013(20%) |
| 2003-04 | 17.12 | 96.83 | 113.95(4.1) | 336,344 (9.6) | 275.30(4.4) | 97,644 (13.5) |
| 2004-05 | 18.24 | 100.35 | 118.59(4.1) | 3,72, 938 (10.9) | 287.55 (4.5) | 1,24,417(27.4) |
| 2005-06 | 19.30 | 104.12 | 123.42(4.1) | 4,18,884 (12.3) | 299.85 (4.3) | 1, 50, 242 (20.8) |
| 2006-07 | 20.32 | 108.12 | 128.44 (4.1) | 4,71, 663 (12.6) | 312.52 (4.2) | N.A. |

Estimate based on Definition prior to enactment of MSMED Act, 2006.

**Note:** Figure in parenthesis indicates percentage growth over previous year.

**Source:** Office of the development commissioner MSME

It is estimated that there are about 128.44 lakhs MSEs in the country as on March 31, 2007 accounting for about 39% of the gross value of output in the manufacturing sector. If modification are effectively made then situations will improve more viably.

❑❑❑

CHAPTER 15

# Industrial Development during the Planning Period

## 15.1 INTRODUCTION

Before the Britishers came into India the industrial base was quite advanced but gradually after the advent of Britishers to India the industrial base of India became weak due to the trade policy. However since independence, the government made all effort to build up a sound industrial base. With the purpose of assisting industrial development, the government granted certain tax concession to industry in 1948-49 and passed the Bill to establish the Industrial Finance Corporation of India. The Industrial policy resolution was also passed in 1948. This had a favourable impact on industrial development. The Official General Index of Industrial output registered a rise of 17.4% over the period 1946 to 1951.

The industrial pattern in India on the eve of planning in India was marked by low capital intensity, limited development of medium sized factory, enterprise, and imbalance between consumer goods and capital goods industries. It would be of interest to examine the extent to which the Five Year Plan have made an attempt to improve the industrial pattern, correct its lopsidedness and develop the capital goods sector.

## 15.2 INDUSTRIAL PATTERN AND THE FIVE YEAR PLAN

### 1. Industries and the First-Five year Plan (1951-56)

During the first plan itself no big effort was contemplated to industrialise the economy rather the emphasis was to build basic services like power and irrigation so that the process of industrilisation is facilitated. A Total investment of Rs. 800 crores was planned for industry, out of which investment in the public sector was to the tune of Rs. 94 crores only. Actual public sector outlay was only about Rs. 57 crores on new projects, replacement and modernisation. Only Rs. 340 crores were actively spent. Thus, there were shortfalls in investment programme. Despite the fact that the first plan only aimed to utilize the existing capacity to the full the general index of industrial production recorded an increase of 39% during the plan or a compound annual growth rate of 7%.

## 2. Industries and the Second Plan (1956-61)

The second five year plan was based on Industrial Policy Resolution (1956) which envisaged an expansion of the public sector. Basic and Heavy industry was given importance. The actual investment in the public sector on organised industry was Rs. 870 crores. Private sector investment was Rs. 675 crores during the second plan, similarly investment in village and small industries was Rs. 265 crores (public and private sector). Taken together total investment in industries was Rs. 1810 crores *i.e.* 27% of the total investment during the second plan.

The second plan was conceived in term of the priorities which were given (*i*) to raising production of iron and steel and of heavy engineering and machine building industries, (*ii*) expansion of capacity in respect of other development and producer good such as aluminum cement, chemical pulp, dyestuff, fertilisers, modernisation of jute, textile and sugar industry. During the second plan a major task in industry was the building up of three steel plants in the public sector *i.e.*, Rourkela Steel Plant in Orissa, Bhilai Steel Plant in Madhya Pradesh and Durgapur Steel Plant in West Bengal. The other programme of industrial development included the manufacture of electrical equipment, expansion of Hindustan Machine goods, expansion of Sindri fertiliser factory and the establishment of a fertiliser plant at Nangal. It also included expansion of Hindustan Ship Yard and Chitranjan Locomotive Factory. It also aimed at development of atomic energy. Most of the investment were in basic heavy industry. In the sphere of village and small industries substantial progress were recorded. About 60 industrial estates comprising 1,000 small factories were set up. Khadi, Handloom and powerloom cloth production increased from 1610 million meters to 2,150 million meters.

The index of industrial production increased from 139 in 1955-56 to 194 in 1960-61. In respect of locational pattern the second plan successfully achieved the dispersal of industries into the backward region.

## 3. Industrial Development during the Third Plan (1961-66)

The third plan made a beginning of long term perspective planning as an instrument to achieve the objective of an integrated growth of industry balanced with agriculture. In order to achieve a self-sustain growth the third plan put emphasis on the development of basic capital good and producer good industries particularly on machine building industries. The third plan tried to build the power and transportation facilities required for industrial development and also tried to activate the process of industrial and technological change.

The third plan finalised the total public sector outlay on industrial development (including small and village industries) to the extent of Rs. 1967 crores which was about 22.9% of the total plan outlay. The third plan accorded top most priority on the completion of ongoing projects initated during the second plan. Moreover the plan also attached importance on the programme of expansion and diversification of production capacity of heavy, engineering and machine building industries. casting and forgings, iron and steel, special steel, alloy metal, ferrous alloy and also for expanding the production of fertilisers chemicals, refinery products, paper, sugar, housing material, cloth, drug etc. During the plan period the projects like heavy electrical corporation, Bharat Heavy Electrical were completed which had a solid base for industrial growth of the country.

## 4. Industrial Development and the Fourth Plan (1969-74)

The fourth plan intended to enlarge capacities in export promotion and import substitution. The fourth plan made an investment of Rs. 3050 crores in the public sector besides this investment in small and village industries in the public sector was planned to be of the order of Rs. 190 crores. However, the actual outlay on organised industry was of the order of Rs. 2700 crores in the public sector. Thus the financial investment was short of the targets set out in the fourth plan. Nearly three-fourths of the total investment was in the core-sector *viz.*, iron and steel, non-ferrous metal, fertiliser, petroleum, petro chemicals iron ore.

The performance was not good. On an average the growth rate in industry was around 5% which was below targeted growth rate of 8 % envisaged in the plan. The main factors responsible for this unsatisfactory situation was lack of raw material, poor industrial relation, low level capacity utilisation, traffic bottlenecks.

## 5. Industrial Development in the Fifth Plan (1974-78)

The fifth plan aimed at achieving self reliance, and growth with social justice. The plan proposed to lay emphasis on the following-

(*a*) Rapid growth of core sector industries by giving high priority to steel, non-ferrous metals, fertiliser, mineral oil, coal and machine building.

(*b*) Rapid diversification and growth of export producing industries.

(*c*) Enlarging the production of industries supplying mass consumption goods *viz.*, cloth, edible oil, vanaspati, sugar, drugs, bicycles.

(*d*) Restraint on the production of non-essential goods.

(*e*) Development of small scale industries by reserving 124 items exclusively for them.

The fifth plan provided a total outlay of Rs. 10,135 crores on organised industry and mining Rs. 9600 crores in the public sector and Rs. 535 crores in villagc and small industries. This accounted for nearly 26% of the public sector outlay of the fifth plan. The plan set a target of annual growth rate of

8.2% in the industrial sector but the annual average growth rate realised during the plan period (1974-75 to 1977-78) was only 6.0% which was much below the target.

## 6 Industrial Development During the Sixth Plan

The sixth plan aimed at structural diversification, modernisation, self reliance. The plan emphasised on the optimum utilisation of existing productive capacities improvement in productivity, raising manufacturing capacities, development of capital goods, electronic industry, improvement in energy efficiency, import of contemporary technology and development of indigenous know-how, export of engineering goods and industrial products and development of backward region through dispersal of industry.

During the 6$^{th}$ plan total outlay on industry and mineral including village industry was Rs. 22200 crores *i.e.* 22.8 of the total outlay of the sixth plan. Besides this for the development of energy Rs. 4,300 crores were to be spent on petroleum and Rs. 2870 crores on coal industry.

A review of the progress of the industrial growth during the 6$^{th}$ plan revealed that as against the target of 7% growth in industrial productions, the growth rate achieved was 5.5%.

## 7. Industrial Development under the Seventh Plan (1985-90)

The seventh plan aimed at "raising growth with justice" and improving productivity. The objectives of the development programme in the industrial sector were.

(*a*) To ensure adequate supply of wage goods and consumer articles of mass consumption at reasonable prices and of acceptable quality.

(*b*) To maximise the utilisation of the existing facilities through restructuring, improved productivity and upgradation of technology.

(*c*) To concentrate on development of industries with large domestic market and export potential to emerge as world leaders in them.

(*d*) To usher in 'sunrise' industries with high growth potential and relevance to our needs.

(*e*) To evolve an integrated policy towards self reliance in strategic fields and opening up of avenues for employment of skilled and trained manpower.

The seventh plan provided for an investment of Rs. 19,710 crores in large and medium industries and Rs. 2,750 crores for the development of village and small industries. Total investment in the industrial sector would thus be of the order of Rs. 22,460 crores or 12.5% of the total plan outlay. The annual targeted growth rate was 8%.

The main element of the seventh plan was commission of four new projects *viz.*, Vizag Steel Plant, the Maharashtra Gas Cracker, the NAL CO Aluminum

Complex and J. Gas Pipe line along with the linked fertiliser plants. Moreover Bongaigaon Petrochemical Complex, and Coaching Aromatics Complex were the two other major projects commissioned during the plan period.

A review of the progress of the seventh plan reveals that the annual growth rate of industrial sector including mining, manufacturing and electricity generation during the seventh plan period was 8.5% which was marginally lower than targeted 8.7%.

## 8. Industrial Development under the Eighth plan (1992-97)

The eighth plan (1992-97) put much stress on the development of the industrial sector. It put stress on the development of small and decentralised manufacturing sector and particularly in respect of the production of consumer goods and manufactured articles for export. The eighth plan has allocated Rs. 46,889 crores on industry and minerals head which accounted to nearly 10.8% of the total plan outlay. The plan envisaged to achieve annual growth rate of 8% for the industrial sector. But during the initial period of the eighth plan *i.e.* during 1992-93 and 1993-94 the annual growth rate attained in the industrial sector were 2.3% and 6.0% respectively. In 1994-95 the industrial sector recorded a growth of 8.6% as compared to 6.0% in 1993-94. Again the overall growth in industrial production in 1995-96 was 13.0% supported by a growth of 9.7% in mining 14.0% in manufacturing 8.2% in electricity. While the overall growth rate in industrial production was 6.1% in 1996-97, 7.3% in manufacturing and 4.0% in electricity and –1.9% in mining (see Table 15.1).

**Table 15.1:** Annual growth rates of industrial production in industry (Base 1993-94-00) per cent.
Annual growth rates to major sectors of industry

| Year (Weight) | Mining (11.76) | Manufacturing (77.11) | Electricity (11.43) | General (100.00) |
|---|---|---|---|---|
| 1981-82 | 17.7 | 7.9 | 10.2 | 9.3 |
| 1982-83 | 12.4 | 1.3 | 5.7 | 3.2 |
| 1983-84 | 11.8 | 5.7 | 7.6 | 6.7 |
| 1984-85 | 8.8 | 8 | 12 | 8.6 |
| 1985-86 | 4.1 | 9.7 | 8.5 | 8.7 |
| 1986-87 | 6.2 | 9.4 | 10.3 | 9.2 |
| 1989-90 | 6.3 | 8.6 | 10.8 | 8.6 |
| 1990-91 | 4.5 | 8.9 | 7.8 | 8.3 |
| 1991-92 | 0.6 | -0.8 | 8.5 | 0.6 |
| 1992-93 | 0.5 | 2.2 | 5 | 2.3 |
| 1993-94 | 3.5 | 6.1 | 7.4 | 6 |

Base: 1993-94=100

| (Weight) | (10.47) | (79.36) | (10.17) | (100) |
|---|---|---|---|---|
| 1994-95 | 9.8 | 9.1 | 8.5 | 9.1 |
| 1995-96 | 9.7 | 14.1 | 8.1 | 13.0 |
| 1996-97 | -1.9 | 7.3 | 4.0 | 6.1 |
| 1997-98 | 6.9 | 6.7 | 6.6 | 6.7 |
| 1998-99 | -0.8 | 4.4 | 6.5 | 4.1 |
| 1999-2000 | 1.0 | 7.1 | 7.3 | 6.7 |
| 2000-01 | 2.8 | 5.3 | 4.0 | 5.0 |
| 2001-02 | 1.2 | 2.9 | 3.1 | 2.7 |
| 2002-03 | 5.8 | 6.0 | 3.2 | 5.7 |
| 2003-04 | 5.2 | 7.4 | 5.1 | 7.0 |
| 2004-05 | 4.4 | 9.2 | 5.2 | 8.4 |
| 2005-06 | 1.0 | 9.1 | 5.2 | 8.2 |
| 2006-07 | 5.4 | 12.5 | 7.2 | 11.6 |
| | | | April - Dec. | |
| 1996-97 | –1.0 | 9.8 | 3.8 | 8.0 |
| 2000-01 | 3.6 | 6.3 | 4.9 | 6.0 |
| 2001-02 | 0.7 | 2.6 | 2.5 | 2.5 |
| 2002-03 | 5.7 | | 4.0 | 5.3 |
| 2004-05 | 5.1 | 9.2 | 6.4 | 8.6 |
| 2005-06 | 0.4 | 8.9 | 4.8 | 7.8 |
| 2006-07 | 3.8 | 11.5 | 7.3 | 10.6 |
| 2007-08 | 4.9 | 9.6 | 6.6 | 9.0 |

**Source:** *Economic Survey, 2007-08, p. 182 CSO, (QE) 1998-99.*

**Note:** *Growth rates from 1994-95 are as per the IIP Base: 1993-94=100 and those for earlier year are for TIIP B 1980-81=100*

## 9. Industries During the Ninth Plan (1997-2002)

The ninth plan envisaged to achieve annual growth rate of 8.5% for industrial sector. But during 1997-98 and 1998-99 the annual growth rate attained in the industrial sector was 6.7% and 4.1% respectively. The overall growth rate in industrial production in 1999-2000 was only 6.7% supported by a growth rate of 7.1% in manufacturing 7.3% in electricity and a growth rate of 1.0% in mining.

In 2000-01 and 2001-02 the growth rate attained in the industrial sector increased to the extent of 5.0% and 2.7% respectively. Finally the overall growth in industrial production during 2001-02 has declined to 2.7% supported by a growth rate of 2.9% in the manufacturing sector, 3.1% in electricity and only 1.2 % in mining. Thus, it is observed that the 9th plan too could not achieve the target.

**Table 15.2:** Industry annual growth rate (per cent)

| Period (weight) | Mining (10.7) | Manufacturing (79.36) | Electricity (10.17) | General (100.00) |
|---|---|---|---|---|
| 1995-96 | 9.7 | 14.1 | 8.1 | 13.0 |
| 2000-01 | 2.8 | 5.3 | 4.0 | 5.0 |
| 2001-02 | 1.2 | 2.9 | 3.1 | 2.7 |
| 2002-03 | 5.8 | 6.0 | 3.2 | 5.7 |
| 2003-04 | 5.2 | 7.4 | 5.1 | 7.0 |
| 2004-05 | 4.4 | 9.2 | 5,2 | 8.4 |
| 2005-06 | 1.0 | 9.1 | 5.2 | 8.6 |
| 2006-07 | 5.4 | 12.5 | 7.2 | 11.6 |
| 2007-08 | | | | |
| (Apr-Nov.) | 4.9 | 9.8 | 7.0 | 9.2 |
| | (4.2[b]) | (11.8[b]) | (7.3[b]) | (10.9[b]) |

**Source:** *Central Statistical Organisation*

[a] Based on Index of Industrial Production. Base 1993-94=100

[b] Figures for April-Nov, 2006-07

(*See* Table 15.2). The CSO estimate of IIP further showed that industrial output fell further to 9.2% during April, 2007 to January, 2008 as compared to 11.6% growth recorded during the period 2006-07. The manufacturing sector grew by 9.8% during the first ten months of 2007-08 as compared to 12.5% in 2006-07. During the same period electricity and mining grew by 7.0% and 4.9% as compared to that of 7.2% and 5.4% respectively during the corresponding period.

## 10. Industrial Development under the Tenth plan (2002-07)

The 10th Plan put adequate stress on the development of the industrial sector. The plan envisaged to achieve annual growth rate of 10% for industrial sector and the break up as envisaged are 4.3% in mining and quarrying, 9.82% in manufacturing sector and 7.99% in electricity gas, water supply. The annual growth rate attained in industrial sector was 5.7%, 7.0%, 8.4%, 8.6% respectively in 2002-03, 2003-04, 2004-05, 2005-06.

The overall growth rate in industrial production in 2006-07 was 11.6% supported by a growth rate of 12.5% in manufacturing, 7.2% in electricity and 5.4% in mining and quarrying (*See* Table 15.2).

The CSO estimate of IIP further showed that industrial output fell further to 9.2% during the period April, 2007 to January, 2008 as compared to 11.6%

growth recorded during the period 2006-07. The manufacturing sector grew by 9.8% during the first ten months of 2007-08 as compared to that of 12.5% during the period 2006-07. During the same period electricity and mining sector grew by 7.0% and 4.9% as compared to that of 7.2% and 5.4% respectively during the corresponding period.

## 15.3 OVERALL RATE OF INDUSTRIAL PERFORMANCES IN INDIA

The Industrial growth rate has not been uniform since 1951. During the first phase (1951-65) Indian industries experienced a steady growth rate of about 8%. After that fluctuating trend was observed in respect of industrial growth. A stagnancy occurred during the period 1966-68. In the phase 1976-77 industrial growth rate became 9.5%. After that the country faced a negative growth rate of -1.4% during 1979-80. In the sixties (1961-80) the average growth rate of industrial growth rate became 5.5% and in the seventies (1971-80) the average growth rate was about 4% per annum. Even during 1980-85 the growth rate of industrial production was 5.5% per annum. During 1985-90 the growth rate had picked up to an average of over 8% per annum and in 1992-97 it declined to 7.3% per annum. The rate of growth of industrial production in the ninth plan was only 5.0% which was less than the target of 8.2% per annum. The performance of industrial sector was highly unsatisfactory during the period second half of 1990s. The industrial sector registered a dismal performance in the last year of the 9$^{th}$ plan 2001-2002, with its rate of growth being just 2.7%. However, it picked up to 5.7% in 2002-2003 and further to 7.0% in 2003-04 due to the performances of the capital goods sector and consumer goods sector [*See* Table 15.3, 15.4].

**Table 15.3:** Annual compound growth rate in index number of industrial production (1980- 2002) - by use-based classification.

| Use Based Classification | 1980-81 to 1991-92 | 1992-93 to 1996-97 | 1997-98 to 2001-02 | 2001-02 |
|---|---|---|---|---|
| Base Good | 7.4 | 6.8 | 4.1 | 2.6 |
| Capital Goods | 9.4 | 8.9 | 4.7 | -3.4 |
| Intermediate Goods | 4.9 | 8.5 | 5.8 | 1.5 |
| Consumer Goods | 6.0 | 6.6 | 5.5 | 6.0 |
| Durables | 10.8 | 13.4 | 10.7 | 11.5 |
| Non-Durables | 5.3 | 4.8 | 3.8 | 4.1 |
| General Index | 7.8 | 7.4 | 5.0 | 2.7 |

**Source:** *Economic Survey 2000-01 p.130. RBI Handbook of Statistics on Indian Economy 2000 p. 409, Economic Survey 2004-05 p. 142.*

**Table 15.4:** Industrial production by use-based classification-growth rates (per cent)

| Sector | (IIP weight) | 2001-02 | 2002-03 | 2003-04 | 2004-05 | 2005-06 | 2006-07 | Apr. Nov. | |
|---|---|---|---|---|---|---|---|---|---|
| | | | | | | | | 2006-07 | 2007- 08 |
| Basic Goods | 35.5 | 2.6 | 4.9 | 5.4 | 5.5 | 6.7 | 10.3 | 9.4 | 8.4 |
| Capital Goods | 9.3 | –3.4 | 10.5 | 13.6 | 13.9 | 15.8 | 18.2 | 17.4 | 20.8 |
| Intermediate Goods | 26.5 | 1.5 | 3.9 | 6.4 | 6.1 | 2.5 | 12.0 | 11.1 | 10.1 |
| Consumer Goods (of which) | 28.7 | 6.0 | 7.1 | 7.1 | 11.7 | 12.0 | 10.1 | 9.9 | 5.2 |
| Consumer durables | 5.4 | 11.5 | -6.3 | 11.6 | 14.4 | 15.3 | 9.2 | 12.4 | – 1.7 |
| Consumer Non-Durables | 23.3 | 4.1 | 12.0 | 5.8 | 10.8 | 11.0 | 10.4 | 8.9 | 7.8 |
| All Index of Indl. Prodn. (IIP) | 100 | 2.7 | 5.7 | 7.0 | 8.4 | 8.2 | 11.6 | 10.9 | 9.2 |

**Source:** Central Statistical Organisation:

[a] Index of Industrial Production, base: 1993-94 = 100

**Table 15.5:** Production figures of selected industries in India

| Commodity | Units | 1950-51 | 1970-71 | 1990-91 | 2000-01 | 2006-07 |
|---|---|---|---|---|---|---|
| Finished Steel | Million tonnes | 1.04 | 4.64 | 13.53 | 29.3 | 50.2 |
| Aluminum | Thousand tonnes | 4.0 | 168.8 | 451.1 | 620.4 | 719.1 |
| Fertiliser (NPK) | Do | 1.8 | 1059 | 9145 | 14770 | 16153 |
| Cement | Million tonnes | 2.7 | 14.3 | 48.8 | 99.5 | 154.7 |
| Petroleum refinery products | Do | 0.2 | 17.1 | 48.0 | 96.6 | 135.3 |
| Machine tools | Rs. Million | 3 | 430 | 7731 | 12263 | 26410.0 |
| Railway wagon | Thousand | — | 11.1 | 25.3 | N.A. | 4.2 |
| Automobiles | Thousand | 16.5 | 87.9 | 366.3 | 784.2 | 2065.6 |
| Paper and paper boards | Tonnes | 116 | 755 | 2088 | 3090 | 4139.0 |
| Jute textile | Do | 837 | 1060 | 1430 | N.A. | N.A. |
| Cotton cloth | Million | 4215 | 7602 | 15431 | 19718 | 26,238.0 |
| Mixed blended cloth | Do | — | 170 | 2371 | 6351 | 68820 |
| Manmade fibre fabrics | Do | 300 | 951 | 5126 | 13606 | 20269 |
| Sugar | Thousand tonnes | 1134 | 3470 | 12047 | N.A. | 28,199 |
| Tea | Millions | 277 | 423 | 705 | N.A. | 949 |
| Vanaspati | Thousand tonnes | 155 | 558 | 850 | N.A. | 12860 |
| Electricity Generated Billion | KWH | 5.1 | 44.8 | 264.6 | 499.4 | 6620 |
| Index of I$^{nd}$ Prod. | | 18.3 | | 212.6 | 162.7 | 247.1 |

Includes output in railway workshop.

**Source:** Economic Survey 2007-2008 pp A-31-34.

The Report on currency and finance 2003-04 attributed that due to improved investment climate, expanding external demand, improved domestic demand, improved domestic demand case and availability of finance and increasing capacity addition in the industrial sector led to an improvement in industrial performances by 5.7 in 2002-03 and 7.0% in 2003-04. In 2004-05 it rose up to 8.4%, 8.2% in 2005-06 and to 11.6% in 2006-07. The growth rate in 2007-08 (April-November) was 9.2% in manufacturing and growth rate of 4.9% in mining, 9.8% in manufacturing and 7.0% in electricity. From a use based classification perspective (*See* Table 15.4) capital good sectors emerged as the most buoyant sector and registered a double digit growth rate during 2005-06 and 2006-07. Within the consumer goods sector non-durables segment posted an increase. The good performance of the capital good sector is an indicator of future industrial growth. Disaggregated industrial profile depicts that out of 17 groups in the manufacturing sector 16 groups registered positive growth rate and industry groups showed growth rate of 10% and above which included beverages and tobacco products (growth rate 12.0%), basic metal and alloy (12.1%) other manufactures (19.8%) Jute and other vegetable fiber textile 33.1%, wood and wood products and furniture and furniture's (40.5%). Leather and fur products 11.7%. Basic chemical and chemical products (10.6%); machinery and equipments 10.4%.

The performances of industrial production has risen up in certain industry as reflected in Table 15.5 and 15.7.

## 15.4 OVERALL RATE OF INDUSTRIAL PERFORMANCE IN INDIA AN EVALUATION

The trend of industrial production has risen up in certain industry. The production of finished steel gradually rose from 1.04 m tonnes in 1950-51 to 50.2 million tonnes in 2006-07 and 15.4 million tonnes in 2008-09. The total production of fertiliser (NPK) has risen from 18 thousand tonnes in 1950-51 to 16153 thousand tonnes in 2006-07. The production of cement rose from 2.7 million tonnes in 1950-51 to 154.7 million tonnes in 2006-07 181.4 million tonnes in 2008-09 paper and paper boards rose from 116 thousand tonnes in 1950-51 to 4139 thousand tonnes in 2006-07 4442 thousand in tonnes in 2008-09. The volume of electricity generated rose from 5.1 billion KWh in 1950-51 to 212.6 billion KWh in 1990-91 and then to 6620 billion KWh in 2006-07. The index of industrial production (base 1993-94=100) has increased from 109.1 in 1994-95 to 145.2 in 1998-99 and then to 247.6 in 2006-07. [For details see appendix]. The performance of six core industrials (*i.e.* electricity, crude petroleum, petroleum refinery products, coal, steel and cement with combined weightage of 26.68% with IIP) is considered as an indicator of the economic health of the economy. Their output registered a growth of 5.6% during 2007-08 as compared to 8.6% last year. This can be seen in Table 15.6.

**Table 15.6:** Growth Rate (%) of six core industries

| | Weight | 2005-06 | 2006-07 | 2007-08 |
|---|---|---|---|---|
| Crude petroleum | 4.3 | –5.3 | 5.6 | 0.4 |
| Petroleum refinery products | 2.0 | 2.4 | 12.6 | 6.5 |
| Coal | 3.2 | 6.6 | 5.9 | 6.3 |
| Electricity | 10.2 | 5.1 | 7.3 | 6.0 |
| Cement | 2.0 | 12.4 | 9.1 | 5.1 |
| Furnished steel | 5.1 | 11.2 | 10.9 | 8.1 |
| Overall | 26.7 | 6.2 | 8.6 | 5.6 |

Thus, we see that the industrial sector has achieved a significant achievement in developing its production capacities in respect of all consumer goods both durables and non-durables. The state of self-sufficiency has already been achieved capital good production has also risen up (*see* Table 15.4). Significant progress has also been achieved in building basic infrastructural facilities Research and Development (R&D) capability project management service consultancy, design and engineering services.

## 15.5 RATE OF INDUSTRIAL GROWTH IN INDIA

The industrial growth has not been uniform since 1951. During the first phase (1951-65). Indian industries experienced a steady growth rate of about 8%. After that fluctuating trend was observed in respect of industrial growth. A stagnancy occurred during the period 1966-68. In the phase 1996-77 industrial growth rate became 9.5%. After that the country faced negative growth rate of minus 1.4% during 1979-80. In the sixties (1961-70) the average growth rate of industrial output was 5.5% and in seventies (1971-80) the average growth rate was about 4% per annum. Even during 1980-85 the growth rate of industrial production was 5.5% per annum. During (1985-90) the growth rate had picked up to an average of over 8% per annum and in 1992-97 it declined to 7.3% per annum. The rate of growth of industrial production in the ninth plan was only 5.0% which was less than the target of 8.2% per annum. The performance of the industrial sector was highly unsatisfactory during the period of the second half of1990. The industrial sector registered a dismal performance in the last year of the 9$^{th}$ plan 2001-02 with its rate of growth being fast 2.7%. However, it picked up to 5.7% in 2002-03 and further to 7.0% in 2003-04 due to the performance of the capital goods sector and consumer goods sector. The Report on Currency and Finance 2003-04 attributed that due to improved investment climate, expanding external demand, improved domestic demand case and availability of finance and increasing capacity addition in the industrial sector led to an improvement in industrial performance in 2002-03 and 2003-04 (*see* table 15.2). In 2004-05 rose upto 8.4%, 11.6% in 2006-07 the growth rate in 2007-08 was 9.2% in general, 4.9% in mining, 9.8% in manufacturing and 7.0% in electricity. From a use based classification perspective (Table 15.4) capital good sectors emerged as the most buoyant sector and registered a double digit growth rate during 2005-07 within the consumer good sector.

## 15.6 CONCLUSION

### 15.6.1 Challenges and Outlook

The industrial sector recorded a robust rate of growth in excess of 8% during 2004-05, 2005-06 and scaled an appreciable 11.6% growth during 2006-07. The current fiscal till, 2007-08 sustained the momentum albeit with a slight moderation in certain sectors. While industrial groups like food products, jute textile, wood products, leather products, chemical and chemical products and other manufacturing have grown at an accelerated pace compared to 2006-07, industries like non-metallic mineral products, cotton textiles and textile product, paper products, metal products have suffered from a significant slackening in growth. The growth of textiles, with very low import intensity, may have been affected adversely by the recent appreciation of the Rupee against US Dollar. The government has promptly taken measures to mitigate the incidence of the slow down. The downslide in consumer durables can be partly attributed to the constrained demand conditions arising from adjustment in policy variables like interest rates. Yet it needs to be appreciated that the automobile segment including passenger cars, jeeps etc. have buoyed down during the current fiscal. In short, the slowdown shown by the available data on consumer durables may not in itself be the cause of concern in the long run provided the overall buoyancy in growth and income is maintained.

There are a number of positive developments that brightens the industrial outlook in the medium term. *Firstly*, there has been a commendable growth in the capital goods sector especially in industrial machinery which along with strong imports of capital goods, augurs well for the much required industrial capacity addition. (*See* Table 15.6) and Figures 15.1, 15.2, 15.3. *Secondly*, the inherent strength of the industrial corporate manifested in the increase in profits and profitability and strong investment plans confirms the strength of the growth prospect in the medium term. *Thirdly*, the investment plan made for infrastructure during the eleventh plan would alleviate the infrastructural constraint to industrial development. Growth in infrastructure not only alleviates the supply side constraint in industrial production but also stimulates additional domestic demand required for industrial growth.

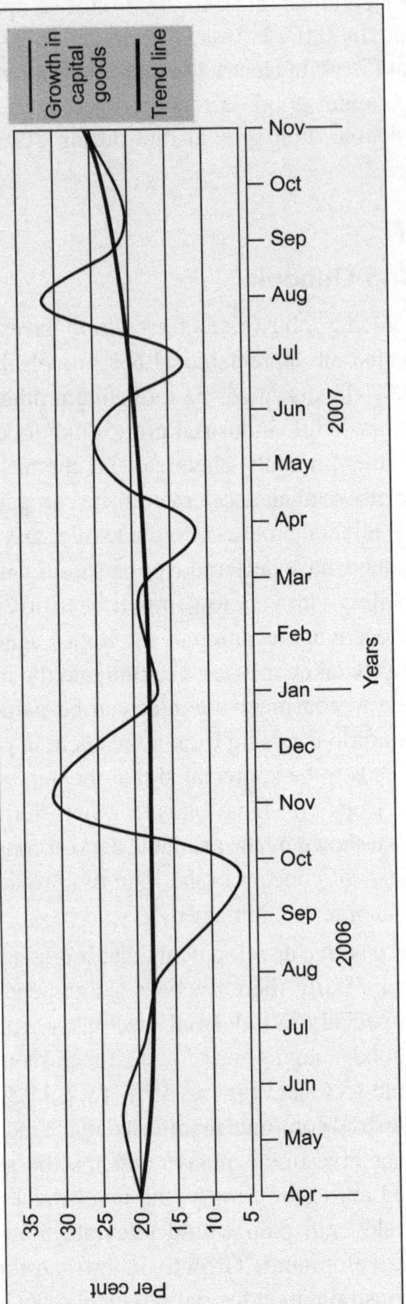


**Fig. 15.1.** Growth in capital goods (month on month).

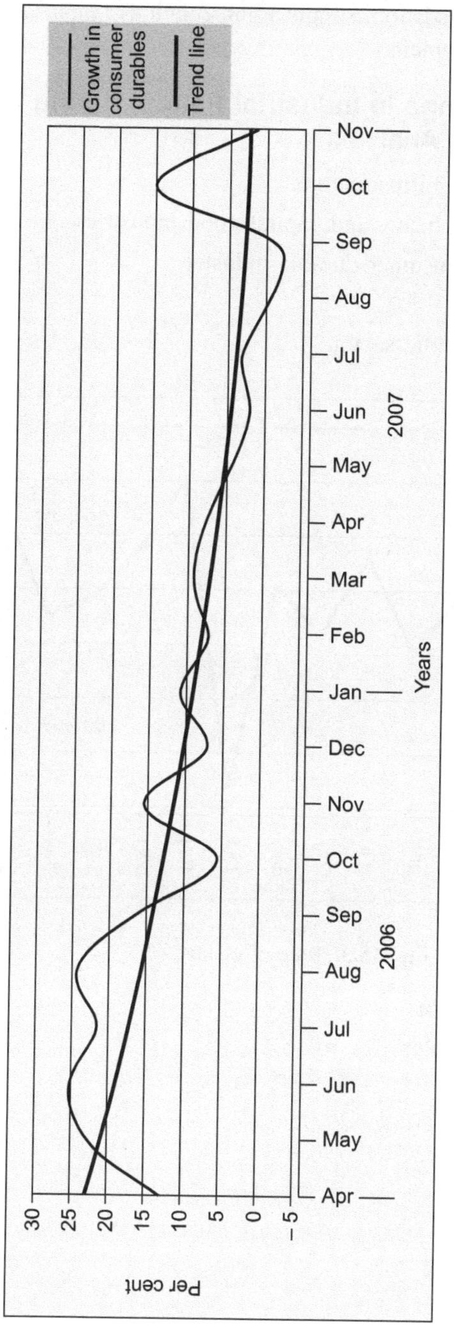


**Fig. 15.2.** Growth in consumer durables (month-on-month).

The eleventh plan document also tailored to address certain issues which were related to skill upgradation, supply argumentation of inputs and promotion of research and development.

### 15.6.2 Overall Change in Industrial Pattern during the Plan Period Brief Analysis

1. Development of infrastructure.
2. Development of heavy and capital good industries.
3. Expansion of consumer durable industry.
4. Rise in G.D.P.
5. Expansion of public sector.

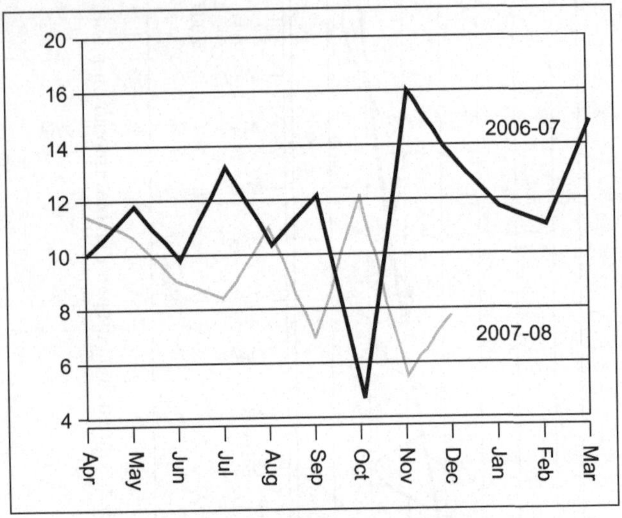


**Fig. 15.3.** Rate of change (%).

### Industrial production

For more detial see Tables 15.7 to 15.11.

**Table 15.7:** Production figures of selected industries in India

| Industry | Unit | 1 950-51 | 1960-61 | 1970-71 | 1980- 81 | 1990-91 | 1999-00 | 2000-01 | 2003-04 | 2004-05 | 2005-06 | 2006-07 | 2007-08 | 2008-09° |
|---|---|---|---|---|---|---|---|---|---|---|---|---|---|---|
| 1 | 2 | 3 | 4 | 5 | 6 | 7 | 8 | 9 | 10 | 11 | 12 | 13 | 14 | 15 |
| **1.** Minning | | | | | | | | | | | | | | |
| 1. Coal (incl. lignite) | Million tonnes | 32.3 | 55.2 | 76.3 | 119.0 | 225.5 | 322.1 | 332.6 | 389.3 | 413.0 | 437.1 | 462.1 | 491.1 | 493.3 |
| 2. Petrolium, crude | -do- | 0.3 | 0.5 | 6.8 | 10.5 | 33.0 | 31.9 | 32.4 | 33.4 | 34.0 | 32.2 | 34.0 | 34.1 | 33.5 |
| (*i*) On-shore | -do- | 0.3 | 0.5 | 6.8 | 5.5 | 11.8 | 11.3 | 11.8 | 11.5 | 11.6 | 11.4 | 11.3 | 11.2 | 11.3 |
| (*ii*) Off-shore | -do- | ... | ... | ... | 5.0 | 21.2 | 20.6 | 20.6 | 21.9 | 22.4 | 20.8 | 22.7 | 22.9 | 22.2 |
| 3. Iron ore | -do- | 3.0 | 10.9 | 32.5 | 42.2 | 53.7 | 77.6 | 80.6 | 120.6 | 145.9 | 154.4 | 172.3 | na | na |
| **II.** Metallurgical Industries | | | | | | | | | | | | | | |
| 4. Hot metal (incl. Pig iron) | -do- | 1.7 | 4.3 | 7.0 | 9.6 | 12.2 | 22.0 | 22.6 | 31.9 | 31.5 | 36.5 | 39.7 | 42.1 | 41.5 |
| 5. Crude Steel (ingots+concast + blooms and stabs) | -do- | 1.5 | 3.5 | 6.1 | 10.3 | na | 29.1 | 30.6 | 38.7 | 43.4 | 46.5 | 50.82 | 53.46 | 54.52 |
| 6. Semi-finished steel (main plants) | -do- | 1.2 | 1.0 | 0.9 | 2.0 | 4.3 | 3.8 | 3.3 | 3.1 | 2.7 | 3.2 | 3.1 | 2.8 | 3.2 |
| 7. Finished steel (incl, secondary producers) | -do- | 1.0 | 2.4 | 4.6 | 6.8 | 13.5 | 29.2 | 31.2 | 38.6 | 41.3 | 44.4 | 52.5 | 56.1 | 56.4 |
| 8. Steel castings | Thousand tonnes | na | 35.0 | 62.0 | 71.0 | 262.0 | 386.9 | 352.4 | 407.8 | 421.7 | 449.5 | 612.0 | 56.7 | 57.0 |
| 9. Aluminium | -do- | 4.0 | 18.5 | 168.8 | 199.0 | 451.1 | 497.6 | 620.4 | 601.2 | 516.4 | 560.5 | 719.1 | 755.7 | 766.7 |
| 10. Copper metal (cathode) | -do- | na | na | na | na | na | 144.7 | 43.3 | 30.6 | 17.0 | 35.6 | 38.5 | 44.7 | 30.0 |
| **III.** Mechanical Engineering industries | | | | | | | | | | | | | | |
| 11. Machine tools | Rs. Million | 3 | 8 | 430 | 1692 | 7731 | 13989 | 12263 | 22225 | 23884 | 26367 | 26410 | 26914 | 24282 |
| 12. Textile machinery | -do- | na | na | na | na | na | 12872 | 125296 | 12559 | 14260 | 21429 | 29100 | 29100 | 29100 |
| 13. Industrial Machinery | -do- | na | na | na | na | na | 26862 | 20046 | 20213 | 23955 | 31107 | 27299 | 35589 | 51543 |
| 14. Broad gauge convered wagons/Passenger carriage | Thousand | na | na | na | na | na | 6.1 | 5.6 | 4.4 | 4.7 | 5.2 | 4.2 | 5.0 | 4.7 |
| 15. Automobiles (total) | -do- | 16.5 | 54.8 | 87.9 | 121.1 | 366.3 | 873.8 | 784.2 | 1283.1 | 1564.5 | 1701.5 | 2065.6 | 2313.0 | 2010.9 |
| (*i*) Commercial vehicles | -do- | 8.6 | 28.2 | 41.2 | 71.7 | 145.5 | 173.5 | 152.0 | 275.1 | 350.0 | 391.0 | 520.0 | 545.1 | 416.5 |
| (*ii*) Cars, jeeps and land rovers | -do- | 7.9 | 26.6 | 46.7 | 49.4 | 220.8 | 700.3 | 632.2 | 1008.0 | 1214.5 | 1310.5 | 1545.6 | 1767.9 | 1825.8 |

| Industry | Unit | 1 950-51 | 1960-61 | 1970-71 | 1980- 81 | 1990-91 | 1999-00 | 2000-01 | 2003-04 | 2004-05 | 2005-06 | 2006-07 | 2007-08 | 2008-09° |
|---|---|---|---|---|---|---|---|---|---|---|---|---|---|---|
| 1 | 2 | 3 | 4 | 5 | 6 | 7 | 8 | 9 | 10 | 11 | 12 | 13 | 14 | 15 |
| 16. Motor cycles, scooters and mopeds/scooterettes | -do- | na | 0.9 | 97.0 | 447.2 | 1842.8 | 3722.5 | 3756.1 | 5624.9 | 6454.8 | 7601.8 | 8436.2 | 8009.3 | 8361.4 |
| 17. Power driven pumps | -do- | 35.0 | 105.0 | 259.0 | 431.0 | 19.0 | 599.2 | 481.9 | 663.3 | 649.2 | 718.3 | 768.7 | 789.8 | 1064.3 |
| 18. Diesel engines (stationary) | -do- | 5.5 | 43.2 | 65.0 | 173.9 | 158.4 | 348.3 | 306.0 | 310.3 | 299.0 | 337.7 | 460.8 | 517.2 | 614.3 |
| 19. Washing/laundry machine | -do- | na | na | na | na | na | 770.2 | 714.9 | 1438.4 | 1588.8 | 1756.6 | 1944.7 | 2168.9 | 2344.5 |
| 20. Bicycles | -do- | 99.0 | 1063.0 | 2042.0 | 4189.0 | 7084.0 | 13734.0 | 14975.0 | 12341.0 | 8030.0 | 8267.8 | 10598.8 | 11397.4 | 11123.4 |
| 21. Agricultural tractors | -do- | na | na | na | 71.0 | 142.2 | 279.7 | 284.4 | 178.9 | 242.3 | 253.8 | 310.7 | 304.4 | 303.3 |
| **IV.** Electrical engineering industries | | | | | | | | | | | | | | |
| 22. Power transformers | Million KVA | 0.2 | 1.4 | 8.1 | 19.5 | 36.6 | 55.7 | 70.7 | 62.7 | 59.5 | 68.3 | 71.4 | 13.2 | 71.9 |
| 23. Electric motors | Million hp | 0.1 | 0.7 | 2.7 | 4.1 | 5.9 | 5.8 | 5.6 | 8.7 | 10.8 | 10.5 | 12.4 | 12.9 | 13.5 |
| 24. Electric fans | Million | 0.2 | 1.1 | 1.7 | 4.2 | 4.2 | 5.8 | 5.2 | 6.4 | 6.0 | 6.9 | 7.7 | 7.9 | 7.7 |
| 25. Electric lamps | -do- | 15.0 | 43.5 | 119.3 | 198.1 | 274.4 | 501.7 | 448.9 | 975.4 | 464.3 | 481.9 | 470.5 | 43.08 | 428.1 |
| 26. Computer system and peripheral | Rs. Million | na | na | na | na | na | 10549.1 | 7914.6 | 18606.4 | 26092.0 | 28887.4 | 31295.2 | 42011.0 | 39591.3 |
| 27. Aluminium conductors | Thousand tonnes | 1.7 | 23.7 | 64.2 | 86.0 | 67.6 | 28.0 | 30.9 | 34.8 | 27.6 | 28.1 | 26.8 | 16.2 | 17.8 |
| **V.** Chyemical and allied Industries | | | | | | | | | | | | | | |
| 28. Nitrogenous fertilizer (N) | Thousand tonnes | 9 | 99 | 830 | 2164 | 6993 | 10912 | 11025 | 10632 | 11340 | 11402 | 11607 | 10902 | 10870 |
| 29. Phosphatic fertilizer ($P_2O_5$) | -do- | 9 | 54 | 229 | 842 | 2052 | 3374 | 3745 | 3567 | 3986 | 4162 | 4546 | 3836 | 3464 |
| 30. Soda ash | -do- | 46 | 147 | 449 | 563 | 1385 | 1514 | 1631 | 1704 | 2026 | 2327 | 2085 | 1981 | 1998 |
| 31. Caustic Soda | -do- | 12 | 99 | 371 | 578 | 992 | 1425 | 1642 | 1600 | 1771 | 1881 | 1929 | 2058 | 2030 |
| 32. Paper and paper board | -do- | 116 | 349 | 755 | 1149 | 2088 | 3459 | 3090 | 3684 | 3848 | 3913 | 4139 | 4260 | 4442 |
| 33. Automobile tyres (Gaint tyre, tractor, two wheeler) | Million | na | 1.5 | 3.8 | 8.0 | 20.1 | 26.8 | 29.3 | 29.7 | 29.4 | 34.4 | 38.6 | 39.9 | 40.5 |
| 34. Bicycle tyres | -do- | na | 11.2 | 19.2 | 27.0 | 24.8 | 12.9 | 12.7 | 50.4 | 75.7 | 95.8 | 93.4 | 95.4 | 86.7 |
| 35. Cement | Million tonnes | 2.7 | 8.0 | 14.3 | 18.6 | 48.8 | 100.2 | 99.2 | 117.0 | 125.3 | 140.5 | 154.7 | 167.6 | 181.4 |
| 36. Petroleum refinery products | -do- | 0.2 | 5.7 | 17.1 | 24.1 | 48.6 | 79.9 | 96.2 | 113.5 | 118.6 | 119.8 | 135.3 | 144.1 | 150.5 |
| 37. Penicillin | MMU | na | na | 190.0 | 337.0 | 25.0 | 487.0 | 822.9 | 1389.0 | 1021.6 | 214.7 | na | 1196.0 | 1831.1 |

| Industry | Unit | 1 950-51 | 1960-61 | 1970-71 | 1980- 81 | 1990-91 | 1999-00 | 2000-01 | 2003-04 | 2004-05 | 2005-06 | 2006-07 | 2007-08 | 2008-09° |
|---|---|---|---|---|---|---|---|---|---|---|---|---|---|---|
| 1 | 2 | 3 | 4 | 5 | 6 | 7 | 8 | 9 | 10 | 11 | 12 | 13 | 14 | 15 |
| 38. Ampicillin | Tonnes | na | na | na | na | na | 354.0 | 293.3 | 829.1 | 817.3 | 512.7 | 709.6 | 556.3 | 688.7 |
| 39. Vitamin C | Tonnes | na | na | na | na | na | 465.1 | 778.8 | 598.2 | 391.5 | 435.0 | 154.8 | 142.1 | 50.0 |
| 40. Vitamin A | MMU | na | na | 38.5 | 59.9 | 220.5 | 64.3 | 77.4 | 65.5 | 97.7 | 81.2 | 88.1 | 83.1 | 95.7 |
| **VI.** Textile Industries | | | | | | | | | | | | | | |
| 41. Cloth | | | | | | | | | | | | | | |
| (*a*) Cotton cloth | Million sq. meters | 4215 | 6738 | 7602 | 8368 | 15431 | 18989 | 19718 | 18040 | 20655 | 23873 | 26238 | 27196 | 26898 |
| (*i*) Mill sector | -do- | 3401 | 4649 | 4055 | 3434 | 1859 | 1105 | 1106 | 969 | 1072 | 1192 | 1305 | 1249 | 1260 |
| (*ii*) Decentralised sector | -do- | 814 | 2089 | 3547 | 4934 | 13572 | 17884 | 18612 | 17071 | 19583 | 22681 | 24933 | 25947 | 25638 |
| (*b*) Mixed/blended cloth | -do- | na | na | 170 | 1270 | 2388 | 5913 | 6351 | 6068 | 6032 | 6298 | 6882 | 6888 | 6766 |
| (*i*) Mill sector | -do- | na | na | 107 | 730 | 698 | 379 | 332 | 253 | 243 | 252 | 330 | 422 | 426 |
| (*ii*) Decentralised sector | -do- | na | na | 63 | 540 | 1682 | 5534 | 6019 | 5815 | 5789 | 6046 | 6552 | 6466 | 6340 |
| (*c*) Man-made fibre fabrics | -do- | 300° | 550° | 951 | 1350 | 5126 | 13725 | 14164 | 18275 | 18691 | 19406 | 20269 | 21941 | 21302 |
| (*i*) Mill sector | -do- | 13° | 3° | 2 | 4 | 41 | 230 | 232 | 212 | 211 | 212 | 111 | 110 | 111 |
| (*ii*) Decentralised sector | -do- | 287° | 547° | 949 | 1346 | 5085 | 13495 | 13932 | 18063 | 18480 | 19194 | 20158 | 21831 | 21191 |
| 42. Spun yam (by cotton textile mills) | | | | | | | | | | | | | | |
| (*i*) Cotton | Million kg. | 533° | 788° | 929 | 1067 | 1510 | 2204 | 2267 | 2121 | 2272 | 2521 | 2824 | 2948 | 2641 |
| (*ii*) Mixed/blended | -do- | na | na | 22 | 144 | 207 | 621 | 646 | 589 | 585 | 588 | 635 | 677 | 590 |
| (*iii*) 100% non-cotton | -do- | 11° | 15° | 65 | 87 | 107 | 221 | 247 | 342 | 366 | 349 | 354 | 378 | 330 |

| Industry | Unit | 1 950-51 | 1960-61 | 1970-71 | 1980- 81 | 1990-91 | 1999-00 | 2000-01 | 2003-04 | 2004-05 | 2005-06 | 2006-07 | 2007-08 | 2008-09° |
|---|---|---|---|---|---|---|---|---|---|---|---|---|---|---|
| 1 | 2 | 3 | 4 | 5 | 6 | 7 | 8 | 9 | 10 | 11 | 12 | 13 | 14 | 15 |
| 43. Filament yam: | (Thousand tonnes) | | | | | | | | | | | | | |
| (*a*) Cellulosic | -do- | ... | 21° | 38 | 43 | 51 | 49 | 55 | 53 | 53 | 53 | 54 | 51 | 42 |
| (*i*) Viscose | -do- | ... | 19° | 36 | 41 | 51 | 49 | 55 | 53 | 54 | 53 | 54 | 51 | 42 |
| (*b*) Symthetic | -do- | na | na | 10 | 32 | 227 | 844 | 865 | 1065 | 1055 | 1126 | 1316 | 1458 | 1377 |
| (*i*) Polyster | -do- | na | na | 1 | 11 | 187 | 818 | 839 | 1034 | 1020 | 1089 | 1284 | 1430 | 1349 |
| (*ii*) Nylon | -do- | na | na | 9 | 21 | 40 | 26 | 26 | 31 | 35 | 37 | 32 | 28 | 28 |
| 44. Staple fibre: | | | | | | | | | | | | | | |
| (*a*) Cellulosic | -do- | na | 22° | 62 | 83 | 160 | 202 | 236 | 221 | 248 | 229 | 247 | 280 | 228 |
| (*i*) Viscose | -do- | na | 22° | 62 | 83 | 160 | 202 | 236 | 221 | 248 | 229 | 247 | 280 | 228 |
| (*b*) Synthetic | -do- | na | na | 5 | 32 | 177 | 633 | 668 | 732 | 774 | 739 | 892 | 964 | 833 |
| (*i*) Polyester | -do- | na | na | 5 | 22 | 135 | 553 | 568 | 615 | 647 | 631 | 795 | 883 | 755 |
| (*ii*) Acrylic | -do- | na | na | na | 10 | 42 | 80 | 100 | 117 | 127 | 108 | 97 | 81 | 78 |
| **VII.** Food Industries | | | | | | | | | | | | | | |
| 45. Sugar° | Thousand tonnes | 1134° | 3029° | 3740 | 5148 | 12047 | 18193 | 18510 | 13958 | 13660 | 19321 | 28199 | na | na |
| 46. Tea | -do- | 277 | 318 | 423 | 568 | 705 | 816 | 827 | 851 | 831 | 893 | 949 | 948 | 968 |
| 47. Coffee | -do- | 21 | 54 | 71 | 139 | 170 | 220.6 | 312.6 | 257 | 296 | 262 | 254 | 265 | 267 |
| 48. Vanaspati | -do- | 155 | 355 | 558 | 753 | 850 | 1320 | 1445 | 1628 | 1899 | 1348 | 1286 | 1243 | na |
| 49. Salt | -do- | na | na | 5568 | 8409 | 12645 | 15585 | 14948 | 15325 | 16662 | 18971 | 17899 | 17845 | 18251 |
| VIII. Electricity Generated° | Billion kWH | 5 | 17 | 56 | 111 | 264 | 480 | 499 | 558 | 587 | 617 | 662 | 704.4 | 723.8 |

**Sources:**

1. Department of Coal.

2 and 36. Minsitry of Petroleum and natural Gas.

9-35, 37-40, 46-49 and VII. Central Statistical Organisation

3. Ministry of Mines

41-44 Minsitry of Textiles

45. Department of Food and Public Distribution, Directorate of Sugar.

na Not available.

*a*. Provisional.

*b*. Includes buses, trucks and tempos, 3 and 4 wheelers.

*c*. Relates to sugar season which is October-September.

*d*. Relates to utilities.

*e*. On a calender year basis

*f*. Relates of calender year 1951.

*g*. Relates ot November-October.

*h*. Realates to November-October.

Economic Survey, 2008-09, pp, A 32-34.

**Table 15.8:** Index of Industrial Production

| Industry group | Industry | Weight 1980-81 | Weight 1993-94 | 1981-82 | 1990-91 | 1999-00 | 2000-01 | 2003-04 | 2004-05 | 2005-06 | 2006-07 | 2007-08 | 2008-09° |
|---|---|---|---|---|---|---|---|---|---|---|---|---|---|
| | | | (Base: 1980-81 = 100) | | | | | | (Base: 1993-94 = 100) | | | | |
| 1 | 2 | 3 | 4 | 5 | 6 | 7 | 8 | 9 | 10 | 11 | 12 | 13 | 14 |
| | General inxed | 100.00 | 100.00 | 109.3 | 212.6 | 154.9 | 162.6 | 189.0 | 204.8 | 221.5 | 247.1 | 268.0 | 274.3 |
| 1. | Mining | 11.46 | 10.47 | 117.7 | 221.2 | 126.7 | 130.3 | 146.9 | 153.4 | 154.9 | 163.2 | 171.6 | 175.8 |
| 2-3 | Manufacturing | 77.11 | 79.36 | 107.9 | 207.8 | 159.4 | 167.9 | 196.6 | 214.6 | 234.2 | 263.5 | 287.2 | 293.8 |
| 20-21 | Food products | 5.33 | 9.08 | 113.5 | 169.8 | 140.3 | 154.5 | 167.9 | 167.3 | 170.6 | 185.2 | 198.2 | 179.2 |
| 22 | Beverages, tobacco and tabacco products | 1.57 | 2.38 | 104.3 | 104.8 | 192.1 | 200.4 | 312.1 | 345.9 | 400.3 | 444.5 | 498.0 | 575.9 |
| 23. | Cotton textiles | 12.31 | 5.52 | 99.7 | 126.6 | 123.7 | 127.3 | 117.4 | 126.3 | 137.0 | 157.3 | 164.0 | 159.4 |
| 24. | Wool, slik and man-made fibre textiles | ... | 2.26 | ... | ... | 197.8 | 209.3 | 240.5 | 249.0 | 248.9 | 268.4 | 281.2 | 280.4 |
| 25. | Jute and other veg. fibre tex. (except cotton) | 2.00 | 0.59 | 95.7 | 101.6 | 105.0 | 105.8 | 103.4 | 107.2 | 107.7 | 90.7 | 120.7 | 108.6 |
| 26. | Textile products and apparel | 0.82 | 2.54 | 96.7 | 103.2 | 156.1 | 162.4 | 184.3 | 219.6 | 255.5 | 285.0 | 295.5 | 306.4 |
| 27. | Wood and wood products, furniture and fixtures | 0.45 | 2.70 | 153.2 | 197.2 | 101.4 | 104.3 | 81.7 | 74.8 | 70.5 | 91.0 | 127.9 | 114.7 |
| 28. | Paper, paper products and printing | 3.23 | 2.65 | 108.3 | 198.0 | 180.5 | 164.0 | 208.7 | 230.7 | 228.6 | 248.6 | 255.3 | 258.6 |
| 29. | Leather and fur products | 0.49 | 1.14 | 128.1 | 194.3 | 135.5 | 150.0 | 147.0 | 156.9 | 149.3 | 150.2 | 167.8 | 156.1 |
| 30. | Basic Chemicals and Chem products | 4.00 | 14.00 | 116.9 | 254.1 | 164.6 | 176.6 | 208.4 | 238.6 | 258.5 | 283.4 | 313.4 | 322.5 |
| 31. | Rubber, plastic, Petroleum and coal products | 12.51 | 5.73 | 119.2 | 174.0 | 137.2 | 153.4 | 187.7 | 192.2 | 200.5 | 226.3 | 246.4 | 242.6 |
| 32. | Non-metallic mineral products | 3.00 | 4.40 | 106.7 | 193.1 | 220.8 | 218.2 | 240.6 | 244.3 | 271.1 | 305.8 | 323.2 | 326.5 |
| 33. | Basic metals and alloy industries | 9.80 | 7.45 | 100.0 | 158.8 | 146.9 | 149.6 | 186.0 | 196.1 | 227.0 | 278.9 | 312.7 | 325.1 |
| 34. | Metal products [a] | 2.29 | 2.81 | 94.6 | 143.1 | 137.8 | 158.5 | 157.3 | 166.3 | 164.4 | 183.2 | 172.9 | 166.0 |
| 35. | Non-electrical machinery and machine tools [a] | 6.24 | 9.57 | 111.1 | 186.9 | 182.5 | 195.8 | 233.3 | 279.4 | 312.8 | 357.1 | 394.4 | 428.7 |
| 36. | Electrical machinery and appliances [a] | 5.78 | ... | 103.9 | 563.6 | ... | ... | ... | ... | ... | ... | ... | ... |

| Industry group | Industry | Weight 1980-81 | Weight 1993-94 | 1981-82 | 1990-91 | 1999-00 | 2000-01 | 2003-04 | 2004-05 | 2005-06 | 2006-07 | 2007-08 | 2008-09° |
|---|---|---|---|---|---|---|---|---|---|---|---|---|---|
| | | | (Base: 1980-81 = 100) | | | | | (Base: 1993-94 = 100) | | | | | |
| 1 | 2 | 3 | 4 | 5 | 6 | 7 | 8 | 9 | 10 | 11 | 12 | 13 | 14 |
| 37. | Transport equipment [a] | 6.39 | 3.98 | 108.1 | 192.5 | 194.1 | 190.3 | 272.6 | 283.7 | 319.7 | 367.7 | 374.4 | 386.7 |
| 38. | Other manufacturing industries | 0.90 | 2.56 | 149.2 | 321.8 | 142.5 | 159.1 | 186.6 | 221.2 | 276.9 | 298.4 | 357.4 | 359.2 |
| 4. | Electicity | 11.43 | 10.17 | 110.2 | 236.8 | 148.5 | 154.4 | 172.6 | 181.5 | 190.9 | 204.7 | 204.7 | 223.7 |

**Source :** Central statistical Organisation (CSO), Industrial Statistics wing, Economic Survey 2008-09, P, A-35.

*a.* Provisional.

*b.* Excludes footwear.

*c.* Excludes repairs.

*d.* Includes parts.

**Note :** The NIC groups 30 and 31 have been interchanged in the Revised Series as compared to 1980-81 series on account of NIC-87.

**Table 15.9:** Gross domestic product at factor cost by industry of origin.

| Year | Agriculture. Forestry & fishing, mining and quarrying | Manufacturing, construction. electricity, gas and water supply | Trade, hotels, transport and communication | Financing, Insurance, real estate and business services | Public administration and defence and other services | Gross domestic product at factor cost (2 to 6) |
|---|---|---|---|---|---|---|
| 1 | 2 | 3 | 4 | 5 | 6 | 7 |
| | | | At current prices | | | |
| 1950-51 | 5155 | 1328 | 939 | 1162 | 1080 | 9664 |
| 1951-52 | 5329 | 1485 | 1017 | 1250 | 1126 | 10208 |
| 1952-53 | 5196 | 1397 | 1024 | 1320 | 1163 | 10100 |
| 1953-54 | 5717 | 1540 | 1087 | 1424 | 1212 | 10980 |
| 1954-55 | 4880 | 1618 | 1117 | 1526 | 1244 | 10385 |
| 1955-56 | 4737 | 1733 | 1157 | 1638 | 1319 | 10584 |
| 1956-57 | 6013 | 2041 | 1337 | 1776 | 1386 | 12552 |
| 1957-58 | 5909 | 2120 | 1480 | 1903 | 1457 | 12868 |
| 1958-59 | 6844 | 2302 | 1618 | 2041 | 1548 | 14352 |
| 1959-60 | 6884 | 2579 | 1747 | 2190 | 1706 | 15106 |
| 1960-61 | 7267 | 3066 | 1926 | 2360 | 1928 | 16546 |
| 1961-62 | 7530 | 3349 | 2082 | 2411 | 2087 | 17459 |
| 1962-63 | 7721 | 3687 | 2279 | 2768 | 2270 | 18726 |
| 1963-64 | 9066 | 4213 | 2550 | 2994 | 2518 | 21341 |
| 1964-65 | 11037 | 4716 | 2992 | 3254 | 2854 | 24851 |
| 1965-66 | 11047 | 5116 | 3245 | 3517 | 3174 | 26099 |
| 1966-67 | 12827 | 5720 | 3772 | 3765 | 3552 | 29637 |
| 1967-68 | 16024 | 6264 | 4311 | 4131 | 3977 | 34707 |
| 1968-69 | 16531 | 6813 | 4590 | 4422 | 4285 | 36641 |
| 1969-70 | 18088 | 7801 | 4954 | 4744 | 4672 | 40259 |
| 1970-71 | 18657 | 8470 | 5458 | 5169 | 5150 | 42903 |

| Year | Agriculture. Forestry & fishing, mining and quarrying | Manufacturing, construction. electricity, gas and water supply | Trade, hotels, transport and communication | Financing, Insurance, real estate and business services | Public administration and defence and other services | Gross domestic product at factor cost (2 to 6) |
|---|---|---|---|---|---|---|
| 1 | 2 | 3 | 4 | 5 | 6 | 7 |
| 1971-72 | 19071 | 9370 | 5919 | 5668 | 5718 | 45746 |
| 1972-73 | 20965 | 10352 | 6528 | 6203 | 6256 | 50305 |
| 1973-74 | 27536 | 12042 | 7814 | 6917 | 7036 | 61345 |
| 1974-75 | 30365 | 15022 | 10319 | 7774 | 8858 | 72338 |
| 1975-76 | 30336 | 16308 | 11701 | 8813 | 9971 | 77129 |
| 1976-77 | 31126 | 18493 | 12673 | 9802 | 10960 | 83054 |
| 1977-78 | 36755 | 20902 | 14258 | 10693 | 11914 | 94522 |
| 1978-79 | 37857 | 23564 | 15635 | 11534 | 13110 | 101701 |
| 1979-80 | 39482 | 26374 | 18042 | 12579 | 14679 | 111157 |
| 1980-81 | 49640 | 30389 | 21298 | 14010 | 17183 | 132520 |
| 1981-82 | 57477 | 35505 | 26125 | 16526 | 19524 | 155158 |
| 1982-83 | 62616 | 39284 | 29818 | 18952 | 22667 | 173337 |
| 1983-84 | 74350 | 46281 | 34636 | 21671 | 25813 | 202750 |
| 1984-85 | 80443 | 52742 | 39878 | 24932 | 29699 | 227694 |
| 1985-86 | 86196 | 59516 | 46567 | 28557 | 33591 | 254427 |
| 1986-87 | 93154 | 66517 | 52636 | 32743 | 38631 | 283681 |
| 1987-88 | 103105 | 76169 | 60107 | 37422 | 44776 | 321589 |
| 1988-89 | 127946 | 89472 | 70968 | 43481 | 51923 | 383790 |
| 1989-90 | 141383 | 106935 | 83065 | 51238 | 59513 | 442134 |
| 1990-91 | 164575 | 124684 | 97313 | 59856 | 68604 | 515032 |
| 1991-92 | 191262 | 137954 | 112119 | 73112 | 79721 | 594168 |
| 1992-93 | 213978 | 160679 | 132191 | 81072 | 92597 | 681517 |
| 1993-94 | 249421 | 184654 | 156202 | 97928 | 103946 | 792150 |
| 1994-95 | 286733 | 225143 | 186425 | 110673 | 116265 | 925239 |

| Year | Agriculture. Forestry & fishing, mining and quarrying | Manufacturing, construction. electricity, gas and water supply | Trade, hotels, transport and communication | Financing, Insurance, real estate and business services | Public administration and defence and other services | Gross domestic product at factor cost (2 to 6) |
|---|---|---|---|---|---|---|
| 1 | 2 | 3 | 4 | 5 | 6 | 7 |
| 1995-96 | 312413 | 276026 | 224259 | 133235 | 137357 | 1083289 |
| 1996-97 | 372938 | 312711 | 264967 | 146991 | 163104 | 1260710 |
| 1997-98 | 399802 | 341711 | 303755 | 167381 | 189284 | 1401934 |
| 1998-99 | 456441 | 385294 | 347864 | 195133 | 231351 | 1616082 |
| 1999-00 | 488109 | 410647 | 387515 | 233549 | 266707 | 1786526 |
| | | | **New series** | | | |
| 1999-00 | 488109 | 410646 | 387514 | 233550 | 266707 | 1786526 |
| 2000-01 | 495271 | 458431 | 428855 | 254772 | 287688 | 1925017 |
| 2001-02 | 534488 | 483661 | 476230 | 292862 | 310485 | 2097726 |
| 2002-03 | 534802 | 535732 | 525968 | 330685 | 334228 | 3261415 |
| 2003-04 | 596224 | 602030 | 604683 | 371452 | 363781 | 2538170 |
| 2004-05 | 637198 | 726302 | 706073 | 405081 | 403047 | 2877701 |
| 2005-06 | 720168 | 849421 | 809870 | 452469 | 450457 | 3282385 |
| 2006-07 | 792069 | 1007283 | 947097 | 524019 | 508917 | 3779385 |
| 2007-08(Q) | 900028 | 1157462 | 1090708 | 594096 | 578598 | 4320892 |

**Source :** Central Statistical Organisation.

P : Provisional estimates. Q : Quick estimates.

Note : For the year prior to 1980-81 totals under col. 7 may not add upto totals of individual item under col. 2 to col. 6 due to splicing technique applied independently at the level of each industry and at the total level.

**Table 15.10:** Annual growth rate of real gross domestic product at factor cost by industry of origin

| year | Agriculture, forestry and fishing. mining and quarrrying | Manufacturing construction, electricity, gas and water supply | Trade, hotels, transport and communication | Financing, Insurance, real estate and business services | Public adminisatration and defence and other services | Gross domestic product at factor cost (2 to 6) |
|---|---|---|---|---|---|---|
| 1 | 2 | 3 | 4 | 5 | 6 | 7 |
| | | | At 1999-2000 prices | | | |
| 1951-52 | 1.8 | 4.5 | 2.7 | 2.3 | 3.0 | 2.4 |
| 1952-53 | 3.1 | -0.1 | 3.2 | 4.2 | 2.1 | 2.7 |
| 1953-54 | 7.5 | 6.3 | 3.7 | 1.4 | 3.1 | 6.0 |
| 1954-55 | 3.0 | 8.6 | 6.4 | 3.7 | 3.6 | 4.2 |
| 1955-56 | -0.8 | 11.3 | 7.3 | 4.0 | 3.1 | 2.6 |
| 1956-57 | 5.4 | 8.9 | 7.4 | 1.6 | 3.8 | 5.7 |
| 1957-58 | -4.2 | -1.3 | 3.3 | 3.8 | 4.5 | -1.4 |
| 1958-59 | 9.9 | 7.2 | 5.1 | 2.8 | 4.1 | 7.7 |
| 1959-60 | -0.8 | 7.1 | 6.3 | 3.8 | 4.3 | 2.2 |
| 1960-61 | 7.0 | 10.6 | 8.5 | 2.1 | 4.9 | 7.2 |
| 1961-62 | 0.3 | 7.1 | 6.5 | 4.3 | 4.7 | 3.0 |
| 1962-63 | -1.5 | 6.3 | 6.0 | 3.4 | 7.1 | 2.1 |
| 1963-64 | 2.4 | 10.6 | 7.0 | 3.1 | 6.6 | 5.1 |
| 1964-65 | 8.9 | 7.4 | 6.7 | 2.7 | 6.6 | 7.6 |
| 1965-66 | -10.2 | 3.1 | 2.0 | 3.0 | 4.0 | -3.4 |

| year | Agriculture, forestry and fishing, mining and quarrying | Manufacturing construction, electricity, gas and water supply | Trade, hotels, transport and communication | Financing, Insurance, real estate and business services | Public adminisatration and defence and other services | Gross domestic product at factor cost (2 to 6) |
|---|---|---|---|---|---|---|
| 1 | 2 | 3 | 4 | 5 | 6 | 7 |
| 1966-67 | -1.3 | 3.5 | 2.7 | 1.8 | 4.6 | 1.2 |
| 1967-68 | 14.3 | 3.2 | 4.4 | 2.7 | 3.9 | 8.3 |
| 1968-69 | 0.0 | 5.2 | 4.6 | 4.9 | 4.5 | 2.6 |
| 1969-70 | 6.4 | 8.0 | 5.4 | 4.2 | 5.5 | 6.3 |
| 1970-71 | 6.5 | 1.7 | 4.8 | 4.2 | 5.5 | 5.0 |
| 1971-72 | -1.7 | 2.6 | 2.3 | 5.2 | 4.5 | 1.0 |
| 1972-73 | -4.6 | 3.5 | 2.5 | 3.9 | 3.3 | -0.3 |
| 1973-74 | 6.9 | 0.9 | 4.2 | 2.4 | 2.6 | 4.3 |
| 1974-75 | -1.3 | 1.2 | 6.2 | -0.3 | 4.7 | 1.2 |
| 1975-76 | 12.9 | 6.3 | 9.0 | 6.9 | 3.5 | 9.2 |
| 1976-77 | -5.4 | 9.3 | 4.6 | 7.9 | 2.8 | 1.1 |
| 1977-78 | 9.7 | 7.3 | 6.4 | 4.9 | 2.7 | 7.4 |
| 1978-79 | 2.3 | 7.8 | 8.1 | 7.1 | 4.3 | 5.1 |
| 1979-80 | -12.2 | -3.5 | -0.4 | 1.0 | 7.3 | -4.9 |
| 1980-81 | 12.9 | 4.2 | 5.7 | 1.9 | 4.1 | 7.6 |
| 1981-82 | 5.1 | 7.5 | 6.2 | 8.1 | 2.1 | 5.6 |
| 1982-83 | 0.4 | 0.5 | 5.4 | 9.5 | 7.7 | 2.9 |
| 1983-84 | 9.7 | 8.7 | 5.1 | 9.8 | 3.7 | 7.9 |

| year | Agriculture, forestry and fishing. mining and quarrrying | Manufacturing construction, electricity, gas and water supply | Trade, hotels, transport and communication | Financing, Insurance, real estate and business services | Public adminisatration and defence and other services | Gross domestic product at factor cost (2 to 6) |
|---|---|---|---|---|---|---|
| 1 | 2 | 3 | 4 | 5 | 6 | 7 |
| 1984-85 | 1.6 | 4.5 | 4.8 | 7.5 | 6.9 | 4.0 |
| 1985-86 | 0.6 | 4.2 | 7.9 | 9.8 | 5.7 | 4.2 |
| 1986-87 | 0.3 | 5.1 | 6.0 | 10.5 | 7.5 | 4.3 |
| 1987-88 | -1.2 | 5.8 | 5.3 | 7.3 | 7.2 | 3.5 |
| 1988-89 | 15.7 | 8.2 | 5.8 | 9.8 | 6.0 | 10.2 |
| 1989-90 | 1.6 | 8.5 | 7.4 | 12.4 | 7.9 | 6.1 |
| 1990-91 | 4.5 | 6.7 | 5.1 | 6.2 | 4.4 | 5.3 |
| 1991-92 | -1.5 | -0.1 | 2.6 | 10.8 | 2.6 | 1.4 |
| 1992-93 | 6.2 | 3.6 | 5.6 | 5.4 | 6.0 | 5.4 |
| 1993-94 | 3.2 | 6.3 | 6.9 | 11.2 | 4.5 | 5.7 |
| 1994-95 | 5.1 | 9.3 | 9.9 | 3.9 | 2.3 | 6.4 |
| 1995-96 | -0.2 | 12.2 | 13.2 | 8.1 | 7.3 | 7.3 |
| 1996-97 | 9.1 | 7.3 | 8.1 | 6.2 | 8.1 | 8.0 |
| 1997-98 | -1.6 | 3.1 | 7.5 | 11.7 | 8.3 | 4.3 |
| 1998-99 | 6.0 | 4.3 | 7.6 | 7.8 | 9.7 | 6.7 |
| 1999-00 | 2.7 | 4.7 | 8.2 | 9.2 | 11.5 | 6.4 |

| year | Agriculture, forestry and fishing. mining and quarrrying | Manufacturing construction, electricity, gas and water supply | Trade, hotels, transport and communication | Financing, Insurance, real estate and business services | Public adminisatration and defence and other services | Gross domestic product at factor cost (2 to 6) |
|---|---|---|---|---|---|---|
| 1 | 2 | 3 | 4 | 5 | 6 | 7 |
| | | | **New Series at 1999-2000 prices** | | | |
| 2000-01 | 0.0 | 6.8 | 7.3 | 4.1 | 4.7 | 4.4 |
| 2001-02 | 5.9 | 2.8 | 9.2 | 7.3 | 4.1 | 5.8 |
| 2002-03 | -5.9 | 6.9 | 9.4 | 8.0 | 3.9 | 3.8 |
| 2003-04 | 9.3 | 7.8 | 12.0 | 5.6 | 5.4 | 8.5 |
| 2004-05 | 0.8 | 10.5 | 10.7 | 8.7 | 6.8 | 7.5 |
| 2005-06 | 5.7 | 10.7 | 12.1 | 11.4 | 7.1 | 9.5 |
| 2005-07 | 4.4 | 11.2 | 12.8 | 13.8 | 5.7 | 9.7 |
| 2007-08(Q) | 4.7 | 8.5 | 12.4 | 11.7 | 6.8 | 9.0 |

**Source :** Central Statistical Organisation, Economic Survey 2008-09, p. A-7.

Q : Quick estimates.

**Note :** For the year prior to 1980-81 totals under col. 7 may not add up to totals of individual item under col. 2 to col. 6 due to splicing technique applied independently at the level of each industry and at the total level.

**Table 15.11:** Tenth plan outlay by heads of development: centre, state and union territory 2006-07 and annual plans. 2002-03 to 2006-07.

| S. No. Head of development | Tenth Plan (2002-07) (Actual) | Annual Plan 2002-03 (Actual) | Annual Plan 2003-04 (Actual) | Annual Plan 2004-05 (Actual) | Annual Plan 2005-06 (Actual) | Annual Plan 2006-07 (RE)[b] | Tenth Plan (2002-07) (Actual) | Annual Plan 2002-03 (Actual) | Annual Plan 2003-04 (Actual) | Annual Plan 2004-05 (Actual) | Annual Plan 2005-06 (Actual) | Annual Plan 2006-07 (RE)[b] |
|---|---|---|---|---|---|---|---|---|---|---|---|---|
| 1 | 2 | 3 | 4 | 5 | 6 | 7 | 8 | 9 | 10 | 11 | 12 | 13 |
| **I.** Agriculture and allied activities | 58933 | 7655 | 8776 | 10794 | 12554 | 7392 | 3.9 | 3.6 | 3.9 | 5.6 | 5.1 | 3.0 |
| **II.** Rural development | 121928 | 19753 | 20729 | 19584 | 25717 | 15643 | 8.0 | 9.4 | 9.2 | 10.1 | 10.4 | 6.4 |
| **III.** Special area programmes | 20879 | 1066 | 1540 | 2351 | 4234 | na | 1.4 | 0.5 | 0.7 | 1.2 | 1.7 | na |
| **IV.** Irrigation and flood control | 103315 | 11965 | 12900 | 19402 | 26332 | 462 | 6.8 | 5.7 | 5.7 | 10.0 | 10.7 | 0.2 |
| **V.** Energy | 403927 | 44710 | 50199 | 22628 | 22043 | 68825 | 26.5 | 21.3 | 22.3 | 11.7 | 8.9 | 28.2 |
| *a.* Power | a | 25281 | 30785 | na | na | 29226 | na | 12.0 | 13.7 | na | na | 12.0 |
| *b.* Petroleum | a | 15806 | 16726 | na | na | 34782 | na | 7.5 | 7.4 | na | na | 14.2 |
| *c.* Coal and Lignite | a | 1911 | 1583 | na | na | 3799 | na | 0.9 | 0.7 | na | na | 1.6 |
| *d.* Non-conventional sources of energy | a | 1712 | 1205 | na | na | 1018 | na | 0.8 | 0.5 | na | na | 0.4 |
| **VI.** Industry and minerals | 58939 | 8776 | 7703 | 5236 | 7898 | 12588 | 3.9 | 4.2 | 3.4 | 2.7 | 3.2 | 5.2 |
| *a.* Village and small scale Industries | a | 2083 | 2186 | na | na | 1670 | na | 1.0 | 1.0 | na | na | 0.7 |
| *b.* Other industries | a | 6692 | 5517 | na | na | 10918 | na | 3.2 | 2.5 | na | na | 4.5 |
| **VII.** Transport | 225977 | 35244 | 35267 | 30026 | 38766 | 49819 | 14.8 | 16.8 | 15.7 | 15.5 | 15.7 | 20.4 |
| a. Raliways | a | 11108 | 13044 | na | na | 24936 | na | 5.3 | 5.8 | na | na | 10.2 |
| b. Others | a | 24136 | 22223 | na | na | 24883 | na | 11.5 | 9.9 | na | na | 10.2 |
| **VIII.** Communications | 98968 | 13057 | 12875 | 737 | 494 | 17851 | 6.5 | 6.2 | 5.7 | 0.4 | 0.2 | 7.3 |
| **IX.** Science, Technology and Environment | 30424 | 4160 | 4356 | 5383 | 6608 | 6774 | 2.0 | 2.0 | 1.9 | 2.8 | 2.7 | 2.8 |
| **X.** General economic services | 38630 | 4995 | 5955 | 4945 | 6084 | 2566 | 2.5 | 2.4 | 2.6 | 2.6 | 2.5 | 1.1 |

| S. No. Head of development | Tenth Plan (2002-07) (Actual) | Annual Plan 2002-03 (Actual) | Annual Plan 2003-04 (Actual) | Annual Plan 2004-05 (Actual) | Annual Plan 2005-06 (Actual) | Annual Plan 2006-07 (RE)[b] | Tenth Plan (2002-07) (Actual) | Annual Plan 2002-03 (Actual) | Annual Plan 2003-04 (Actual) | Annual Plan 2004-05 (Actual) | Annual Plan 2005-06 (Actual) | Annual Plan 2006-07 (RE)[b] |
|---|---|---|---|---|---|---|---|---|---|---|---|---|
| 1 | 2 | 3 | 4 | 5 | 6 | 7 | 8 | 9 | 10 | 11 | 12 | 13 |
| **XI.** Social Services | 347391 | 56954 | 62726 | 67981 | 92350 | 61768 | 22.8 | 27.1 | 27.9 | 35.2 | 37.4 | 25.3 |
| *a.* Education | a | 11603 | 13069 | na | na | 18840 | na | 5.5 | 5.8 | na | na | 7.7 |
| *b.* Medical and public heath | a | 4340 | 4649 | na | na | 2884 | na | 2.1 | 2.1 | na | na | 1.2 |
| *c.* Family welfare | a | 3735 | 4230 | na | na | 6421 | na | 1.8 | 1.9 | na | na | 2.6 |
| *d.* Housing | a | 7685 | 8476 | na | na | 7450 | na | 3.7 | 3.8 | na | na | 3.1 |
| *e.* Urban development | a | 6524 | 6704 | na | na | 345 | na | 3.1 | 3.0 | na | na | 1.2 |
| *f.* Other social services | a | 23066 | 25597 | na | na | 23127 | na | 11.0 | 11.4 | na | na | 9.5 |
| **XII.** General services | 16328 | 1868 | 1801 | 4074 | 4098 | 542 | 1.1 | 0.9 | 0.8 | 2.1 | 1.7 | 0.2 |
| **XIII.** Total (I to XII) | 1525639 | 210203 | 224827 | 193114 | 247178 | 244230 | 100.0 | 100.0 | 100.0 | 100.0 | 100.0 | 100.0 |
| *a.* Central Plans | 893183 | 126247 | 132262 | 80526 | 104658 | na | 58.5 | 60.1 | 58.8 | 41.7 | 42.3 | na |
| *b.* State Plans | 632456 | 78430 | 86756 | 112616 | 142519 | na | 41.5 | 37.3 | 38.6 | 58.3 | 57.7 | na |
| *c.* Union Territory Plans | na | 5526 | 5809 | na | na | na | na | 2.6 | 2.6 | na | na | na |

**Source :** Planning Commission, Economic Survey, 2008-09, A-45. Re Revised Estimates na Not Available

*a.* Tenth Plan Allocations have been made broad sector-wise

*b.* Allocation for UT Plans is included in State Plan.

**Table 15.12:** Eleventh plan (2007-2012) outlays by heads of development centre, states and union territories, 2007-08 and 2008-09.

| S. No. | Head of development | Amount (Rs. Crore) | | | Percentage distribution | | |
|---|---|---|---|---|---|---|---|
| | | Eleventh Plan 2007-12 Projected (At 2006-07 prices) | Annual Plan 2007-08 (RE) | Annual Plan 2008-09 (BE) | Eleventh Plan 2007-12 Projected (At 2006-07 prices) | Annual Plan 2007-08 (RE) | Annual Plan 2008-09 (BE) |
| 1 | 2 | 3 | 4 | 5 | 6 | 7 | 8 |
| **I.** | Agriculture and allied activities | 136381 | 8544 | 10075 | 3.7 | 2.9 | 2.7 |
| **II.** | Rural development | 301069 | 17511 | 18972 | 8.3 | 6.0 | 5.1 |
| **III.** | Special area programmes | 26329 | na | na | 0.7 | 0.0 | 0.0 |
| **IV.** | Irrigation and flood control | 210326 | 454 | 411 | 5.8 | 0.2 | 0.1 |
| **V.** | Energy | 854123 | 72230 | 93815 | 23.4 | 24.7 | 25.0 |
| | *a.* Power | a | 34354 | 45238 | na | 11.8 | 12.0 |
| | *b.* Petroleum | a | 33174 | 42450 | na | 11.3 | 11.3 |
| | *c.* Coal and lignite | a | 3644 | 4922 | na | 1.2 | 1.3 |
| | *d.* Non-conventional sources of energy | a | 1059 | 1205 | na | 0.4 | 0.3 |
| **VI.** | Industry and Minerals | 153600 | 17953 | 28836 | 4.2 | 6.1 | 7.7 |
| | *a.* Village and small scale Industries | a | 1869 | 2218 | na | 0.6 | 0.6 |
| | *b.* Other industries | a | 16084 | 26618 | na | 5.5 | 7.1 |
| **VII.** | Transport | 572443 | 68930 | 84177 | 15.7 | 23.6 | 22.4 |
| | *a.* Railways | a | 29893 | 36726 | na | 10.2 | 9.8 |
| | *b.* Others | a | 39037 | 47450 | na | 13.4 | 12.6 |
| **VIII.** | Communications | 95380 | 16599 | 21937 | 2.6 | 5.7 | 5.8 |

| S. No. | Head of development | Amount (Rs. Crore) | | | Percentage distribution | | |
|---|---|---|---|---|---|---|---|
| | | Eleventh Plan 2007-12 Projected (At 2006-07 prices) | Annual Plan 2007-08 (RE) | Annual Plan 2008-09 (BE) | Eleventh Plan 2007-12 Projected (At 2006-07 prices) | Annual Plan 2007-08 (RE) | Annual Plan 2008-09 (BE) |
| 1 | 2 | 3 | 4 | 5 | 6 | 7 | 8 |
| **IX.** | Science, Technology and Environment | 87933 | 7741 | 9283 | 2.4 | 2.6 | 2.5 |
| **X.** | General economic services | 62523 | 3043 | 6052 | 1.7 | 1.0 | 1.6 |
| **XI.** | Social services | 1102327 | 78798 | 100778 | 30.2 | 27.0 | 26.8 |
| | *a.* Education | a | 23073 | 31420 | na | 7.9 | 8.4 |
| | *b.* Medical and public health | a | 3332 | 5201 | na | 1.1 | 1.4 |
| | *c.* Family welfare | a | 8717 | 9677 | na | 3.0 | 2.6 |
| | *d.* Housing | a | 9714 | 12848 | na | 3.3 | 3.4 |
| | *e.* Urban development | a | 4808 | 5674 | na | 1.6 | 1.5 |
| | *f.* Other social services | a | 29154 | 35959 | na | 10.0 | 9.6 |
| **XII.** | General services | 42283 | 533 | 1150 | 1.2 | 0.2 | 0.3 |
| **XIII.** | Total (I to XII) | 3644717 | 262336 | 375486 | 100.0 | 100.0 | 100.0 |
| | *a.* Central Plans | 2156571 | na | na | 59.2 | na | na |
| | *b.* State Plans | 1488147 | na | na | 40.8 | na | na |
| | *c.* Union Territory Plans | na | na | na | na | na | na |

**Source :** Planning Commission, Economic Survey 2008-09, P. A-46.

BE Budget Estimates

na Not Available

RE Revised Estimates

*a.* Tenth Plan allocations have been made braod sector-wise.

CHAPTER 16

# Nature of Industrial Sickness

## 16.1 INTRODUCTION

Industrial sickness a byword in the corporate world has become a part and parcel of the industrial scene in our country during the past two decades. As it has been spreading at alarming pace profitable units turned unprofitable, an erosion of their reserves and capital took place and ultimately they had to close their door or had to operate on the verge of subsistence just biding time for the last breath.

According to **Oxford English Dictionary** 'Sickness' means the state of being sick or ill' or the conditions of suffering from some malady. Sickness is a symptom of ailment and not an ailment in itself. It indicates that everything is not well but it does not in itself show what is not well in that everything. The **R.B.I.** has defined 'a sick unit as one which has incurred cash loss for one year and in the judgment of bank it is likely to continue to losses in the current year as well as the following year and which has an imbalance in the financial structure such as current ratio of less than 1:1 and worsening debt equity ratio.[1]

According to the Sick Industrial Companies (special provisions) Amendment Act, 1994, "sick industrial company" means an industrial company (being a company registered for not less than five years) which has at the end of any financial year accumulated losses equal to or exceeding its entire net worth. The definition is for the purpose of application of the Act which covers only registered companies which have been in existence for at least seven years[2]. Common symptoms of industrial sickness include failure to pay statutory liabilities like provident fund, E.S.I. contributions, failure to pay timely installment of capital, interest on loan taken from financial institution and through public deposits increase in inventories with a large number of slow or non-moving items, high rate of rejection of goods manufactured, low capacity utilisation and frequent industrial disputes.

1. *Report R.B.I. Trend and Progress of Banking in India* (1977-78) p 25.
2. *The Sick Industrial Companies (Special Provisions) Amendment Act* (12 of 1994).

**Table 16.1**

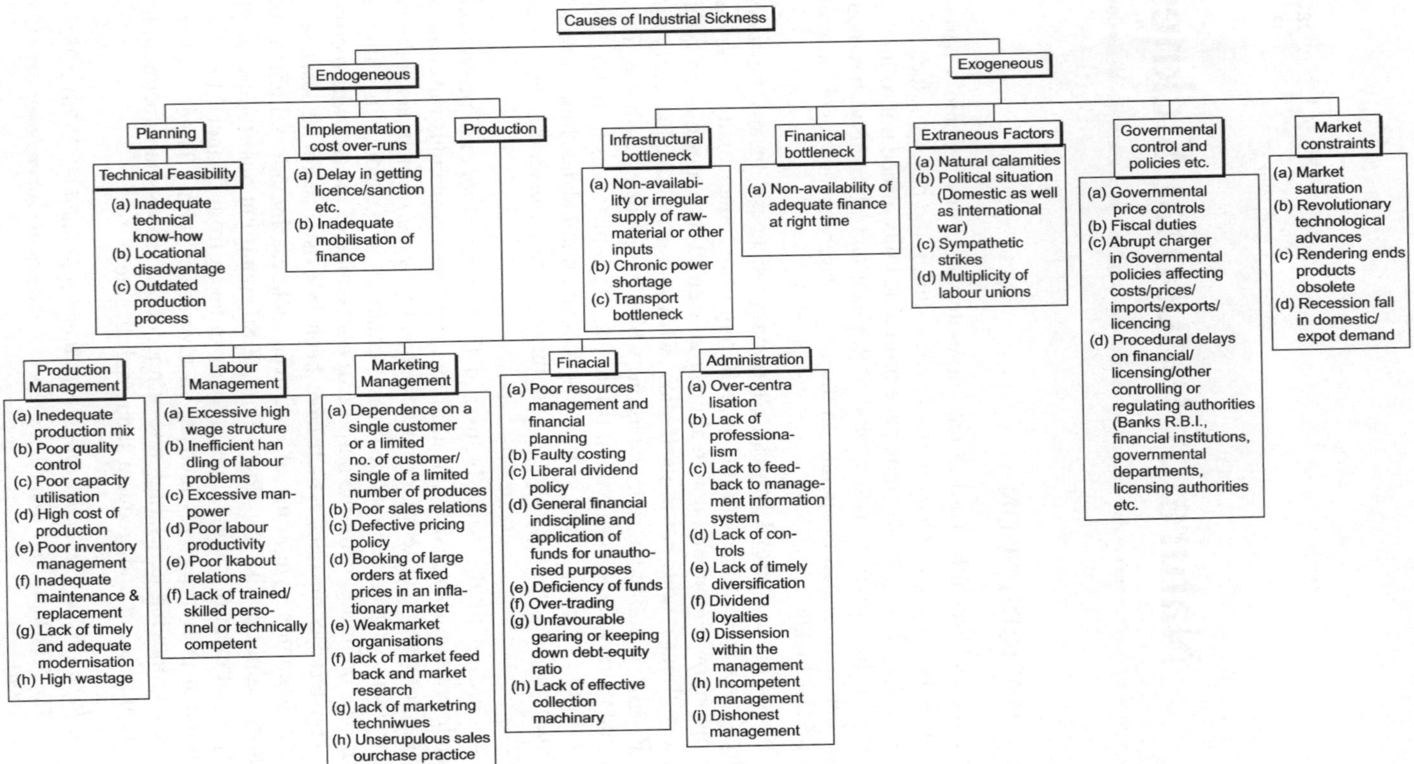


**Source:** S.K. Seth, Industrial Sickness p. 6.

## 16.2 CAUSES OF INDUSTRIAL SICKNESS AND MAGNITUDE

Various studies had been conducted in the recent past to analyse the key causes behind sickness in industrial undertakings. The study conducted by R.B.I. underlined the fact that managerial deficiency and out right management is the single largest cause of sickness in large industrial enterprise[3] while the Development Commission of Small Scale Industries conclude that the non-availability of raw material, price hike of raw materials, shortage of working capital and marketing problems are the causes of sickness in small scale sector[4].

The causes of sickness of an enterprise are as such attributed to a complex of factors which may be either due to internal disorders in the functional area or due to external disruptions that is either due to endogenous factors or exogenous factors. The endogenous factors may be function related which are very much within the control of the managements of the industrial enterprise, while the exogenous factors are related to factors like government policies pertaining to production, distribution and price changes in investment pattern, shortage of power, transport, raw materials and fall in industrial relations. Industrial units are at times born sick or achieves sickness or have sickness thrust upon them[5] (as reveled in Table 16.1).

### 16.2.1 Sickness from Inception

Certain industrial units are said to be born sick in the sense that they are destined to face problems from their very inception. They may arise either due to faulty project planning, wrong project selection, lack of experience of the promoters, paucity of funds and faulty financial management etc. At times due to delay in the supply of equipment, locational problems, faulty selection of technology or wrong assessment of the market potential may lead to the birth of sick units. According to a study conducted by the Institute of Economics, Hyderabad it found that 50% of the dead units closed within three year of opening. This proved that these units never had any reasonable survival prospect right from birth[6].

---

3. Roongto A.L. " Why sickness in Industry Yojna Vol 28 No. 19 Oct 16-31, 1984, P. 25:
4. Development Commissions, Small scale Industries: Diagnostic Survey regarding sickness in small scale units New Delhi 1985, pp 47m-61.
5. V.N.N. Nadkarni, Sickness in Industries its effect on Banking, SBI Monthly Review, June 1983 245-246.
6. V.N. Nadkarni, "Sickness in Industry and its effect on 'Banking," State Bank of India, Monthly Review, June 1983. p. 247.

### I. Endogenous Factors

The Sixth Plan after making a careful analysis of the factors leading to sickness concluded that "However perhaps the most important of all causes of sickness is the incompetence or the cupidity of the management [7]. As such the various factors traceable to managerial ineffectiveness in different aspects can be listed as such:

1. Bad management which "covers a wide range from in experience inefficiency, lack of professional expertise, neglect and internal squabbles to delinquency and dishonesty"[8] is an important cause of industrial sickness. According to the Tiwari Committee Report, 1984, the factor most often responsible for industrial sickness can be identified as 'management'. This may take the form of poor production management, poor labour management, poor resources management lack of professionalism, dissensions within the management or even dishonest management. The committee found that 65% of the large sick units were affected by this problem.
2. Unwarranted expansion and decision of resources may also result in sickness. Due to lack of resources and managerial ability it may land the units in trouble.
3. Lack of alertness to environmental changes requiring modernisation of machinery, product innovation and review of product mix and making mix.
4. Failure to deal with persistent labour-management conflicts leading to low morale and productivity.
5. Inefficiency in sort of operating management in functional areas production, marketing, finance etc. As such persons with poor managerial talent that is poor supervisory ability, intelligence initiative and maturity, lack of proper human relations are unable to resolve the problems[9].

### II. Exogenous Factor

Sickness may be caused due to factors beyond the control of an industrial unit. Some of these external factors are:

1. Energy Crisis arising out of power cuts or shortage of coal, and oil have been a serious problem for many industrial units in India.

---

7. Planning Commission Draft five years plan (1978) p 186.
8. V. Nadkarni "Sickness in Industry and its effect on Banking "State Bank of India, Monthly review June 1983 P. 247.
9. Chawla M.H. "Industrial Sickness in India and Role of BIFR" Chartered Secretary (Sept 1988) pp 789-790.

2. The units are not able to achieve optimum capacity due to shortage of raw material, due to production set back in supply industries poor agricultural output due to natural reasons, changes in import condition etc.
3. Infrastructural problems like transport bottleneck.
4. Credit Squeeze is another important factor responsible for industrial sickness. According to Tiwari Committee 24% of the large sick units were affected by shortage of working capital or liquidity constraints.
5. Artificial economic constraint also make their contribution to the growing industrial sickness. Government controls on the product mix and prices caused serious problems for certain industries. Sometimes it is not possible to rationalise due to unfavorable government policy/ labour attitude.

Thus the causes of industrial sickness are numerous and varied. At macro level, the causes are external on which the unit had hardly any control and at micro level the internal factors are wrong choice of location, mismanagement lack of adequate information and reporting system[10]. It is therefore not unusual to say that an industrial unit which is sick is beset with more than one adverse factors. As such industrial sickness which may arise from the incipient stage to the grave situation needs real and quick remedy for once it is pronounced it would be difficult to control it. The steps for revival should be coordinated between the bank, financial institution, government labour and management.

### 16.2.2 Extent/Magnitude of Sickness

The extent of the problem of sickness of Indian Industry has been growing alarmingly. According to Economic Survey 1989-90" Growing incidence of sickness has been one of the persisting problems faced by the industrial sector of the country. Substantial amount of loanable funds of the financial institution is locked up in sick industrial units causing not only wastage of resources but also affecting the healthy growth of the industrial economy".

10. S.K. Seth. Industrial Sickness p. 9

**Table 16.2:** Magnitude of industrial sickness in India-end March 1991 and end of March 2003

| Category | | Number of Units | | Amount Outstanding (Rs. Crores) | |
|---|---|---|---|---|---|
| | | 1991 | 2003 | 1991 | 2003 |
| 1. | SSI sick Units | 2,21,472 | 1,67,980 | 2792.04 | 5,706.00 |
| 2. | Non SSI sick units (covered under SICA, 1985) | 1,461 | 3,396 | 5,105.57 | 29,109.00 |
| 3. | Non SSI weak units (not covered under SICA) | 876 | | 2,870.21 | |
| **Total** | | **2,23,809** | **1,71,376** | **10,767.82** | **34,815.00** |

**Source:** *Government of India, Economic Survey 2006-07, p 135 and RBI report on CURRENCY and FINANCE, 1997-98, RBI, Hand book of Statistics on India Economy 2003-04.*

At the end of March 2003 there were nearly 1.71 lakh sick/weak industrial units on the rolls of scheduled commercial bank. More than 1.67 lakh of these units were in small scale sector which constituted about 98% of their total number. Non small scale units covered under SICA 1985 was 3396 at the end of March 2003. Total outstanding bank credit locked in all these 1.71 lakh sick unit was to the extent of Rs. 34,815 crores out of which the amount involved in SSI sick unit was Rs. 5706 crore. The outstanding bank credit locked in non SSI sick unit was Rs. 29,109 crores. The total number of non-SSI weak unit (not covered under SICA) stood at 420 at the end of March 1997 and their amount of outstanding credit was to the extend of Rs. 1564 crores. At the end of March 2003 although small scale industries accounted for 98.0% of the total sick and weak but their share in the aggregate locked up bank credit was only 16.4% in respect of sick SSI units. The bank credit outstanding at the end of September 1991 accounted for nearly 16.2% of the total credit to small scale industries. But for sick or weak large and medium scale industries units the ratio was 17.9%. Out of 2427 non SSI sick and weak industrial units in 1996, (*i.e.* about 81%) units were in the private sector which locked 72.7% of the total outstanding bank credit to non SSI sick/weak units.

Industrywise analysis revealed that (see Table 16.3) five industries *viz* textile, engineering, iron and steel, electrical and chemical accounted for about 56% of total outstanding bank credit by 31st March 1997. If non SSI sick and weak unit are taken together then the five industries stated above accounted for a total locked up bank credit of Rs. 5956 crore. (*i.e.* 58.5% of the total outstanding bank credit in such units). Total bank credit locked up in 2368 sick and weak units of the non SSI sector was Rs. 10,178 crores as at the end of March 1997.

**Table 16.3: Industrywise classification of non SSI weak sick unit and non SSI weak unit as on 31st march 1997**

| Unit | Non SSI Sick Units | | | Non SSI Weak Units | | | Sick and Weak | |
|---|---|---|---|---|---|---|---|---|
| | Number | Out standing bank credit | % of toal | Number | Out standing bank credit | % of total | Outstanding Bank credit | % of Total |
| Textile | 380 | 1418 | 16.5 | 65 | 130 | 8.3 | 1548 | 15.2 |
| Engineering | 212 | 1181 | 13.7 | 35. | 82 | 5.2 | 1263 | 12.4 |
| Chemical | 190 | 838 | 97 | 42 | 157 | 10.0 | 995 | 9.8 |
| Iron and Steel | 137 | 672 | 7.8 | 22 | 171 | 10.9 | 843 | 8.3 |
| Electrical | 88 | 906 | 10.5 | 14 | 401 | 25.6 | 1307 | 12.8 |
| Metal | 75 | 429 | 5.0 | 21 | 96 | 6.1 | 525 | 5.2 |
| Paper | 111 | 227 | 2.6 | 9 | 21 | 1.3 | 248 | 2.4 |
| Cement | 52 | 300 | 3.5 | 14 | 45 | 2.9 | 34.5 | 3.4 |
| Sugar | 21 | 99 | 1.1 | 7 | 12 | 0.8 | 111 | 1.1 |
| Jute | 27 | 163 | 1.9 | 3 | 5 | 0.3 | 168 | 1.7 |
| Rubber | 33 | 93 | 1.1 | 8 | 12 | 0.8 | 105 | 1.0 |
| Misc | 697 | 2288 | 26.6 | 180 | 432 | 27.6 | 2720 | 26.7 |
| Total | 1948 | 8614 | 100.00 | 420 | 1564 | 1000 | 10178 | 100.00 |

**Source:** *Compiled and computed from the Data given in RBI report on currency and Finance (1997-98).*

**Table 16.4:** State wise analysis of industrial sickness in India as on 31st March 1997

| Unit | Number of Units | | | Outstanding Bank Credit/Rs. Cr. | | | Total | % of total |
|---|---|---|---|---|---|---|---|---|
| | Non SSI sick | Non SSI weak | SSI sick | Non SSI sick | Non SSI weak | SSI sick | | |
| Textile | 380 | 1418 | 16.5 | 65 | 130 | 8.3 | 1548 | 15.2 |
| Maharashtra | 340 | 59 | 19360 | 1615 | 220 | 764 | 2599 | 18.8 |
| W. Bengal | 216 | 27 | 53451 | 1033 | 53 | 372 | 1458 | 10.6 |
| U.P. | 170 | 32 | 23286 | 916 | 65 | 299 | 1280 | 9.3 |
| A.P. | 225 | 39 | 15460 | 1061 | 126 | 214 | 1401 | 10.2 |
| Gujarat | 174 | 39 | 6510 | 584 | 81 | 197 | 862 | 6.2 |
| Tamil Nadu | 141 | 34 | 9809 | 623 | 103 | 203 | 929 | 6.7 |
| Karnataka | 110 | 49 | 6937 | 556 | 468 | 399 | 1423 | 10.3 |
| Sub Total of (1 to 7) | 1376 (70.6) | 134813 (57.3) | 6388 (74.2) | 1116 (71.4) | 2448 (67.8) | 9952 (72.2) | 72.2 | |
| Kerala | 64 | 17 | 8908 | 409 | 84 | 168 | 661 | 4.8 |
| Haryana | 66 | 12 | 2574 | 304 | 24 | 64 | 392 | 2.8 |
| Bihar | 55 | 9 | 22702 | 117 | 74 | 121 | 312 | 2.3 |
| M.P. | 91 | 20 | 12070 | 300 | 65 | 151 | 516 | 3.7 |
| Orissa | 55 | 7 | 3408 | 261 | 24 | 45 | 330 | 2.4 |
| Rajasthan | 67 | 17 | 14561 | 250 | 27 | 98 | 375 | 2.7 |
| Punjab | 51 | 11 | 2466 | 146 | 55 | 84 | 285 | 2,1 |
| | | | 10133 | 166 | 1 | 54 | 221 | 1.6 |
| Others | 85 | 45 | 23397 | 273 | 94 | 376 | 743 | 5.4 |
| Total | 1948 | 420 | 235032 | 8614 | 1564 | 3609 | 13787 | 100 |
| | (100.0) | (100.0) | (100.0) | (100.0) | (100.0) | (100.0) | (100.0) | |

**Source:** *Compiled and computed from the data give in RBI, Report on Currency and Finance (1997-98).*

**Note:** Figures in brackets (are % of the total of the respective column.)

Statewise analysis of industrial sickness revealed that Maharashtra has the maximum number of (340 units) followed by West Bengal (216), A.P. (225 units) industrial Non SSI sick units and the lowest is in Assam which was 38 units. Thus it is seen that states like Maharashtra and West Bengal together accounted for 28.5% of the total number of sick units in the non SSI category and 30.7% of the total credit outstanding. In case of SSI sick units Maharashtra and W. Bengal accounted about 30.9% of the total sick units under this category and the total credit outstanding in these two states at the end of March 1997 was to the extent of Rs. 1136 Crore. These regions faced greatest cases of sickness because of the existence of textile engineering goods and jute industry.

As regards SSI sick unit (67.8%) and 72% the total outstanding bank credit of such units was concentrated in the first seven industrially advanced states of India in 1997.

As per information compiled by RBI from commercial bank as on 31st March 2001 there were 252947 sick/weak units consisting of 2,49,630 units in the SSI sector and 3317 units in the non SSI sector. Among these 3317 units private sector, public sector, joint sector accounted for 2942 units, 255 units and 106 units respectably the number of sick SSI units has decreased from 304235 units to 249630 units but the number of sick/weak units in the non SSI sector has increased from 3164 to 3317. However there is an overall increase of 10.4% in total number of non SSI sick/weak units as compared to that of previous year. The total bank credit blocked in the sick units has increased from Rs. 23656 or (as on March 31, 2000) to Rs. 25,775 or (as on March 31, 2001). They accounted for around 6.7% of the total bank credit and 13.3% of the total bank advances to industry. The small scale sector has Rs. 4506 crores (17.5%) blocked in its units while the non SSI sector has Rs. 21270 crores (82.5%) Bank credit blocked in the non SSI sector in private public, joint sector was Rs. 17,705 crores Rs. 2986 crores and Rs. 537 crore/42 crore respectively.[11]

## 16.3 CONSEQUENCES OF INDUSTRIAL SICKNESS

The impact of industrial sickness on the Indian economy can be listed is such:

1. **Setback to Employment Prospects:** Closure of industrial unit would render workers unemployed.
2. **Fear of Industrial Unrest:** Trade Union of other industries are likely to oppose retrenchment of labour of the closed unit and resort to widespread industrial sickness. The peace and tranquility of the industrial environment will be threatened resulting in industrial losses and set back to production in a number of units.
3. **Wastage of Resources:** Stoppage of production in sick units leads to blockade of valuable savings and capital equipment.
4. **Adverse Impact on Related Units:** An industrial unit is linked with other units. Therefore sickness in one unit is likely to affect adversely a number of other units.
5. **Adverse Effects on Investor and Entrepreneurs:** Closure/ liquidation of a large sick unit creates a psychology of despair among investors. The share price of that unit will tumble down and the prevalence of gloomy market condition would adversely affect the entire stock market. Not only this failure of a unit acts as a disincentives to other entrepreneurs who were planning to launch

11. Economic Survey 2000-2001 p./82

production in the same lines. Such industrial climate is not conducive for industrial development.

6. **Losses to Bank and other Financial Institution:** Closure of units causes losses to banks and financial institution which had granted loans to these units to set up their plant and machinery and commerce production.

Finally it also leads to loss of governmental revenue central, state and local government.

## 16.4 REMEDIAL MEASURE

Since, Industrial sickness causes loss of production very often leading to unemployment and resulting in blocking of scarce resources of the banks and financial institution, revenue to the exchequer. The magnitude and incidence of industrial sickness are matters of serious concerns for the central and state Governments, Reserve Bank of India banks and financial institution not merely due to the above factors but also because such a trend undermines public confidence in the functioning of the organised sector with repercussions on the investment of the economy. Several measures have therefore been taken by the government and financial institutions to detect the symptoms of sickness and to prevent or cure sickness to the extent possible.

1. **Steps taken by the Banks**

   Inorder to revive and rehabilitate the sick industrial units, the commercial banks granted various concession of these units which include:

   (*a*) Granting additional working capital.

   (*b*) Recovering proper moratorium on payment of interest.

   (*c*) Recovery of interest at reduced rates.

   (*d*) Freezing a portion of the outstanding in accounts etc.

   Besides, banks have also taken various steps on the organisational front by setting up sick industrial undertaking cell, state level inter-institutional committees a standing coordinating committee (constituted by RBI) from coordinating various issues related to commercial banks and term lending institution and a special cell within rehabilitation finance division of IDBI.

2. **Policy framework of the Government**

   In order to deal with the problem of industrial sickness the government laid down various guidelines. They are:

   (*a*) The administrative ministers in the government have been given specific responsibility for taking remedial action and preventing industrial sickness.

(*b*) In order to take corrective action for preventing incipient sickness the financial institution will strengthen the monitoring system and may take over the management of unit for its revival.

(*c*) Whenever the banks and other financial institution fail to prevent sickness of a sick unit thereafter reporting the matter to the government they recover their outstanding dues with normal banking procedures.

(*d*) In order to nationalise the undertaking the management of the unit may be taken over under the provision of Industries (Development and Regulation) Act 1951 for six months period.

(*e*) The government could also consider steps such as restructuring, merger with healthy units etc to rehabilate the sick unit. Where revival did not seem possible the government could denotify the unit resulting in its closure.

**3. Concession Granted by Government**

Certain concession were also provided by the government to assist revival of sick units without intervention. For instance the Income Tax Act was amended in 1977 by addition of section 72 A which provided for the grant of tax benefit to healthy units when they took over the sick units by amalgamation with a view to receiving them. On January 1st 1982, a scheme for provision of margin money to sick units in the small scale sector at safe terms was introduced to enable them to obtain necessary funds from banks and financial institution and to implement their revival scheme. This was followed by the introduction of a liberalised margin money scheme in June 1987 to supplement the efforts of the state government in reducing sickness in the small scale sector. The amount of money was raised from Rs. 20,000 to Rs. 50,000. In October 1989, the government announced a scheme for the grant of excise loans to sick/weak industrial units. Under this scheme selected sick units were eligible for excise loans not exceeding 50% of the excise duty actually paid for 5 years.

**4. Steps for early detection of sickness**

In order to detect sickness of those companies not covered under SICA 1985 at an early stage, the Reserve Bank has taken various measures like advising the bank to take necessary steps in respect of any industrial unit and monitoring certain industries through its standing committee where sickness is widespread.

**5. Industrial Reconstruction Bank of India**

This Bank was established to assist the rehabilitation of mostly the non SSI sick units with an authorised capital of Rs. 200 crores and paid up capital of Rs. 50 crore. At the end of March 1991 total amount of assistance sanctioned by IRBI was Rs. 1262 crore out of which Rs. 923 crore was disbursed.

**6. Sick Industries Companies Act**

Sick Industrial companies Act 1985 aimed at:

(*a*) The timely detection of sick and potential sick companies owning industrial undertaking.

(*b*) The speedy determination by a Board of Experts of the preventive, ameliorative revival and other measures which need to be taken with respect to such companies.

(*c*) The expeditions enforcement of the measure so determined and for matters connected therewith or incidental thereto.

According to the SICA amended in 1993 a sick industrial company meant an industrial company (being a company registered for not less than 5 years) which had at the end of any financial year accumulated losses equal or exceeding its entire net worth.

**Board of Industrial and Financial Reconstruction (BIFR)** was set up in **January 1987** under the Sick Industrial Companies (Special Provision Act 1985) inorder to revive potentially viable companies. The decision of BIFR is final as it has its binding an all concerned, from 15th May 1987 the Board became operational. In December 1991 public sector enterprises were brought within the purview of BIFR through an amendment of the SICA. Since the inception of the Board and upto the end of September 2006 the BIFR has received 6991 references under section 15 of SICA. Out of these 1573 cases were rejected, on scrutiny of the 5418 references registered 1707 cases were dismissed as not maintainable, revival schemes were also sanctioned or approved in 760 cases and 1303 cases were recommended to the concerned High Court for winding up, 485 companies are declared no longer sick and discharged from the purview of SICA. During the year 2006-07, the gross disposal of cases reached to 4115.

The BIFR has so far received 7158 references under the SICA 1985. These references include 297 from central and state public sector undertakings (CPSU's and SPSUs). Out of the total references received 5471 were registered under section 15 of the SICA 1857 references were dismissed as non-maintainable under the Act 825 rehabilitation schemes were sanctioned and 1337 companies were recommended to be wounded up of the 297 references for public sector undertaking the references of 92 CPSUs and 122 SPSUs were registered upto December 31$^{st}$, 2007.[12] It was further received that maximum sick companies were registered from the western region (563) followed by southern region (558 cases), the northern region (447 cases) and the eastern region 283 cases. Among the states Maharashtra had the majority

12. Economic Survey 2007-08 p. 204

of cases at (290), followed by Andhra Pradesh (250), U.P. (191) and W. Bengal (177). About 47% of the sick companies registered with the board were from these four states. Textile sector alone accounted for 301 cases followed by paper and pulp sector with 138 and chemical with 118 cases. The RBI has also been laying emphasis on the deflection of sickness and timely formulation of rehabilitation package in respect of sick/weak non SSI units which are found to be potential and commercial viable.

## 16.5 CONCLUSION

The working of the BIFR has been subject of debate and criticism that is due to the reasons that there are considerable delays in the BIFR process. Such inordinate delays make it difficult for a sick company to turn around successfully and rehabilate itself. Because of delay in decision taking by BIFR, banks stopped giving working capital to these PSU's. Thus compounding the crisis the parliamentary standing Sub-committee therefore called for speeding up work of the BIFR to make it cost effective. It also suggested decentralising the BIFR with the creation of regional branches in the state, where the incidence of industrial sickness is quite high.

❑❑❑

# Bibliography


1. Bhagoliwal T.N. — Personal Management and Industrial Relations.
2. Bauer & Yamey — The Economics of Under Developed Countries.
3. Barthwal R.R. — Industrial Economics.
4. Cherunilam Francis — Industrial Economics — Indian Perspective.
5. Chang P.K. — Agriculture and Industrialisation.
6. Cherunilam Francis — Business Environment.
7. Chawla M.H. — Industrial Sickness in India and Role of BIFR
8. Dhingra I.C. — Indian Economic Environment.
9. Datt Ruddar & Sundaram K.P.M. — Indian Economics
10. Gadgil P.G. and Gadgil — Industrial Economy of India
11. Hanson A.N. — Public Enterprise and Economic Development
12. Jha Bishwambhar — Fundamental of Industrial-Organisation and Management.
13. Jhingan M.L. — The Economics of Development and Planning.
14. Kuchall S.C. — Industrial Economy of India.
15. Kulshestra-Raghubir-Sahay — Industrial Economics.
16. Kaicker P.S. — Sick Industrial Companies Act 1985.
17. Lal B.B. — Industrial Productivity & Economic Growth.
18. Lokanathan P.S. — Industrial Organisation in India.
19. Lekhi R.K. — The Economics of Development and Planning
20. Monappa Arun — Industrial Relations

**21.** Mishra Banarasi — Monitoring of Industrial Sickness

**22.** Mishra S.K. — Sickness in Industries and Key to Revival from it.

**23.** Mehta M.M. — Structure of Indian Industries.

**24.** Mishra and Puri V.K. — Indian Economics.

**25.** Mishra and Puri V.K. — Economics of Development and Planning

**26.** Mehrotra S.N. — Labour Problem in India

**27.** Pahwa H.P.S. — Sick Industries and B.I.F.R.

**28.** Roongta A.H. — Why Sickness in Industry

**29.** Sharma A.M. — Industrial relation Conceptual and Legal. Frame Work

**30.** Sinha V.C. — Industrial Economics

**31.** Seth S.K. — Industrial Sickness

**32.** Shivayya and Das — Indian Industrial Economy

**33.** Sudarshan Lal — How to Prevent Industrial Sickness

**34.** Virmani B.B. — The Sick Industrial Companies Act.

**35.** Vakil C.N. — Industrial Development of India 1974.

# Reports and Journals

- Economic and Political Weekly
- Economic Survey — Various Issues
- India — A Reference Manual, Ministry of Information and Broadcasting
- Government of India, Labour Year Book
- The Hindu — Survey of India Industry
- Indian Economic Journal
- Mainstream
- Kulshetra
- Ministry of Labour, Report of the National Commission on Labour
- Southern Economist
- Yojna
- Report on Currency and Finance

# INDEX

## J



## K



## L



## M



## N



## O



## P



## R



## S

## T



## U



## V



## W